IN SEARCH OF A FUTURE

BOOKS BY MAURICE HINDUS

IN SEARCH OF A FUTURE
THE BRIGHT PASSAGE
THE COSSACKS: THE STORY OF A WARRIOR PEOPLE
MOTHER RUSSIA
RUSSIA AND JAPAN
HITLER CANNOT CONQUER RUSSIA
TO SING WITH THE ANGELS
SONS AND FATHERS
WE SHALL LIVE AGAIN
GREEN WORLDS
MOSCOW SKIES
THE GREAT OFFENSIVE
RED BREAD
HUMANITY UPROOTED
BROKEN EARTH
THE RUSSIAN PEASANT AND THE REVOLUTION

MAURICE HINDUS

In Search of a Future

PERSIA, EGYPT, IRAQ, AND PALESTINE

Doubleday & Company, Inc., 1949

GARDEN CITY, NEW YORK

Awake, awake, put on strength.
—ISAIAH 51:9

THE AUTHOR GRATEFULLY ACKNOWLEDGES PER-mission from the publishers to use the following material:

The quotations from Hafiz are from *Hafiz, Fifty Poems,* by Arthur J. Arberry, professor of Arabic in the University of London. Cambridge University Press, 1947.

The quotations from Saadi are from *Tayyibat, the Odes of Sa'di,* translated by the late Sir Lucas White King, Kt.C.S.I., LL.D., sometime professor of Arabic and Persian in the University of Dublin. Published by Luzac and Co., London, 1926.

Foreword

THIS IS A BOOK ABOUT PERSIA (IRAN),[1] EGYPT, Iraq, and Palestine—countries in search of a future. Essentially it is a book about people and land, only incidentally about cities and culture.

It is the author's judgment that Jewish Palestine, now known as Israel, provides a workable blueprint for the development of the other nations with which this book is concerned. Indeed, unless, in one way or another, to suit the character of their peoples and the physical conditions of their lands, the Mohammedan nations in the Middle East avail themselves of the example Israel has set in pioneering for a new way of life in desert and neglected country, their future is weighted with dire consequences. Anything may happen there, including violent revolution. Let it be emphasized that in 1946, Persian Azerbaijan, Persia's largest and most populous province, actually witnessed the dress rehearsal of such a revolution.

Until a generation ago, the part of Palestine that now consti-

[1]Throughout the book I have used the words Persia and Iran interchangeably, even as did the people whom I met wherever I journeyed and as do foreign, particularly the British and American, residents of the country.

tutes Israel was almost as much aslumber with stagnation as was Arab Palestine. Since then a spectacular process of rejuvenation has taken place. Israel has already achieved a well-defined blueprint for the course of its internal development. Its overwhelming concern is with outside pressures, particularly from Great Britain. The Mohammedan countries in the Middle East, while as yet secure from foreign encroachment that may threaten their statehood, are still darkly groping for a way of national regeneration.

I am writing neither a political polemic nor a historical treatise. I am concerned with the philosophies neither of Zionism nor of Arabism, but rather with Persians, Egyptians, Arabs, and Jews as human beings and as peoples I came to know during several journeys in the Middle East. Other men have written ably and brilliantly on the political controversies, the historical issues, the international embroilments that the very word Palestine suggests. The Report of the Palestine Royal Commission (known also as the Peel Commission) of 1937 is one of the most searching and most illuminating documents on these subjects. Sumner Welles's *We Cannot Fail* is such a terse and highly documented account of Zionism, of British commitments and British reversals, of American promises and American defaults, of the legal claims and historical contentions between Jews and Arabs over Palestine, that a discussion of these subjects would be repetition of a performance which I cannot hope to rival.

Besides, whatever the future of Israel, even if the Foreign Office in London and the Imperial General Staff were to bring forth a fresh arsenal of diplomatic or military weapons with which to snuff out the Jewish Community or smother it into impotence, the record of pioneering it has already attained, the facts and conclusions about desert farming and desert life it has already demonstrated would shine forth like the summer waters of the Mediterranean on the shores of Tel Aviv. They would still constitute a hopeful and viable example for the internal regeneration of Persia and the Arab world.

It was my good fortune to know the late Wendell Willkie. In the course of a conversation about the backward peoples of Africa and Asia, many of whom he had visited in 1942, I heard him make this significant pronouncement: "If the millions and millions of peasants had land enough to enable them to buy one suit of clothes a year, one pair of shoes, a couple of suits of underwear, shirts, and socks, think how much business we could do with them."

Himself the owner of five well-managed farms in his native state of Indiana, Willkie was transcendently land-minded, as few Western statesmen are. In laggard and backward Africa, as well as in meagerly developed and thickly populated Asia, he glimpsed intuitively the relationship between the landlessness of the multimillioned peasantry and their unspeakable poverty.

In this landlessness of the farming population, and in the absurdly primitive mode of tillage that accompanies it, lurk the chief causes of the turbulence that, like the smoke of a brewing volcano, hover over so large a part of the world. Persia, Egypt, Iraq, and the other Arab countries are only a segment of the Asia and Africa that are shrouded with uncertainty and threatened with upheaval. In Israel internal peace may be menaced by violent minorities, but even in moments of crisis its land policies and its highly developed agriculture, the health and the hopefulness of its rural population are certain to prove a Gibraltar against forces of disunity and disintegration. Yet there is nothing Jewish Palestine has achieved that the Mohammedan nations of the Middle East cannot attain. Difference in historical heritage does not necessarily preclude similarity of effort and identity of accomplishment.

Let a casual incident speak for itself. During my visit to the Jewish village of Givat Brenner, as I was sauntering around the many-laned and hilly fields, I was suddenly attracted by what from a distance appeared to be a scuffle between Jews and Arabs. Pointing to a small crowd of black-robed Arab women and ragged Arab children who seemed to have besieged a Jewish wagon, I asked the village secretary who accompanied me, "A race riot?" "Oh no," he said, "this is a daily occurrence. Arab women and children wait on the highway for our garbage wagon, and when it starts out for the garbage pit, they rummage around for the scraps and rags that may be of use to them." He glanced at the loud scene before us and added sorrowfully, "It is a pity, a great pity, that this should be so."

The sordid incident need never have happened, or might have been exceptional instead of commonplace, had the Arabs, in the centuries they have lived in Palestine, achieved an equitable distribution of the land and acquired a knowledge of scientific farming.

No Moses guided by divine inspiration has struck with a rod, for the Jews of today, a rock out of which flows water for parched throats and parched lands. The Jews have hunted for water, have dug for it, have drawn it to the surface. They have cleared the pestilential swamps, all but one, and have vanquished the malaria-carrying mosquito which for centuries has been the scourge of the Arab population of the country.

They have toiled and sweated over desert sands, rocky hills, have spent large sums of money—chiefly contributions from the outside—and have achieved a supreme agricultural triumph. They have few if any equals as desert farmers in Asia or Africa. They have demonstrated as have no other people on these continents that neglected and damaged land can be redeemed and freshened and be made to bear bread and fruit. Their triumph in the regeneration of deteriorated livestock, sheep and goats, poultry, and above all cattle, has been as spectacular as their redemption of unproductive lands, a triumph without which the Mohammedan countries in the Middle East cannot hope to stabilize, strengthen, and enrich their newly acquired and ardent nationhood. Though the Jewish farmers know no opulence, the annual suit of clothes and pair of shoes and shirts and underwear and socks of which Willkie spoke are not—as in Persia, Egypt, and Iraq—a dream or a legend, but an everyday reality.

Since this is a book primarily for American readers, I have deliberately devoted more space to Persia than to any other country. One of the most fascinating countries I have ever visited, Persia may not be "America's baby," as a foreign resident in Teheran expressed himself; yet, if only because it is the key to the Russo-American conflict in the Middle East, it is "America's baby" more than anyone else's. "Power in Persia," writes A. C. Edwards, a British author, "means only too often the support of the British or Russian Embassy."[2] I should dispute the writer's use of the present tense; America has superseded Russia and Great Britain as the chief foreign influence in the Land of the Lion and the Sun. The fact that an American Military Mission has been entrusted by the Iranian Government with the responsibility of helping to reorganize the army, and that American army officers have been engaged to rebuild the Iranian gendarmery, or internal police, tells its own story of the position America now holds.

Justifiably or not, friends and foes of America credit America more than their own government with the victory of Teheran over the autonomous regime in Azerbaijan in December 1946, and with the resoluteness with which the Majlis (Parliament), in October 1947, braced itself out of its fear of Russia and voted down Russia's clamorous demand for an oil concession in the northeastern provinces, which Ahmad Ghavam, the Prime Minister, had previously promised Moscow.

Despite America's prestige, Iran remains one of the most vexing problems on Washington's doorstep. Meanwhile, whatever America's future policy and influence in Teheran, Washington has, I believe, been more expertly supplied with full-bodied and authentic information about Iran than about any other Mohammedan land in the Middle East. Under the ambassadorship of George Allen, himself a former newspaperman, who has an eye for color and an ear for fact, hardly a phase of Iranian life escaped the searching attention of his staff of assistants and re-

[2]"Persia Revisited," *International Affairs* (London: January 1947).

searchers. The 800-odd-page report of the Morrison-Knudsen Engineering firm of Boise, Idaho, is a treasure house of information. Invited by the Teheran Government, a staff of experts representing the firm made a comprehensive survey of Persia's economic ills and economic potentialities and proposed remedies for the removal of the one and the realization of the other. To the best of this writer's knowledge, no other such scientific and lucidly digested analysis of Persia, or of any other Mohammedan country in the Middle East, has ever been made.

Neither the State Department in Washington nor the American Embassy in Teheran has, at this writing, released to the press this highly significant report. But the governor of the Teheran National Bank lent me his copy, and it made exciting reading. For detail and massiveness of information it has not its equal in any of the volumes that have been published on that little-known land. Whatever America's future position in Iran, whatever the conflicts that may arise between Washington and Moscow over Iran's destiny, in the light of the studies made by the Embassy during George Allen's term in Teheran, and particularly the Morrison-Knudsen engineers, no American President or diplomat, and neither congressman nor senator, can ever ascribe errors or failures, should they occur, to scant or false information on the Persian land and the Persian people.

Yet it is impossible to escape the conclusion that Israel, despite all its harassments and imperfections, is the only country in the world that offers Iran a scientifically drafted blueprint for the solution of the ever-present and ever-pressing ailments with which it is afflicted. And what is true of Iran is true of Egypt, Iraq, Syria, and the other Arab lands in the Middle East. I shall not presume to assert that this blueprint can be literally and bodily applied to these other nations. Of course it cannot be. But there is nothing else in the world, and particularly in their part of the world, from which these nations can learn so much of ways and methods of rejuvenating their lands and of uplifting their peoples.

Almost thirty years ago Lawrence of Arabia, in writing of Jewish achievement in Palestine, then still in its infancy, said: "The success of their scheme will involve inevitably the raising of the present Arab population to their own material level, only a little after themselves, in point of time, and the consequences might be of the highest importance for the future of the Arab world."[3]

However deep their enmity for Israel at the moment, the Arab leaders can no more disregard its successful solution of problems identical to their own than a sick man can disregard the penicillin a physician prescribes for him because it cured a neighbor with whom he has quarreled.

MAURICE HINDUS

[3]T. E. Lawrence, *Oriental Assembly,* p. 93 (New York: E. P. Dutton, 1940).

Contents

CHAPTER I

City at the End of the World

I LEFT FOR THE ORIENT FROM GENEVA, SWITZER-
land. By the time I finally reached Teheran, capital of Persia (or,
more officially, Iran, as the country is now called), I felt as
though I had come to the end of the world. Teheran is the largest
and most modern Persian city; its population is 750,000. Yet the
swift-flying, four-motored airliners that cruise the globe rarely
stop there—there is not enough traffic to warrant the expense of
a landing. On no American airline could I book direct passage to
Teheran.

Air mail from America reaches the city in from two to four
weeks, ordinary mail in as many months or more. No American
newspapers and no European newspapers save those from nearby
Russia are hawked in the street or sold on newsstands, and the
scarcity of world news—written as news, displayed as news—in
the Russian dailies makes them unattractive even to those who
have mastered the language. By the time European or American
newspapers arrive, they are museum pieces—nothing to get excited about, merely something to take to bed and fall asleep over.
In no other city in the Middle East did I feel so out of touch with
the daily stream of events.

Only when I visited the American or some other embassy did I learn what was happening in the world. In addition to each having their own news sources, the embassies subscribe to the competent daily bulletins of Pars, the Persian news agency, which reprint quite fully the important stories of the best news-gathering agencies of the world. There are also short-wave radios, which receive news and other broadcasts from foreign countries. But one must have access to an embassy or to some privileged Persian functionary to avail oneself of these services. For the foreigner, there is no news in the air. He lives in a world of hazy uncertainty and sensational rumor. Not even the *Journal de Tehran,* the French daily, despite all its journalistic virtues, presents an adequate picture of the happenings of the world. Twice during my stay in Persia, I was told that Russia and America had gone to war.

Teheran is the East, barely shaken by the tumults, yet ruffled by the triumphs of the West, and sundered from it by more than distance.

One perceives something of the mood and the temper of the city by observing its dogs and its beggars. The dogs are the tamest and most unaggressive, the beggars the humblest and most genial I have met anywhere in Africa or Asia. The beggars are many, the dogs are few, for Mohammedans spurn the companionship of "man's best friend." Not that the Prophet had excoriated the dog. The *kalbon moallam*—the "educated" dog, such as the hunting dog, the sheep dog, the watchdog—he esteemed, and for it he urged kindly treatment. He disapproved of the pet dog, Persian Moslems explained to me, not only because it was a consumer of food, of which there was a scarcity in the Arabian Desert, but also because it was a carrier of disease. In time, as with so many other precepts of the Prophet, the original attitude, with its sharp distinction between the educated and the pet dog, degenerated into a contempt for all dogs.

Branded as unclean, the dog is supposed to defile everything he touches with his feet, including the rugs on which people kneel in prayer. Everything he licks with his tongue must be washed seven times before it is cleansed of desecration.

The dog is the untouchable in this land. Except among those Persians who are completely emancipated from Moslem usage, the family pets are cats, canaries, here and there a nightingale in a cage, and above all pigeons. Teheran dogs seem to know their lowly position. They rarely obtrude their attention upon man, either in affection or in resentment. They live their own lonely lives like the spirits that are supposed to be sent down to the earth to expiate their sins in homeless wandering. Unleashed and unmuzzled, the dogs roam the streets and scavenge in gutters and courtyards, eagerly snapping up the bone or the morsel of bread that a kindly shopkeeper or a merciful child rarely tosses to them. When they have had their fill of food, they seek out a shady spot on the sidewalk, or under a tree or a mud wall, and fall asleep utterly oblivious to the roar of traffic about them. They arouse neither pity nor hate. They are just dogs—a nuisance to be tolerated. When they breed too fast and too many of them rove the streets, there is always someone who will roll strychnine into a bit of bread, and the creature passes out of life as unobtrusively as he came into it.

Though timid and aloof, a dog may infrequently be goaded by hunger or rage into turning on a tormentor or even on an innocent passer-by. Yet for some mysterious reason rabies is uncommon in Teheran (even as, for an equally mysterious reason, is infantile paralysis).

It was with some astonishment, then, that on entering the home of Princess Ashraf Pahlevi, the Shah's twin sister, for an interview with her, I found myself surrounded by a pack of clean and friendly dogs ranging from a spunky cocker spaniel to a dignified St. Bernard. "Yes, I love dogs," the princess said. One of the most beautiful and emancipated women in Moslem Persia, her example of kindliness to animals may yet help dissuade Persians, especially the youth, from the harsh treatment they accord to dogs and to other dumb creatures.

Beggars are a conspicuous feature of the human procession in Teheran. As in all cities in the East whose piety and poverty have barred the infiltration of modern hygiene, the blind, the maimed, the halt are everywhere in evidence. Stumbling on crutches, sliding legless along the sidewalks, leaning against a tree or wall, or sitting huddled up on a street corner, they moan and mutter as if to themselves their pleas for mercy. Sometimes they stretch out on the sidewalk and go to sleep, rarely failing to set their rumpled felt skullcaps open beside them as a reminder to hurrying pedestrians that just because they are asleep they should not be neglected. Only once did a beggar accost me the full length of a block, chanting an amusing invocation which, no doubt, an American GI had taught him: "Baksheesh, johnny, baksheesh goddam."

It was in cheering contrast to Cairo, where beggars approach a foreigner with a whisper and a whimper and, if ignored, end with a shout and a curse. Teheran beggars have not yet learned the sly art of shaming or incensing the outsider into bribing them to silence.

Teheran is not so much a city as it is a civilization, or rather a jumble of civilizations that, like plants in a field unevenly watered, rise to varying levels of growth and efflorescence. Here are the bazaars, Persia's ancient trade marts, securely roofed and sealed against the blazing sun and the fierce downpours. The murky retreats, the labyrinthine lanes, the clutter of shops, the gleams of charcoal fires, the fumes and the smells, the clangs and the chants evoke a primeval antiquity. Yet outside the cavernous enclosures, radiating in all directions, are avenues as broad and as shiny with asphalt as those of any modern metropolis. The rows of shade trees, a delight to the eye, are a welcome protection in summer against the withering sun.

Then one sees and hears loud-voiced vendors dispensing glasses of drinking water from a goatskin, and one suddenly grows aware that the capital is without piped water. Milk is transported in goatskins and it sours quickly; butter melts easily by the time it reaches the city. Wise Europeans and Americans touch neither the milk nor the butter, for either may induce one of the many virulent fevers that rage in the Mohammedan Middle East.

For the first time in its history, Teheran now has an up-to-date taxi service—not the squeaky and sputtering jalopies of the war years, which were the despair of the foreign visitor and the butt of racy, often ribald GI witticisms, but a fleet of flashy baby cabs, fresh from Great Britain's assembly lines. They are the joy of Teheran, of everybody but the ever-wailing droshky drivers, who look like relics of a forlorn age. The new cabs constantly cruise the streets and are always available. They are cheap, safe, and fast; and, miracle of miracles, there is no tipping. I know of no other city in the Middle East where taxi service is so reasonably priced and so efficiently organized. Here is more than a moderate measure of the discipline and comfort of the West.

Yet as one drives about the city one passes or cuts across caravans of donkeys or, on the outskirts of Teheran, of camels, a mile long or longer, hauling on their backs, as in ancient times, the freight of the country—barley, wheat, fruit, vegetables, lumber, and even cut straw, which Persians still use in a mixture with mud to seal roofs against rain.

In reality, Teheran is a city with a European face and an Asiatic body, and the incongruity is striking and thought-provoking. The face is new and bright, the body is old and untidy. The face was forcibly grafted onto the city by the late Riza Shah, father of the present king. Like Peter the Great of Russia, Riza Shah was so appalled by the backwardness of his country that he set out to re-create it in the image of Europe. He tore down the old city, with its mud walls, its mud huts, its narrow and crooked streets, its stagnant pool, its foul smells. He brooked no opposition, any more than Peter had done; he struck it down no less ruthlessly. He shocked and frightened and infuriated his people even as Peter did, and like Peter, though on a much less

5

lavish scale, he swept them into the stormiest ordeal they had known in over a thousand years. Riza Shah tore the turban off the heads of men and the loose, flowing garments off their bodies. He forced men into European clothes: jacket, trousers, collar and tie, hat or cap—and pajamas! He ripped the veil off women's faces and sought to shame or lure them into modern dress.

It was only in 1928 that Persian women were first permitted to attend motion pictures and to visit cafés, and at the beginning only the brave took advantage of these liberties. But on January 6, 1936, in a spectacular gesture of defiance of Moslem customs, the formidable king appeared at the commencement exercises of a Teheran girls' high school, and with him were his wife and his two older daughters, unveiled and in European dress. The act of impiety caused a rumble of indignation. It shocked the populace, but it produced a permanent revolution in manners.

In the new and modern part of Teheran a veiled woman is to-day so rare, even among the poor and the pious, that passers-by stare at her and wonder whether the gauze over her face is a cover for an unsightly skin disease or a disguise for an assignation.

Yet some of the old customs still linger. Men and women do not walk arm in arm in public. Nor will young people, except perhaps college students with a flair for Westernism, who deliberately seek to attract attention in the hope that passers-by will suppose that they have lived or studied in Europe or America. The hunger for social elevation is as deep-rooted in the Persian as in any Westerner, and it finds its own mode of expression, however petty or trivial it may seem to the foreigner.

Only men hold one another by the hand—not, as some foreigners imagine, as an expression of sexual affinity, but out of pure comradeship, as with Russians and other Slavs or Frenchmen who kiss one another on the cheeks in public. At parties and in her home, in gardens and restaurants, the emancipated girl, who speaks at least one foreign language, usually French, is as free and comradely with men as any European or American girl.

Yet if she is well born, she will not be seen in the street with a male acquaintance, however well she may know him, unless a brother or her father or some other near relative acts as an escort.

"Will you not even go to the cinema with a man who is no relation of yours?" I asked the daughter of an eminent lawyer.

"Not even to the cinema."

"Not even with your fiancé?"

"Not even with him. If I did, people would talk and say I am spoiled and immoral, and such talk is bad for a girl."

"So you are a good girl?"

"Sometimes—not so good!"

When the foreign visitor reaches Teheran, he is impressed by the face of the city. Its plan, the array of resplendent buildings, the broad and shiny boulevards, the flourishing trees, the well-dressed and well-drilled police—these remind him of Europe. Yet beneath the captivating façade he soon glimpses the ancient body, bound down with torpor and ineptitude. With all his modern-mindedness, the bold Riza Shah never gave a thought to the importance of a sanitary sewage and water system for the capital. The water that surges down from the mountains flows through the city's streets in open channels, called *jubes,* gathering in its course no end of pollution. Children wash their feet and bathe in the *jubes*. Men and women wash their socks and shirts in them. Dogs and donkeys, sheep and goats quench their thirst in them.

No Europeans touch the *jube* water, not even for bathing, unless it has first been boiled. Persians who can afford it obtain their water from peddlers, who in turn obtain it, cool and pure, from the city's underground canals and deliver it in metal-barreled carts and wooden casks all over the city. Yet foreigners are in error, as was the late Wendell Willkie, when they conclude that the water in the *jubes,* with all its daytime pollutions, is the only water the overwhelming mass of the population of Teheran must use for drinking and cooking as well as for washing themselves. Every courtyard in Teheran has an *ab-anbar,* a cellar

7

reservoir, and the water that pours into it comes from the flow of the *jubes* late in the night, usually between two and five in the morning, when it is least contaminated. Salt and charcoal are put into it, and sometimes goldfish, to destroy impurities. It is not as pure as the water from the underground canals, but neither is it as foul as the daytime flow in the street canals. Teheranis are water-conscious, and no housewife, however poor, would dip up water for household purposes from the open *jubes*. But they do not hesitate to rinse their fruits and vegetables in the courtyard pools, as stagnant as they are scum-covered, which are a constant source of disease. Only now, after years of planning and discussion, has a British engineering firm been engaged to lay underground pipes for water and sewage in Teheran.

Despite the contrasts in the everyday scene, as the antique yesterday and the modern today intertwine like weeds and flowers in an uncultivated garden, the individual Persian displays no lethargic or defeated traits—not in Teheran. He walks with a short brisk stride, hands swinging at the sides, head held high, with no hint of slouchiness in bearing or of vulgarity in manner. Ever aware of his innate decorum, he has neither the hardy chunkiness of the Slav nor the listless sullenness of the Arab, two of his most troublesome and most embarrassing neighbors. Lithe, small of frame, and sharp-featured, with brilliant and deep-set black eyes and a particularly strong nose, he has something of the aliveness of the Frenchman. This may be one reason why he has responded to the French more enthusiastically than to any other Western culture. French is the one language which, if he is to be educated, he considers it his duty to master.

The Persian gesticulates as he speaks, not as dramatically or expressively as the Slav, but with the easy grace of the Italian or the Frenchman in addition to a vivid jerkiness of his own. There is nothing morose or melancholy about him. Wretched as he may appear, ragged as he may be, he wears no expression of gloom, not even when he is sitting cross-legged on the floor of his shop or his home, listening to the plaintive melodies that pour out of his radio. (I have yet to hear a gay tune—gay to. the Western ear—come out of the Persian radio.)

A fat man in the streets of Teheran is so rare that, when seen, passers-by turn with a grimace of amusement or a chuckle. When I spoke of it to a Persian university professor, he smiled and said, "All our fat men are in Parliament." He meant that the deputies in Parliament are overwhelmingly merchants and land-lords, who have the leisure and the means to indulge luxurious appetites. Lean and wiry, the average Persian is tough in spirit. There is barely a shred of sentimentality in his richly emotional nature.

"Is there any suicide in your country?" I asked a noted Te-heran author.

"Not to speak of," was his reply. "Our people have endured so much hardship and struggle, our deserts and mountains have made life so painful an ordeal, that no personal conflict, however shattering, rouses the sense of futility that leads to suicide. We go on living."

Yet attempted suicide is one of the more melodramatic fea-tures of Teheran social life, among poor as well as wealthy and cultivated families. Girls between seventeen and twenty are the chief performers in these family scenes. A quarrel with a father or mother over a boy friend, over the meaning of the word free-dom, over such things as proper dress or proper make-up or some other purely personal privilege or obligation often so dis-concerts a girl that she will swallow a stick of opium, not neces-sarily with the intent of bringing her life to an end, but to frighten a recalcitrant parent into sanction or acquiescence in her desires. Invariably the victim of these family conflicts will ingest a large dose of the drug, because a larger amount is slow to be absorbed, and will wash it down, not with an alcoholic beverage, which might prove fatal, but with water. Invariably she will commit her revengeful act in a place where she can easily be discovered, by parent or servant. Invariably the frightened father or mother will instantly inquire whether the portion consumed was large or small or whether it was washed down with water or an alcoholic drink. If the portion was large and was washed down with water, the panicky parent will breathe easy. Prompt medical attention will save the delinquent daughter or son. In the municipal hospitals of Teheran there are special opium-suicide rooms in which these cases are effectively treated. Thus, when reason fails, melodrama often rewards a disenchanted or lovesick girl or boy with triumph.

And how the Teherani works! In Cairo, as I passed the crowded sidewalk cafés, I often asked myself, "When do Egyptians work?" In Teheran, as I roamed the streets I asked myself, "When do the Persians rest or play?" Because of the blistering sun in summer, most shops close for several hours during the hottest interval in the afternoon. Otherwise people are always busy, and the capital is a booming beehive of activity. Work is in the blood of the Persian. He is always banging or clattering away at something—unless he happens to be a gentleman.

The *gentleman* regards work as beneath his dignity and his person. Not only the landowner, but the engineer, the owner of a prosperous garage, the importer of foreign tools or foreign machines, will not soil his hands with anything suggestive of physical labor. Always there is a servant to perform the menial task. The gentleman will not even be seen carrying a parcel. He must always think of his decorum and his social position. He must ever be aware of what other gentlemen, and ladies too, and ordinary folk, including his own servants, will say about him. Not the least reason for the inertia which is so flagrant a trait of the Persian capitalist—merchant or landlord—is this disdain of physical labor. The shirt-sleeve capitalist is as alien to Persia as the factories and industries that symbolize his presence in America.

During the war years Persians were shocked when they saw American lieutenants, captains, majors leap out of their jeeps and trucks and with their own hands repair a stalled engine. They still talk about it. "A Persian gentleman would never do it," a Persian poet said to me dolefully. "That's one of our misfortunes."

The gentleman's attitude toward labor dramatizes with startling vividness the contrast in the sociology of Persia's ancient Zoroastrian civilization and its confused society of today. Zoroaster (660–583 B.C.) glorified labor. Clearing land, digging for water, growing crops, planting trees, tending live stock were extolled as the height of human nobility, acts of divine command and divine fulfillment. "He who sows ground with care and diligence," proclaims the Zend-Avesta, "acquires a greater stock of religious merit than he could gain by the repetition of ten thousand prayers." The letter and the spirit were one, in man's attitude not only toward labor but also toward women, animals, and truthtelling. Out of the cornices of the Zoroastrian Temple in Teheran, which non-believers are not permitted to enter, there loom the sculptured heads of cows—animals useful to man and therefore deserving of man's respect and gratitude. The dog was honored. Abusing a dog was an outrage and a sin. A funeral procession was headed by a man leading a dog. The horse was venerated. All animals which contributed to man's welfare were accorded comradely and affectionate treatment. This virtue has long since atrophied in the Persian; the Moslem creed, in the instance of the dog, specifically castigates it.

And how immeasurably higher and more noble was man's relation to woman in the Persia of twenty-five hundred years ago! None of the frustrations and inferiorities of Islam were foisted on her. Concubinage prevailed among the kings and the well-to-do, but polygamy such as Mohammedanism sanctions did not exist. Women enjoyed equality with men, which—despite all the emancipation that has come in the wake of Riza Shah's reforms and the infiltration of Western manners by way of Western education and even more by Hollywood motion pictures—the Persian woman of today is still struggling to attain. The saint of the Magi religion was obliged not only to toil with his hands but

11

"to beget children." The mother, therefore, had an especially honored position in Zoroastrian society.

Zoroastrianism glorified truthtelling and branded the lie as the grossest of transgressions. Ahriman, the principle of evil, was associated with lying, and every follower of the faith was enjoined to battle Ahriman as man's greatest enemy. Zoroastrianism damned the liar unto eternal torment, for liars were the villains who corrupted and destroyed all goodness and all life. In his *The Persian Wars,* Herodotus relates that Persians instructed youth between the ages of five and twenty in three things: "to ride, to draw a bow, and to speak the truth." Persians, according to Herodotus, regarded it a disgrace to involve themselves in debt, "because a debtor is obliged to tell lies." Persian kings ruthlessly punished men who falsified the truth.

The decay of Zoroastrian morality in Persian life today is dramatically in evidence at every hand. "The first thing you want to remember about Persians," an English-educated Persian said to me shortly after my arrival in Teheran, "is that they are monumental liars."

"Are you a liar?" I said, laughing.

"I am a Persian," he retorted, but he did not laugh.

"How do you explain it?" I further asked.

"You have to know our history to understand it. We have been kicked about so much by conquerors and foreign diplomats, by our own shahs and our own police, that the lie became the most natural and the most effective weapon of security and self-preservation. I don't expect you to agree with me, unless you study the plight of our people since the fall of our great kings, especially since the Arab conquest."

One of the most admirable traits of the educated Persian is his readiness to acknowledge the failings of his people. In this one respect he has not his equal in the other Mohammedan countries. A. C. Milspaugh, formerly an economic adviser to the Teheran Government, quotes the Parliament Deputy Ali Dashti as declaring: "We should not praise ourselves by saying that once upon a time Cyrus the Great conquered the whole world . . . In what other country can you find so many traitors, adulterators and embezzlers, all immune from punishment?"[1] Sickened of the intrigue and falsehood that has permeated the political life of the country, another deputy once lamented privately, "Only my dog doesn't lie to me."

I have met university professors and other intellectuals who dream of the day when Zoroastrian morality will be revived and exalted. "We shall never be a great people until Zoroaster again rules our minds and our hearts," a noted writer once exclaimed.

"But did not Zoroastrianism decay with the centuries?" I asked.

"Quite true, it did," came the solemn answer. "But if a house totters it can be rebuilt. Zoroastrianism was our Persian house, our Persian temple of goodness, put together with our own hands, out of spiritual materials we found in our own land. We are not and never were a desert people like the Arabs, and Mohammedanism, with all its virtues, which are great, is the religion of a desert people. Our poets, even when they were pious Moslems like Nizami and Saadi, were too life-loving, too romantic, too civilized, I should say—civilized in the modern meaning of the word—to yield to the soul-stifling rigidities of Mohammedanism. Their soul was always their own, a lofty Persian soul."

Nor was this an outburst of chauvinism. A people like the Persians, with a gift for eloquent self-criticism, who not only lament but laugh at their frailties, are too mature, too sophisticated, too cynical, to elevate self-respect into jingoistic self-glorification. The revival of Zoroastrianism such as my companion contemplated may be only a poetic dream, a nostalgic delusion, but the Zoroastrian emphasis on hardihood and uprightness, on love of labor and of animals and of truthtelling, was one of the most notable attributes of Persia's ancient civilization.

[1] A. C. Milspaugh, *Americans in Persia* (Washington: Brookings Institution, 1946).

The perversities in Persian social life are further attested by certain expressions that shock the Westerner when he first hears them. "You must come to one of my villages," a landlord said to me in 1942, when I visited the country for the first time. "Do you mean you own villages?" I asked. "Of course," was his reply. "I own twenty-two villages." Nor did he show unhappiness or any spirit of wrongdoing. Of course there is no slavery in Persia. Landlords cannot dispose of peasants as of wheat, barley, rice, or silk. But since they own the land in the villages, or at least 80 per cent of it, they have accustomed themselves to the expression "owning villages." The dissatisfied peasant may leave whenever he hopes to improve his condition elsewhere. Some of them do leave, and settle in towns, or in another landlord's village. Sometimes they acquire an education and rise to an eminent position. There are no social bars to advancement. "From one point of view," wrote Lord Curzon, in his monumental work on Persia, "Persia is the most democratic country in the world. Lowness of birth or station is positively not the slightest bar to promotion or office of the most exalted nature."[2] Riza Shah, trained originally as a Cossack by Russian officers, was of lowly origin.

But the majority of *dahati* (village folk) stay on in a landlord's villages from generation to generation and suffer the disabilities with which they are burdened, including the compulsion, not readily dodged or defied, to cast their vote for the deputy to the Majlis designated by the landlord's agent. This alone invests the very word democracy, as Westerners interpret it, with absurd connotations. To speak of democracy in such countries as Persia, Egypt, or Iraq, where the mass of the peasantry is illiterate, is like speaking of medical science in the villages in which they live, in which charmers and sorcerers do so much of the healing.

Shortly after my arrival in Persia on my last journey there, in 1947, a literary friend invited me to attend a performance in one of Teheran's few amateur theaters. As we were waiting for the

[2]Lord Curzon, *Persia and the Persian Question* (London: Longmans Green & Co., 1892).

curtain to rise, a friend of my companion, who spoke excellent English, came over to greet us. Glancing around the audience, which was whiling away its time cracking pistachio nuts, he remarked, "They are all third-class people." He did not speak offensively. He only wished me to realize that "first-class" people like himself would not behave in so ill-mannered a fashion in a theater. Yet the expression struck me with special force. To repeat, though there is no hereditary caste system in Persia as there is in India, and the son of a peasant or an artisan may, by dint of good luck and superior gifts, advance himself to the highest level of achievement there is in the country, there are nevertheless "first-class" people and "third-class" people. Never did I hear anyone speak of "second-class" people. There are none, or else there are so few that they automatically fall into the categories of firsts or of thirds. Persian society would seem to consist of an upper and a lower level, with nothing between to leaven the one or the other or to serve as a binding link between the two.

Nothing big or complicated is ever produced in Teheran, not even in its factories. Only little things are fashioned there, chiefly by hand, using the simplest and crudest of tools. The Persian can improvise or "master-mind" an extraordinary number of objects of immediate utility and of supreme beauty. He has the patience and the tradition of craftsmanship. The handsome bodies of the new busses that breeze around the city are made by hand. The displays of carved bronze and of silverware, of rugs and carpets, of woodwork and miniatures in the more fashionable shops on the Lelazar or in the bazaar excite the eye and captivate the imagination.

Ancient Persia was a nation of craftsmen whose workmanship earned them universal praise and renown. Modern Persia is still a nation of artisans. Though many of the old skills and old inspirations perished with the glories of the Persia that was, many others, such as the Isfahan samovar makers, or the Shiraz silversmiths, or the rug weavers everywhere, have but few equals anywhere in the world.

Because not the machine but the hand, the strong and nimble Persian hand, accomplishes most of the work in the country, Teheran's economy is crudely unintegrated. An American officer once wisecracked that out of the three quarters of a million people in the capital, 750,000 of them were in business for themselves. The exaggeration only lights up the truth. The economic processes involved in the making and disposing of goods are splintered into infinitesimal units.

There are fashionable shops in the Lelazar but not a single department store. Ask a grocery man for powdered milk or for rice and he is likely to roll his eyes in astonishment and advise you that not he but the druggist sells powdered milk, not he but the cereal man sells rice. The sidewalks of Teheran, especially late in the afternoon and after dark, swarm with "businessmen," men and boys—never girls or women—who stride up and down shouting and chanting their wares, from safety pins and chewing gum to silks and satins, from tumblers of ice water or of fruit juice to chased silverware and fine woodwork, from exquisite rugs to photographs of Hollywood stars.

Unlike Cairo, which, largely because of its foreign groups and its own great university, teems with foreign bookshops, Teheran, despite its large population, has very few. There are about eight shops that sell books in foreign languages. Despite excellent laws that make education compulsory, broad literacy is still an intention of tomorrow rather than an achievement of today. According to Dr. Sadigh, the Minister of Education, in the year 1946 only 336,882 pupils attended primary schools, while 1,200,000 of primary-school age were deprived of such instruction. The same year witnessed the completion of primary-school education by 16,894 pupils. Only 1,593 completed lycées (high schools) and primary normal schools. In all Iran, incidentally, which is presumed to have a population of over sixteen million, there are seventeen hundred physicians, of whom only six hundred are licensed practitioners.

The oldest and largest newspaper in the capital and by far the most reliable, *Ettelaat,* has a daily circulation of thirty thousand. A publisher who manages to build up a sale of four thousand daily copies considers himself quite successful.

Yet the intelligentsia, particularly university students and graduates, eagerly snatch up foreign works on philosophy and psychology, though they barely glance at foreign works of fiction, however up-to-date and exciting. It is true that *Gone with the Wind,* which has been rendered into Persian and is also available in French, has swept the literate population of Persia as it has that of Europe, but I could discover not a single other volume of modern American or British fiction that has won favor among large numbers of Persian readers. About three quarters of a century ago, at the instance of the monarch, Naser-od-Din Shah, much French fiction from Alexandre Dumas and Balzac on was liberally and enthusiastically rendered into Persian. More than two thousand novels, chiefly French, have since found their way into the Persian language.

The educated youth does not neglect the imaginative works of foreign writers. When he first discovers them he is so fascinated with the depiction of life in Western lands that he reads volume after volume. But as he grows older and more mature he reaches out for a more intellectual interpretation of the modern world and of modern man. That is why books on philosophy and psychology—chiefly German during the prewar years but now essentially French, British, and American—are snatched up as swiftly as they are placed on the shelves. "Why," I asked a noted Persian author, "are you intellectuals so absorbed in the study of philosophy and psychology?"

Slowly and meditatively, as though weighing each word, he replied, "Because we are still learning, still groping for the truth." And after a long and significant pause he added, "For the old and the new truth."

Proud of their ancient poets and prophets, almost any Persian peasant or herdsman, however illiterate and impoverished, knows by heart and loves to recite for the edification of himself and his neighbors passages from the nation's classical poetry. Mothers often lull their babies to sleep to the sound of the rhythmic verses of some ancient ode or epic. The more prosperous *gahve-khanes* (teahouses), even in the villages, will invite or engage a *nakkal,* a professional taleteller, to entertain the guests with recitals of folk tales and of passages of classical poetry. Usually the *nakkal,* even when he is illiterate, is a gifted elocutionist, with a dramatic fervor for his calling, and his repertoire is likely to be so rich that he can render a new program day after day, evening after evening.

Persia is a country in which classical poetry is the priceless heritage not solely of the intelligentsia but of the people. Yet the young intellectuals who read French or English or German, or who have studied in a foreign university, know only too well that the verses of yesterday, however brilliant in imagery, noble in sentiment, rich in philosophy, and strong in inspiration, lack the formula for new deeds of national heroism and national salvation. The new age is upon them; it beats on the ancient land from the East and the West as relentlessly as the blazing summer sun. The Persians are used to their sun. They have lived with it and under it for thousands of years. They have learned to tame its fiercest terrors. The peasant's mud hut, with its thick walls and domed roof, affords escape and protection. The landowner and the wealthy merchant have their fabulous gardens, set with trees and a wealth of flowers, with spouting fountains and tinkling pools, that give forth all the refreshing coolness they may seek.

But the new age is too new and too overpowering. It is a challenge and a promise, a torment and an inspiration. Philosophy —not only William James and John Dewey, Bergson and Eddington, but Karl Marx—as well as psychology, particularly the highly specialized studies of American psychologists, are to the Persian intelligentsia keys to the understanding of the new age. They know they can neither escape nor exorcise it. Nor do they want to. They also know that if they are to escape another conquest, whether by military force or by a powerful idea, they must tame it and make it their own, even as they have tamed the fierceness of their sun.

Teheran is remote from the great speedways of the world. Yet Teheran is astir with more reflection and apprehension, more dreams and vexations than it has known in perhaps all its history.

CHAPTER II

House of Wisdom

KNOWN AS THE "HOUSE OF WISDOM," SHIRAZ IS PER-
sia's most beloved city. The province of which it is capital, Fars,
is the cradle of the Persian nation, and from its name the word
Persia was derived. Teheran and Isfahan, Hamadan and Meshed
may twit one another gaily or rudely about their respective
foibles and failings, but no Persian anywhere will utter an irreverent word about Shiraz. Its name is as sacrosanct as though it
were a shrine of holy dedication.

Though it has the distinction of being the birthplace of Seyed
Ali Mohammed, known as Bab, precursor to Bah-Ul-Dah,
founder of the religion of Bahaism, the fame of Shiraz in the Persian mind is associated not with religion or any act of divine
revelation but with literature. It was the home of Saadi and
Hafiz, Persia's best-known and best-loved poets. Both were born
in Shiraz, and though Saadi, who lived almost one hundred
years, was an inveterate traveler, while Hafiz rarely stirred from
his birthplace, both are buried there.

Their tombs outside the city are national shrines, to which
Persians pay humble and joyful homage. Shiraz therefore is a
symbol of beauty and romance, of wit and wisdom, of earthly
bliss and poetic dedication, and of something more, of philo-

sophic rebellion against the rule of the clergy. Fittingly enough, the dining room of the Saadi Hotel, in which I was staying, was decorated with a portrait of Omar Khayyám, painted by a Persian artist. It depicted the famed bard in his old age, with flowing white beard, a white turban on his head, a jug of wine beside him, and on his arm a beautiful girl with dark tresses strumming a stringed instrument and singing. "He is the real Shirazi," a Persian remarked as we were examining the portrait, "though he lived far away in Nishapur."

> *Shiraz, city of the heart,*
> *God preserve thee!*
> *Pearl of capitals thou art,*
> *Ah, to serve thee.*

Such was Hafiz's tender tribute to the city of his birth.

"Shirazis," said a Teheran poet, "are different from any Persians you have ever met."

They were. On my arrival I met a young businessman, and almost immediately after I was introduced to him he asked:

"Do you write poetry?"

"No," I said. My words perplexed him. "Do you?" I asked.

"Of course. We all write poetry in Shiraz." To him it seemed almost sacrilege that a literate person should not compose poetry.

I drove out to the tombs of Hafiz and Saadi. They are close to one another, on high hills that command an entrancing view of the city. The tomb of Hafiz is more ornate than Saadi's, and its gardens are set with more trees and flowers, with sculptured pillars and two sparkling lagoons. But both tombs, in their settings, appeared more like pleasure parks than burial places. People came there not to mourn but to relax and rejoice. Little parties were gathered on rugs on the ground, eating, drinking, laughing, often with a steaming little samovar before them, while someone strummed a *taar* (a Persian stringed instrument) and chanted an old lyric or ode. "You should come here on Fridays," said the Persian who drove me out. "They are our most popular picnic grounds."

Saadi died in 1291, Hafiz in 1389, and throughout the centuries their verses have been passed from generation to generation, far more by word of mouth than by printed page. They have been diversion and hope, escape and inspiration. And they have been the arbiters of vexing dilemmas and of haunting conflicts. Should a man make the journey he contemplates? Would he make or lose money? Should he marry the girl who has stirred his fancy, divorce the woman who has ceased to please him? The poets, Hafiz in particular, almost as much as the sacred Koran, will render the decision by means of the so-called *fahl,* or mystic augury. With eyes shut, one opens the book at random and places one's finger on the page. The printed text under the finger offers the much-desired counsel and guidance. Rich and poor, peasant and townsman, merchant and statesman often have recourse to the *fahl;* and Shirazis, as if to profit from the closeness of his spirit, prefer to perform the act on the very tomb of Hafiz. Both poets of Shiraz are remembered and revered by the elite and the lowly as no shah and no statesman has ever been in Persian history.

One reason for the incomparable popularity of the poets, not only Saadi and Hafiz, but Firdausi and Nizami and all the others, is that despite their Moslem faith, which was imposed on Persia by the Arabs in the seventh century, they rebelled against the behests and intolerances that Islam had foisted on their own and their people's life-loving natures. Saadi, one should add, was not the rebel that Hafiz was. A conformist, he upheld the *status quo* of his day, religious and political. Yet even he, like Hafiz and Omar Khayyám and other poets, exalts the purely earthly pleasures of living, of wine and song, of nature, and man's love for woman— one woman. As if in angry protest against the Moslem permission of polygamy, Saadi cries out, "A heart cannot be attached to two sweethearts, nor can it admit two loves!" Despite his well-known piety, Nizami, who lived about a century earlier, not in the balmy and sun-drenched South but in the more severe northern province of Azerbaijan, and who prided himself on his religious orthodoxy, writes no less movingly on the subject. "Do not ruin the harvest of thy life by marrying several wives," he counsels. "A son as pure as a gem can only be born when the mother and father are united in one heart." This was the universal sentiment of Persian poets. "What are the rights of fidelity?" asks Nizami. "The observance of fidelity," is his rapturous answer.[1]

However devout and mystical-minded they may have been, the poets spurned the concept and deprecated the custom of the veiled face and the Moslem discouragement of romantic love. "Who says it is a sin to look at a lovely face?" exclaims Saadi. If such be the command of religion, he will have none of it. "O believer," he intones, "I have no patience away from a fair face; ye have your religion and I have mine." He will not be denied a love that is the all-consuming rapture and the all-rewarding right of mortal man. Without it, all is gloom and desolation. "Pleasant is the malady I suffer when the beloved comes near to pay a sick visit: those who are afflicted with this kind of pain do not desire any other remedy." And if it be a sin thus to indulge one's sentiments, then he, Saadi, is a sinner and welcomes with free heart the penalties the sin incurs. "If I were offered a choice on the Day of Judgment . . . what I wanted, I should reply, 'Give us the Beloved and let the delights of Paradise be yours.' "

Hafiz, whom literary Persians regard as their most eminent poet and their most exquisite stylist, echoes and re-echoes the glowing sentiments of Saadi, whom he worships as his master. To him too there is no greater recompense than love for one woman.

> *When thou dost see the well-loved face*
> *Be lost at last to time and space. . . .*

[1] G. H. Darab, *The Treasury of Mysteries of Nezami of Ganjeh* (London: Arthur Probsthain, 1945).

And again:

> *Could those stern fools who steal religion's mask*
> *And rail against the sweet delights of Love,*
> *Fair Leila see, no paradise they'd ask,*
> *But for her smiles renounce the joys above.*

A lover of mankind, regardless of racial origin or religion, Hafiz mocked and scorned the fierce disputes of rival faiths and the rival promises of salvation. "Excuse the war of all the seventy-two sects: as they have not seen the truth, they have plundered on the highway of legend." Man is man, God's own creation, and it is not for one man to say to another that, unless he accepts his particular faith, he is doomed to everlasting torment. "The fire and deceit of hypocrisy will consume the barn of religion."

To Hafiz mankind is one, God is one, salvation is beyond the right and the power of mullah or priest to dole out as though it were a merchant's goods solely within his gift to dispense.

He castigates the vindictive partisanship which the Moslem, or indeed any faith, inculcates, and no less the harsh asceticism which on pain of punishment the Moslem or any religious doctrine seeks to enforce. Alien to him are the long fasts, the self-laceration, and the anguished mourning which the Shiite wing of the Moslem faith demands of its followers. "Let wine on the prayer mat flow," Hafiz sings, and again:

> *Drink, Hafiz! Revel, all your cares unbend,*
> *And boldly scorn the mean dissembling knave*
> *Who makes religion every vice defend.*

Nor—like all other Persian poets—has he any use for the Moslem ban of the musical instrument.

> *Then let sorrow's wailing cry*
> *Be drowned in floods of melody.*

With their glorification of the good life as it is lived on this earth, the Shiraz poets are the antithesis of the mullahs. Those Moslem teachers interdict music and wine, which to the poets spell unending joyfulness, and they canonize man's prerogative over woman, making her an object of man's lust, which the poets believe pollutes and throttles romantic love. The Prophet's limitation of the number of a man's wives to four may have been an advance for the desert Arab, who at that time cherished no respect for the person or individuality of women. "Whoever hath a daughter," reads one of the sayings of Mohammed, "and doth not bury her alive, or scold her, or shew partiality to his other children, may God bring him into Paradise." But Persians were not Arabs. In the pre-Moslem centuries under the Zoroastrian dispensation, they revered women. The very thought of burying a daughter because she could not bear arms or might precipitate a family scandal would have horrified the Zoroastrian.

The outcry of the Shiraz poets against Mohammedan social and emotional severities impelled Edward Gibbon to remark, "The wine of Shiraz triumphed over the laws of Mohammed." This is not quite true, yet it is expressive of the inner rebellion, of the poets especially, against the frustrations and self-denials which Mohammedanism imposed on the Persian's life-loving soul. Nothing could more eloquently express the spirit of this rebellion than the epitaph, lightly inserted in one of his most joyful poems, over Hafiz's tomb. "When thou passeth the head of our tomb," it reads, "pray for inspiration. It shall be the place of pilgrimage of all the libertines of the world."

Though the glorification of the personal life and of personal bliss is a perennial theme of the Shiraz poets, there is no lack of social purpose or spiritual elevation in them. If ever a fighting progressive movement sweeps Persia, its leaders, should they be so minded, can cull from Hafiz alone many a brilliant verse for use as an inspiring slogan of the moment. Hafiz sings of the good life to which, in his view, not the select few but all men and women are born. He spurns the ideas and the usages that have cloven mankind into hostile or exclusive groups and societies. Indeed, hearing literary Shirazis and other literary Persians discourse on Hafiz as a social prophet—which aspect of his writings, they say, Western literary critics have ignored or underestimated—was one of the most stirring experiences I had in the Land of the Lion and the Rising Sun.

Shiraz is a city of 130,000. Despite its poverty, the worst I have observed anywhere, it is one of the liveliest and most agreeable cities in Persia. Rimmed around with mountains, its very setting seems intended for the literary capital of the country. Only a mile outside, one comes on all manner of wild life—boars, deer, jackals, leopards, and other beasts as well as a variety of birds. The cypresses of Shiraz are noted the world over. Tall, straight, and dense, with superbly shaped branches, they often rise with a cathedral-like splendor above the desolate streets. Its roses are as beautiful and as fragrant as in the days of the poets, and the nightingales still build their nests in the gardens. The incomparable climate—high elevation, invigorating air, brilliant sun, cool night breezes from the mountains—adds to the charm and the geniality of the city.

The people of Shiraz are more unbending and more vivacious than those of any city of the Middle East I visited. Rare is the woman who veils her face. Here is one city in which the mullah's effort once more to enshroud women in the funereal black *chadur* appears barren of results. As illiterate as the women of Isfahan and Tabriz, they yet resist the exhortations to conceal their faces from the light of day and from the sight of strangers.

They are the purest of Persians. Nowhere else in the country will the foreigner observe such comely women. "Dress our girls in European and American clothes," said a young editor, "and what beauties they would be." Even in their wrinkled, often ripped and patched cotton dresses, and their bare feet, they charm the passer-by. Poverty has not tarnished their clear-cut features, their large, luminous dark eyes, and their exquisite white teeth, nor dampened the vivacity of their expression.

27

In no other city did I see so many women engaged in trade. Most of these traders are peasant women from nearby villages who come peddling fruit and vegetables, eggs and sheep's-milk curds, or city women selling toilet articles and other pretty wares. The men of Shiraz, unlike those of Rasht, Tabriz, and Isfahan, regard it neither a social transgression nor a defiant intrusion on masculine privilege for women to compete with them in business. I paused and stared when I passed an elderly woman, her hair freshly hennaed, puffing a cigarette and crouching over a little stand cluttered with gimcrackery. Not even in impious Teheran had I observed so open a defiance of social convention by a woman of her years. Even the professional prostitute in Shiraz does not affect piety by draping herself in a black *chadur*. Confidently she approaches the foreigner and with a coquettish smile requests a cigarette, which, even as in Europe, is her way of proclaiming her profession.

Despite its ancient glories, the beauty of its natural surroundings, the liveliness of people, the city is facing the severest crisis it has ever known. Its onetime affluence has dried up almost as completely as the waters in the Ruknabad River of which the poets sing with such rapture. Some twenty years ago, when the late Riza Shah closed the port of Bushire on the Persian Gulf, he signed the death warrant of Shiraz prosperity. Older people speak longingly of the days when traffic to and from Bushire passed through the city, bringing with it a surge of activity that kept the population, except its throngs of habitual beggars, busy and contented. Having cut off the chief source of its livelihood, the relentless Shah, himself a sturdy northerner, was so preoccupied with the modernization and enrichment of the North that he did nothing to lift Shiraz out of the distress to which he had callously condemned it. There is talk in Shiraz and in Teheran of reopening the port of Bushire. So far nothing has happened. Nor is anything so promising likely to take place in the foreseeable future. Nowhere else in Persia is the former Shah remembered with such hatred and execration.

To an outsider it becomes manifest that the local citizenry—
the landowners and the merchants in particular—must share
some of the blame for the misfortunes of the city, no less than the
late and ill-willed Shah. It is true that they are more public-
spirited than the wealthy of other communities: by their own
efforts, and largely with their own money, they undertook the
broadening and repaving of the main avenue and the installation
of a new water system. But they have not begun to exploit the
resources of the province. With a population of two million, Fars
is one of the largest and, in agriculture, richest domains of the
country. Blessed with a superb climate—mild winters in the
north, year-round sun in the south, and frost nowhere nipping
the earth for more than two months of the year—the province is
like a garden. There is hardly a crop that cannot be grown in
luxurious abundance—wheat, barley, rice, cotton, sugar beets,
and the choicest of fruits, including oranges, figs, dates, and even
bananas. The one overwhelming obstacle is the lack of water.
This at least is the universal lament.

Vision and enterprise could long ago have effectively removed
this obstacle. In spring, water streams down from the mountains.
In winter, the rains are often heavy. So far little has been done to
impound and conserve the spring and winter flow for the long
rainless season. There is also water underground—how much
nobody knows, for no geological survey has ever been made.
During my visit to Shiraz the British engineers who had been
engaged to install a water system drilled the first well. It proved
a gusher, spouting forth at the rate of twenty thousand gallons
an hour, pure water that any city might covet. The water has
always been there; nobody had ever made an effort to bring it to
the surface. Of Shiraz, as of so many other parts of Persia, it may
well be said, "Water, water, everywhere, nor any drop to drink."

Beggars swarm the streets of Shiraz. There is no respite from
them and their appeals for mercy. Here are not only the lame,
the halt, and the blind, but fathers with sons, mothers with

daughters, women with broods of little children, and hosts of boys and girls of school age, with shining eyes and melodious voices and a cheery, real Shirazi disposition. They all must beg or die. Of the fifty thousand persons classed as workers, less than two thousand are employed in factories, three thousand (twice the number necessary) work in government institutions, some thirty-five thousand eke out a dismal existence in home industries, and the remaining ten thousand, according to the information of the Labor Department, are without any source of livelihood.

Despite the matchless literary tradition and the passion for poetry of the people of Shiraz, not more than one tenth of the population is literate. There are only two motion-picture theaters in the city and one amateur theatrical group, composed of educated youths, which now and then stages a production. The combined circulation of its eight journals—weekly, semiweekly, and one issued three times a week—is a little over thirteen thousand. The several lycées—high schools—in the city are the only institutions of higher education. There is no college. The Anglo-Iranian Institute, sponsored by the British consul, is the chief promoter of the culture of the modern world. One of the busiest institutions in the city, it has not, like the Institute of Isfahan, been transformed into a rich man's club. The library and the social rooms are open to all members, whereas in Isfahan students and schoolteachers who cannot afford the high dues of regular members may make use of the library but are barred from the main social lounge, where entertainments and lectures take place.

Shortly after my arrival, a group of young men, graduates of the British Anglican college in Isfahan or of the American Presbyterian college in Teheran, arranged a garden party for me. They spoke English and French and were well versed in Western social movements and in Western culture. One of them, a tall, sturdy, and handsome youth, was a city magistrate. The son of an

eminent family of Teheran, he had resolved, he said, to enforce
the law without favor to anybody, friend or foe. He would have
no traditional Persian corruption in Shiraz. But when he caused
the arrest of two high-finance officials for embezzlement of
public funds, two of their friends, citizens of some eminence in
the city, called on him. They requested first and then demanded
the immediate release of the embezzlers. Neither cajolery nor
threats of retribution nor fistfuls of notes offered as bribes availed
them. The offenders, the young magistrate insisted, must stand
trial. If innocent, they would be released. If guilty, they would
suffer the full penalty the law prescribed for the misdeeds of
which they were accused.

Indignant and angry, the callers left, threatening vengeance.
The threat materialized a few days later in the form of a com-
munication the young magistrate received from the Ministry of
Justice in Teheran, informing him that he was transferred from
Shiraz to an obscure town on the Persian Gulf. Outraged at the
success of his enemies, the young crusader journeyed to the capital and enlisted the aid of his highly influential father and of
another public-spirited citizen. The vigorous protestations they
made to the Ministry of Justice resulted in the annulment of the
transfer. "That's what we young law graduates are facing all the
time," he said. "Men of wealth and power who have friends in the
Cabinet want the old evils to go on, so they can get still richer and
still more powerful. But some of us stand up against them, and
lick them, too."

"Only some of them, and how rarely," said another young
man, a close friend of the magistrate.

When the party was over, this young man and I went walking.
It was still much before midnight, but the streets, which a few
hours earlier had thronged with promenaders, were now as deserted as a village. Only pariah dogs skulked around, and here
and there on a street corner a beggar or a party of beggars still
loitered about.

"Yes," said my companion, "Shirazis go to bed early, there is so little entertainment. After they have had their promenade they go home and go to sleep. There is nothing else for them to do." He was not happy about it, but it was the truth.

We talked of books and foreign countries and finally drifted into a discussion of religion. He had studied in both the Anglican college at Isfahan and the Presbyterian college at Teheran. He had read books on Christianity, read and pondered them and often discussed them with his Christian teachers. But he preferred to remain a Moslem. It was a great religion, and Westerners did not really understand it. It drew no color or race distinctions. It made men charitable toward one another, for almsgiving is one of the main tenets of the faith. A man could commune with God anywhere without benefit of priest or mullah. God would heed him and bless him. Moslems were not beholden to priests, and that was good: they could think for themselves. He did. He prayed five times a day. Whenever he was busy with his duties in the office and missed the noon or afternoon prayer, he made up for it afterwards. The Moslem faith permits the recital of two prayers together, one immediately after the other. He had never yet missed the prescribed number of prayers, any more than the ablution before sitting down to a meal. Yes, he was happy to be a Moslem, very happy, and when he had been ready to be married, he had not deviated from the orthodox custom of using a relative as a matchmaker. He had seen the girl he wanted to marry, but had never spoken to her or been introduced to her. He knew her family, she knew his, their fathers were friends. When he told his father he wanted to marry her, the father gave his approval. His mother had died when he was young, so his father consulted another woman, a relative, and she acted as matchmaker. The girl and the family accepted the proposal and they were married. "Sounds odd to you, doesn't it?"

"Did you love your wife," I asked, "when she came to live with you?"

Solemnly he answered: "To tell the truth, I didn't know whether I loved her. I wasn't, as you say, crazy about her. But from day to day I loved her more and more, and now we are happy, very happy, we couldn't possibly be happier. That's not the way marriages are arranged in America, I know. I went to the American college and during the war years I met many Americans, and I have read American books. In your country young people know each other well before they marry. But"—and with the innate decorum and sensitiveness that is natural to the highly cultivated Persian, he went on—"please do not feel offended, for I intend no offense—are your young people happy? Is your Christian system so superior to ours? Why then have you so many divorces in your country? I can assure you, I'll never divorce my wife. I'd sooner die."

We walked on under a brilliant moon, while a chill wind blew from the mountains. For some moments my companion was silent, nor did I speak. I pondered the difference between Persians and other Moslems in the Middle East. Here in Shiraz, as in Teheran, Isfahan, and Rasht, Persians, when one made friends with them, were engagingly and astonishingly frank. Their talent for self-scrutiny and self-criticism was matched only by the eloquence with which they expressed themselves. At the party which I had attended, the young intelligentsia of the city, in the midst of the gaiety and the revelry, were as if sitting in judgment of their city and their people. They related incident after incident of shocking malefaction, perpetrated not by the poor and the ignorant but by the elite and the powerful—by officers, gendarmes, merchants, high government functionaries.

"Do you know something?" my companion resumed. "Good Moslem as I am, I never go to the mosque."

"Why not?"

"Because I don't like the mullahs. There are exceptions, to be sure. There is one in Shiraz, a close friend of mine, one of the saintliest men in the world. He is a real priest, a great priest, modest, kind, moral, and noble. But he is an exception. Maybe in all Shiraz, of the hundreds of mullahs, about five, six, at most a dozen are good men, wonderful men. But the others——" He paused as though the subject was painful to discuss or as though he felt impelled to restrain himself in the presence of a foreigner.

"I wish you'd continue," I said. "I haven't met an educated young man in your country who has your religious fervor. Usually the educated young men cease to be religious. Am I right?"

"It's true of most of them, yes, it is. And I tell you the mullahs are to blame. Have you ever read the Koran?"

"Not carefully," I said.

With heightened emotion, he said: "The Koran, such a wise and wonderful book, says that if a man fears that he is unable to treat all his wives—at most four—with equal justice, which means in everything, in food, shelter, clothes, gifts, yes, and in intimate relationships, he should marry only one. And do you know what an authoritative commentary says? I'll tell you in my unliterary English: 'This is conditioning a legitimate act to an impossible situation,' which is another way of saying that it is illegitimate."

"Finespun logic," I said.

"And so true. No man can possibly love really more than one woman, and do you think our people don't know it? They do. We are an intelligent people and there isn't much polygamy in our country. But mullahs should be the last people to forget the Prophet's words and the Mohammedan commentaries. But they do; not all, of course. Even if a few of them marry more than one wife, or divorce an older wife for a young girl, or take a *sighe*— a contractual wife for a limited time—in addition to the women they have married, they set a terrible example for our young people. They are not good Moslems and they are so greedy and hypocritical. They don't mind falsifying things, telling poor people fanatical stories which never do anybody any good. That's why I don't go to the mosque."

Again we fell into silence. There was nothing I could say, and I waited for him to resume the conversation. Presently he did.

"Do you know something else? I am seriously thinking of leaving the country."

"Where would you go?"

"Anywhere. Australia maybe, South America, your country, Canada—anywhere. You see, it is all so discouraging here, so terribly discouraging."

He was a brokenhearted young man. There are many like him in Persia. Some of them flee abroad and never return. Others flounder about, talk, argue, hope, and long for a return of a popular movement like Tudeh, but one divested completely of Russian and all other foreign influence. They would join such a movement. They would fight for such a movement. But it must be an all-Persian movement, dedicated to the redemption of the Persian people. Still others get tired of fighting and hoping, and they succumb to the ways of their fathers, their uncles, their cousins. They live their own free and dissolute lives, with no thought of anyone else, least of all of the public good.

We shook hands and parted, and as I walked along a deserted street I heard the whine of an animal. I glanced around and saw a little brown-coated puppy with a white star on its face, struggling to rise out of a small pit into which it had fallen or been dropped by someone who wished to get rid of it. Near by was a pool, and had the dog succeeded in scrambling out of the pit, it might easily have fallen into the pool and drowned. I lifted it and held it in my hands and wondered what to do with it. Looking around, I saw only a few steps away a legless beggar sitting on the sidewalk beside a charcoal fire, sipping tea. I walked over and, with aid of gestures and the few words of Persian I had picked up, asked if he wanted the puppy. I had no hope he would take it. In a country where there was no love of dogs, it was too much to expect that a beggar would adopt a homeless puppy.

The beggar thought and thought, and offered me a cup of tea. And then he called aloud. Out of a dark, cellarlike room came a man, yawning with sleep. He introduced himself as the beggar's brother. He took the puppy and caressed it, exchanged some words with the beggar, and then disappeared inside the cellar.

35

Soon he returned with a piece of Persian flap-bread and offered it to the puppy. The little dog bit at the bread but could not eat it—it was too hard. I knew the Persian words for meat and milk, and I asked if he had any of those to give to the puppy. He shook his head and, accompanying his words with expressive gestures, indicated he had no money to buy milk or meat. He was only a workingman and his brother a legless beggar. I gave him some money and he bowed and thanked me and with words and gestures assured me he would take care of the little animal. I left wondering whether he would be as good as his word. Poor as they were, I thought, it would be easy for them to keep the money and do away with the puppy.

The next evening I stopped by the cellar. As on the previous evening, the beggar was sitting on the sidewalk beside a charcoal fire, drinking tea. He recognized me and smilingly pointed to a little pile of rock against the wall of the cellar which was his and his brother's home. Under the pile, in a little house that was built for it, the puppy lay fast asleep. Again the beggar called and the brother came out. He greeted me and pointed with pride to the little house and to the sleeping puppy inside. I gave him some more money and left.

Several days passed and I thought no more of the incident. On the morning I left Shiraz, as I was on my way to the bus station, I remembered the puppy and strolled over to find out what happened. Lying beside one another on the bare sidewalk, the beggar and his brother were asleep. Near by, with a string for a leash, tied to a hook in the cellar door, was the puppy. Visibly larger than when I had picked it up, it lay there, curled up and as sound asleep as its masters.

There was a farewell party and a "little entertainment," as my host expressed himself, of a sort in which Shiraz specializes—a concert in Persian poetry. The entertainers were two Jewish youths from the city, one a baritone, the other a tenor, the one strumming a *taar,* the other beating with his fingers a *donbak* (a

Persian drum made of walnut wood with a vaselike neck, a keg-like body, and a goatskin tightly drawn over the bottom).

There are about two hundred such Jewish performers in Shiraz, and their specialty is singing the odes and lyrics, the romances and the epics of Saadi, Hafiz, Nizami, Omar Khayyám, and other poets. The performers at this party, though untutored, were excellent musicians. Their repertoire seemed inexhaustible. It appeared strange that, though they had lived in Persia over two thousand years and had completely assimilated the Persian tongue and culture, Jews should be the only professional singers of Persian poetry in a city like Shiraz, the literary capital of the country.

When I asked my host why no Iranians cultivated professionally the art of singing, which must not be confused with the art of reciting classical poetry, his reply was illuminating. "Some of them are beginning to do so," he said. "But you must remember that even in Shiraz we are Moslems, and the Moslem faith bars the use of the musical instrument, while the Jewish faith doesn't. So the people don't learn to play instruments as in your country. Education is changing all this, but most of our people have no education. Besides, Persians, as you know, look down on professional entertainers. It isn't considered a respectable profession. But Jews are different. They love music and poetry and they don't think it is a disgrace to be professional entertainers."

For over two hours the young Jews sang and played with a pathos and a fervor that communicated itself to the listeners, including myself, to whom the language and the melody were equally alien. "You have to be a Persian to understand what our great poetry means to us," whispered a young lawyer. "It makes us so happy and so sad."

One need not be a Persian to feel admiration for a people who, despite misfortunes past and present and despite the dark uncertainty that broods over their land, cherish an abiding love for the men who lived long ago and composed the most exquisite poetry of their day.

CHAPTER III

Power in the Saddle

"SO YOU WANT TO GO AND VISIT THE KASHGAIS?" said Hussein Kashgai, one of the four brothers who rule the tribe and whose family has for a long time borne the tribe's name. Educated in England and Germany, Hussein spoke excellent English and German. He was in Teheran representing his tribe in Parliament.

"Yes," I said, "I am going to Shiraz, and I'd like to make a trip to your tribe."

I had heard that the Shah was averse to Americans visiting the Kashgais and had told the brothers not to invite or encourage Americans to go there. I wanted to make certain that there would be no political interference with my journey to Firuzabad, in the province of Fars, which is headquarters of the tribe. Without confirming or denying the story of the Shah's protestations, Hussein said:

"I'll arrange it. When do you want to go?"

It was like a Kashgai chief to dismiss as irrelevant the possible opposition of the king. Teheran and Firuzabad are enemies that speak to one another when they have to, and fight one another with guns when speech fails. The Kashgais have not forgotten the forcible attempts of the father of the present Shah to suppress the tribe. He had arrested and jailed their father and older brother, Naser Khan. In prison, one evening after a meal, the elder Kashgai, in the presence of his son, who was his cellmate, curled up and died. The brothers are convinced their father was poisoned. Nor was so unheroic a method of taking the life of an enemy an uncommon practice in Persian court circles.

In the summer of 1946 the Kashgai tribe had its fierce revenge. It staged an uprising against the Teheran Government. The tribesmen fought so successfully that they overpowered the regular army of the Shah, which was neither large nor strong in the province of Fars. After a three-day battle they seized the port of Bushire on the Persian Gulf. They moved up to Kazaroon and captured it and then marched up to Shiraz. They drew a ring around the capital of the province of Fars and would have seized it had not the inhabitants appealed to the oldest brother to spare them the agony of an occupation.

They were fighting, the Kashgai spokesman said, to compel the Teheran Government to put an end to the Azerbaijani rebel regime and to wrest from it concessions for the province of Fars, in return for the high taxes its population were paying to the capital. Whatever the origin and the instigation of the Kashgai rebellion, the tribesmen's triumph over the regular army was as painfully distasteful to the Teheran generals as to the young Shah. Reinforcements which the Teheran Government had sent might have defeated the tribe, even as Riza Shah had done, but for some mysterious reason Teheran chose to come to terms with the Kashgais.

On my arrival in Shiraz, a representative of the tribe called and we agreed on the time for the journey to Firuzabad.

When we arrived there after a hair-raising automobile ride over narrow and precipitous mountain roads, I imagined myself, more than I had in any place I had yet visited, thrown back to biblical times. I was away from cities, from factories, from machines, from all the mechanical paraphernalia of modern civilization. I was in a land of sun-scorched desert, of tents and sheep. Rings of mountains, overlapping one another, rose on all sides like gigantic fortresses. No doubt the leaders of the tribe had chosen this particular country for the excellent military advantages it afforded. A sudden invasion, whether by another tribe or by the regular Persian Army, was as impossible as the sudden leveling by human power of the gigantic mountain ranges.

There are about two hundred thousand tribesmen, and they spurn the appurtenances of modern civilization, the plow as well as the home. They live now as they did centuries ago, and as did the Hebrew tribes in the days of Abraham. They are as primitive as they are picturesque, as unshakable in the emulation of their own verities and virtues as they are inhospitable to the voices of the outside world. With their flocks of sheep, their donkeys, their camels, they wander in the direction of the sun— to the Persian Gulf in winter, and back north in summer, over a distance of four hundred miles. They must always have sun for themselves and grass for their flocks, even if only the prickly and withered camel's-thorn.

As I observed the men on their spirited horses, I thought of their rebellion a year earlier. Warrior-like, every man had a gun slung over his shoulder, ready for any emergency, and their horsemanship made me think of the Russian Cossacks. They were in complete mastery of the spirited steeds they were riding. Now and then I heard a gun go off. There is game all around, jackals, boars, wolves, leopards, wild birds, and the Kashgais are passionate hunters. When they get bored with tent life, they mount their horses and take off for their favorite sport. That is why they cherish their guns more than any gift within their possession, and as long as they have guns, not only Teheran but Moscow, London, and Washington must take cognizance of their presence in the Persian land.

Daring horsemen, crack marksmen, devout Moslems, they regard themselves, despite the Turki dialect they speak, as among the truest sons of Persia. Nothing riles them more than the charge often flung at them in Teheran that their exclusiveness and their possession of arms stamp them as Persians in name only. Invariably they hurl back with pride the retort that no other group in the country is more ready to lay down its lives for the Persian fatherland. Their perpetual quarrel with Teheran, especially over disarmament, on which issue they have only partially compromised, is only one of the internal vexations with which the unhappy capital is beset.

Yet the tribesmen look neither wild nor uncouth. Uniformly lean and hard, with piercing dark eyes, their sun-scorched faces bring vaguely to mind the American Indian, with whom they have no blood relationship. Though unlettered, they are extraordinarily courteous. They speak in low, measured voices, like men to whom refinement is a natural gift. Since I had come to the reservation with one of their leaders, they treated me as a guest, with marked magnanimity. Any pleasure within their power—a gun, a horse, a hunting trip in the mountains—was mine for the asking. The home of Naser Khan himself, oldest of the brothers, who was in Teheran at the time, was opened for me—a newly built cottage in a grove of date palms and orange trees, adorned with precious rugs and stocked with European liquors and a kitchen service rivaled hardly anywhere in the country.

Since I had come to acquaint myself with the life of the tribesmen, I preferred to visit among the black half-open tents and observe how they lived. I had no more than stopped at the first cluster of tents than I perceived a gulf as immense as the mountain barriers I had crossed, separating the Kashgais from the civilization of the rest of Persia.

A delegation of tribeswomen was starting for the home of a bride, carrying gifts from the bridegroom. The bearer of the gifts was a tall, stately woman attired in a resplendent costume. Balanced on her head was a large parcel neatly wrapped in gaily colored cloths. A crowd of lively children followed in her footsteps, and a brigade of older women, likewise garbed in ornate costumes and mounted on sprightly saddle horses, was her official escort.

I watched the festive procession make its way over the sun-baked, breeze-blown desert, and I marveled at the freedom which the Kashgai women were enjoying. Nowhere else in Persia did I observe women of their age riding, and riding saddled mounts, at that. Only a few of the younger and more emancipated women in Teheran indulge in the sport. The Kashgai women made a brilliant sight, and they radiated a stateliness and self-confidence that are utterly alien to the overwhelming mass of women in the Mohammedan world. They seemed a symbol of a type of civilization Persia long ago lost and has not yet recovered. The mountain fastnesses that girdled Firuzabad and that clove the sky with their bleak barrenness protected the tribe not only against a military invasion but against all mullah dispensation and intimidation.

I walked around the tents, bare of furniture but stacked high with hand-woven rugs. With pride the women unrolled the rugs, and the gay hues gleamed in the brilliant sun with a beauty that was expressive of an appreciation of nature which I had not observed in the peasant villages. The women were as open-faced as in any Western country and mingled with men inside and outside the tents with no less freedom. A wedding feast was in preparation, and while the men built fires in big holes in the earth, poured water into huge, smoke-blackened copper kettles, and skinned the freshly slaughtered and blood-dripping sheep, the women seemed only too happy to have a stranger in their midst and to exhibit before him the precious things they had fashioned with their own hands. They talked animatedly of their work and their life. There was neither diffidence nor aloofness about them. The children, barefooted and unwashed, clustered about their mothers, the little ones clinging to their skirts, and quietly listened to the talk. Neither in their movements nor in their speech did the women disclose the lethargy that weighs like a pall of darkness over the Persian villages in the very province of Fars in which they were living. Sunny-natured and sunburned, they gloried in their femininity, and the very style and color of their dresses testified to the pride and enthusiasm with which they sought in their own fashion to enhance and embellish their appearance.

"It seems incredible," I said to the Kashgai leader who came with me from Shiraz, "that these are Moslem women."

He translated my words and they all laughed.

Of course they were Moslems. They would fight for their Moslem faith with no less fierce a passion than any Arab. But the Kashgais, it seemed, never permitted the Moslem compulsions and austerities to obtrude into their original folkways. Mullah power and influence got stranded somewhere in the gorges and mountain passes which one must cross to reach the Kashgai country. The one book the Kashgais carry with them in their wanderings is the sacred Koran. Those of them that are literate can read it in the original Arabic, because there is slight difference between the Arabic and Persian alphabets. The sacred book sanctifies the home, even though home may be only a tent of hand-woven black cloth. It is a protection against the evil spirits that haunt the earth. But though they cherish the Koran, they will interpret its teachings in their own way. They have no mullahs in their widely scattered outdoor colonies, most of which at the time of my visit had already started their migration south. They will go to the mullah in some nearby village for the performance of an indispensable rite. They will have their Moslem faith on their own terms and none other.

Though the Moslem faith permits four wives to a man, monogamy has been the Kashgai creed and practice, and not even the khans, wealthy as they may be, would impugn the one or violate the other. Nor do they readily avail themselves of the masculine prerogative in the matter of divorce. Triumphantly, leader after leader assured me that divorce had been nonexistent or rare in the tribe for three centuries.

One reason the Kashgais do not like to see their women marry outside the tribe is that they might be divorced, and the brothers and fathers would feel it incumbent on themselves to avenge the insult. That would mean bloodshed. Men, however, do not disdain to marry outside the tribe. Nor is there a ban on it, though its practice is quite infrequent. Only the eldest of the Kashgai brothers is married, and his wife, despite all his worldliness, is a Kashgai woman.

Early marriage is the rule. Girls younger than sixteen often become wives, though boys rarely accept marital responsibilities so young. A widow rarely remarries, and then only the brother of her deceased husband. The unmarried man is such an anomaly that when I met one, a high functionary with a somewhat modern education, I asked him why he was single. "Because," he said, "I want to be free." When I pressed him for an explanation of his concept of the word freedom, he cheerfully explained, "With me it is a choice between a wife and a gun, and I prefer the gun." He was neither light-minded nor facetious. A passionate hunter, he chose to remain free from marital bonds so he could indulge unhindered the hobby he loved.

Every family has at least one gun and usually one horse, and every boy and man is as skilled with the one as with the other. Though women ride, they rarely shoot. Their domestic duties, which include help in the tending of the flocks, crowd their time.

I had the fright of my life when, passing a bride's home outside which lingered a crowd of tribesmen, the young Kashgai who was with me fired twice in the direction of the crowd. I expected someone to fall dead and to find myself embroiled in a shooting affray. But the burst of smiles and shouts from the crowd attested not to condemnation but to acclaim of this demonstration of exuberance. Puzzled by the action, I asked my companion, "Why did you shoot?" "For fun," he said. "We always do it when there is a celebration."

With rare exceptions, the Kashgais are good enough Moslems to abstain from alcoholic drinks. Otherwise the faltering hand might easily convert the fun into a funeral.

The Kashgai women indulge their love of bright colors at every opportune occasion. Their gay-colored kerchiefs are bordered with gleaming coins that jingle melodiously as they walk. Their necklaces are shiny with beads, blue, green, red, yellow, and with more coins, now and then of gold. Their long-sleeved, ample waists and their long skirts, puffed out by an assemblage of petticoats underneath, are reminiscent of women's dress in the peasant villages of central Europe. Indefatigable workers, they do their own designing, and they are among Persia's most skilled rug weavers. Possibly it is because they live so much of the time in bright sun, wintering in the South and summering in the North, that they are given to flashy ornateness, though merchants who buy their rugs for American export sometimes complain that the colors are too loud and too gaudy for American taste.

Because they follow an outdoor life and are usually in a sunny climate, they are among the healthiest people in Persia. Neither typhoid nor smallpox plagues them as much as they do city or village folk. Malaria, which is Persia's number-one scourge, is nowhere endemic among them to the degree that it is among the peasantry. Nor is trachoma, which causes so much blindness in the country. Venereal ailments are likewise much less prevalent than in towns. But tuberculosis is frequent. The hardships involved in the journeys over mountain passes, and the storms that often blow over them, with strong winds and violent rains, render the tribespeople susceptible to the ravages of this disease.

Among the Kashgais there are none of the nervous and mental derangements that are so much in evidence in the highly organized modern community. Their appetites are hearty and simple. Their wants are elemental and limited. Sugar and tea are the greatest luxuries, and they rarely have enough of either, principally because some of the chiefs who receive the rationed allotments for the tribe dispose of the coveted commodities in their own way and for their own enrichment. When I asked a khan if there was any suicide among them, he stared at me puzzled and somewhat bewildered, as though I had heaped insult on him and the tribe. "Of course not," he said. "Why should there be? Men do away with themselves because they are disappointed in love or because they are in trouble. Our Kashgais suffer neither from the one nor the other. And when a tribesman is in trouble his khan or his relatives or his neighbors will come to his rescue. If he is poor, someone lends him a few sheep and he starts life anew. He never starves." He did not add that the impoverished or improvident Kashgai often makes forays on peasant villages and obtains by loot what he may have lost by misfortune.

Unencumbered by the irritations and frustrations which the machine age has brought in its wake, the Kashgai considers so unnatural an act as self-destruction both monstrous and absurd.

Because the Kashgais, like some of the other tribes, are among the hardiest people in the country—natural fighters, with "war in their blood," as a Kashgai khan expressed himself—American advisers counseled their acceptance into the gendarmery officers' schools. That would have been a means of merging their fighting strength with that of the regular police and eventually that of the national army. But Persian generals would not venture so risky a measure. They do not trust the tribes and more particularly the Kashgais, the mightiest of them all. They are conscripted neither into the army nor into the police. They are their own army and maintain their own fighting strength. They wage their own wars for their own aims and purposes. They are a state within a state, a formidable little state of their own.

During my stay in Shiraz, I was invited by a descendant of one of the oldest families to tea in his garden, one of the most beautiful I saw in a land that prides itself on its beautiful gardens. It was a pleasant occasion, and once more I was impressed by the great gifts cultivated Persians possess for civilized companionship, luxurious living, brilliant conversation, and aesthetic appreciation of nature. Only after I had bidden my youthful and highly educated host and hostess farewell did I learn that, a few hours earlier, their home had been raided by a party of Bahramjats, one of the most undisciplined and lawless tribes in Persia. There are about fifty thousand of them in the province of Fars, and they make frequent forays both on villages and on the wealthy residents of Shiraz. The raiders had somehow broken inside the high-walled compound and had looted precious possessions and for fun smashed furniture and shot bullets into the mirrors before which they posed to see their reflection.

"Our host did not want to disappoint us," said one of the guests who drove me to my hotel. "Otherwise he would have called off the party."

"Do such raids happen often?" I asked.

"More often than we like to think," was the reply.

All over the province of Fars, as one drives along the highways, one must stop at barriers—a pole or a barrier of rocks across the road. From a lone mud hut atop of which floats the Persian flag, a gendarme or several of them, with guns on their backs, come out to inspect the traveler. They are ever on guard against smugglers and against bandit tribesmen who infest the mountains of the province. The bandits make automobile travelers their chief victims on the highways, because only people of means travel in automobiles. Travel at night in the province of Fars is always a danger.

The only exception is the Kashgai country. Other tribesmen will not venture into Kashgai territory without permission. They know that they cannot escape pursuit and discovery however deep in the mountain country they have their lairs. Kashgais would murderously avenge the insult of an attack in their territory by outsiders. Kashgais themselves, though the best disciplined tribe in Persia, do not disdain to raid villages. The Kashgai brothers, two of whom were educated in England and Germany and one in the American college at Teheran, emphatically deny that their tribesmen engage in plunder, but too many citizens in Shiraz dispute the assertion for it to be accepted as valid. The only time I ventured into night travel in the province of Fars was when I stayed in Kashgai territory or was traveling with Kashgais who always carry their guns with them. No tribesman, however desperate, would dare touch a Kashgai, especially a khan.

"Have you any hospitals?" I asked a Kashgai leader.
"No."
"Any doctors?"
"No."
"Any schools?"
"No."
"Any radios?"
"No."
"I suppose it is even absurd to ask if there are any cinemas among you," I finally said.
"Quite right, we have no cinemas."

Yet some Kashgais do obtain an education. The man with a large flock of sheep will engage a tutor for his son or sons, though not for his daughters. The sons may go to town, may even be impelled to leave the tribe, but daughters remain with fathers and mothers and marry into the tribe, and, according to tribal belief, neither need nor want any education.

Kashgais are barely aware of the outside world. They know nothing of and care even less for the diplomatic scrimmages in their own country and in other lands. They are content to be left alone. There is not much in their life to ruffle their nerves or upset their equanimity. They have their songs and sometimes even musical instruments. But music is not a talent they have cultivated with marked enthusiasm or even relish. Marriages are an occasion of gaiety, and the celebrating sometimes lasts fifteen days. Nor do they bother about cemeteries. When a Kashgai dies, he is buried somewhere on a height so that the sun will always warm the earth in which he is interred.

Though unlettered, they glory, as do all Persians, in poetry. The *Shahnamee* (Book of Kings), by the poet Firdausi, is their favorite literary work. Many of its celebrated passages they know by heart. The vivid descriptions of battles, the legendary powers of real and imaginary national heroes, the passionate spirit of patriotism rouse their imagination and their fighting spirit.

"Last year," said a Kashgai leader, "when we were fighting the Persian army, some of our women stood by the side of the men in the mountains and chanted heroic passages from the *Shahnamee*."

"Weren't they afraid of getting killed?"

He laughed. "Not our women."

From faraway America a new influence has already made a deep inroad into one ancient aspect of Kashgai civilization—men's clothes. For centuries the Kashgai men wore their distinctive garb: a long, loose-fitting, light-colored smock with a voluminous white cloth loosely tied around the waist. Now they are taking with a vengeance to pieces of khaki American Army outfits and to secondhand American business suits. The American clothes, they say, are much lighter in weight, fit the body more snugly, and permit much freer movement on horseback, whether pleasure-bound, hunting, or fighting. The tight-fitting light brown felt hat, with upstanding flaps which flutter like the wings of a bird when a Kashgai horseman is galloping, is the only outward mark of tribal identity to which they still uniformly cling.

It would be easy for an outsider like myself to become romantic about so primitive and so lusty a tribe as the Kashgais. Theirs is a free life. Hugging the earth, living off nature in its rawest state, away from the complexities of modern civilization, with wants few and simple and amply gratified, their life has its compensations. "It is so wonderful to be with them at night," a British journalist rhapsodized. "Above are the moon and the stars and below the desert is agleam with the little fires on which the women cook the evening meal. It is an enchanting sight." One need be neither poet nor painter to become enraptured with so idyllic a scene. Yet with the world what it is, with science and the machine age pressing directly and indirectly on all primitive peoples, and with nations arrayed against one another as unreasonably and as vehemently as ever before in all history, one wonders about the future not only of the Kashgais but of the other tribes in Persia.

In the absence of reliable figures, it is reasonable to assume that, out of Persia's population of some sixteen million, between three and four million are tribesmen, a comparatively small number of whom have been tamed and acclimated to a sedentary or settled life. The others are still pursuing a nomadic existence, and the effort of the former Shah to break down their tribal exclusiveness and to integrate them into the nation's social and economic life has borne but scanty and bitter fruit. It has inflamed a fresh resentment against the Teheran Government and against the gendarmes and the army, which were the instruments by means of which the late Shah strove to coerce the tribes into an abandonment of their nomadic existence. There is no state of war between the national government and the tribes, but neither is there a state of peace. The tribes pay no taxes and do no military service. Though they are the best fighting men in the country, Teheran never can depend on their loyalty. With bribery and corruption deep-rooted and with international intrigue rife, agents of foreign powers that may seek advantage for themselves can contrive ways to stir up tribal rebellion and make it an instrument of their own policy and their own desires.

Wise statesmanship combined with a policy of firmness may heal the political breach between the national government and the tribes. Appeal to their martial spirit may in time make loyal soldiers out of them, provided of course that army officers are restrained from the custom of squeezing bribes out of rank-and-file soldiers and from subjecting them to punishment and humiliation for failure to pay bribes. Army-minded as he is, the young Shah, with or without the aid of foreign advisers, may integrate the fighting and adventure-loving tribesmen into the army.

More difficult of fulfillment is the breakup of their nomadic existence, with all the havoc it brings to the land. Their sheep and their goats, grazing in the open the year round, have been among the most predatory destroyers of forests and watersheds. Reforestation is impossible, because sheep and goats nibble saplings to death. As long as the tribes live off their sheep and their goats, a large part of Persia is doomed to erosion and agricultural stagnation. Millions of acres have already been despoiled even of grass.

Fresh from my journey to the Kashgai country, on my return to Teheran, I searched out Naser Khan, the oldest of the Kashgai brothers, the real leader of the tribe, and the only one with no modern education and no knowledge of foreign language. When I asked him what future there was for a tribe so primitive as the Kashgai, whose name his family bears, he said:

"You have traveled in our country. You have seen how our people live. Don't you agree that the Kashgais are better off than the average Persian? They are free. Their women are not repressed. They are healthier than any people in the country. They fear nobody, neither landlord nor gendarme." (All of which was indisputably true: a gendarme would find himself with barely enough breath for flight were he to attempt extortion in the Kashgai country.) "When our country reaches a stage of development which offers the plowman all-steel plows, electric lights, doctors, hospitals, good homes, good water, and freedom from police arrogance, then it will be time for our people to think of settling down."

"But they live such a wasteful life," I argued. "Think of the millions of acres of land which they use up for grazing only, land that might grow wheat and barley, fruits and vegetables, and think of the sheep that die because of the strenuous wanderings and the lack of veterinary care."

In Teheran I learned that at least two million sheep die annually in the country. This is about one tenth of all the flocks, and the monetary loss, conservatively estimated, is twenty million dollars.

"Quite true," was Naser Khan's answer. "We have no veterinaries for our sheep and no doctors for our people. Herbs and roots are the medicines our tribesmen chiefly use. A lot of sheep die. A lot of people when they get seriously sick do not easily recover. But we have no beggars in our midst. Our old people are never left at the mercy of fate. Their children always care for them. When our girls marry, they know it is for life. Their husbands can neither send them away nor cast them off."

There was no disputing Naser Khan's words—the easy, adventurous, indolent life of the tribesmen, free from the frets and frivolities of civilization and the repressions of the hated gendarmerie, is infinitely superior to the bleak existence of the peasantry.

Yet even as the American Indian succumbed to modern civilization, so in time must the Kashgais and the other tribes of Persia.

CHAPTER IV

A Rice Village

"PERSIANS DO NOT NEED TO BE TAUGHT COUR-tesy," said a foreigner who had lived in Persia for over a generation. "They are born with it."

I thought of this observation when, accompanied by a young Persian, scion of an old landlord family, who had graduated from Cambridge University, I drove into a courtyard in a Caspian village, a "rice village." Two sturdy and barefooted girls, who were flailing a sheaf of grain in front of the house, instantly stopped working. Hurriedly they brushed the dust off their faces, tidied up their red kerchiefs, and greeted us with a smiling and embarrassed salaam. Our arrival was unannounced, and like farm girls in a European village when "company" suddenly appears, they grew conscious of their dowdiness and fluttered away.

As if from nowhere, a band of children loomed up before us, the cleanest and healthiest I had seen in a Persian village; the little girls wore tiny strings of green beads in their ears. They all welcomed us with a loud, sprightly salaam. For them, precisely as for children in a European village, company from the city was an adventure, and they would not conceal their delight in greeting us. Bright-eyed, with lively expressions, they stood

55

around, silent but not overawed, and listened to the conversation, the little girls as intent and as composed as the boys.

Presently the father came out of the house, a slender-bodied, alert man, with a thin, brownish stubble on his face, and once more we were greeted with a dignified bow and an air of respectful solemnity—the hand over the heart, as is the fashion of Persians. The mother followed with still another salaam, cheerful though diffident.

Soon the two girls reappeared, their faces washed, their hair combed, their kerchiefs neatly tied. Each carried a chair, a piece of furniture the family never uses and which is reserved for special occasions such as a visit of the *rowze-khan,* a religious performer who comes to mourn the martyrdom of Ali and his sons, beloved heroes of the Shiite Moslems, or a visit of the landlord and his friends or of strangers like my companion and myself. The mother whispered something to the girls. Smilingly they nodded and once more disappeared, but not for long. Soon they came out, one bringing a little table which she set before our chairs and the other glasses of tea. Hardly had we exchanged a few words with the man of the house, when the mother, who had gone indoors, came out again with a honeydew melon carved into large and gleaming slices.

There is more than sentiment in this ancient rite of hospitality. There is sense and logic in it. A sip of tea and a bite of food break down the barrier of strangeness and create an atmosphere of friendliness between host and guests. A pleasurable ceremony, it facilitates acquaintanceship and the flow of conversation.

Everything around me was in marked contrast to the villages of the South. Here in the region of the Caspian Sea was the richest subtropical vegetation. Fruit trees and shade trees, gnarled and untrimmed, thick with foliage and heavy-limbed, lined the immense courtyard. Fences were not of mud but of reeds and brush. Houses were not lumped together, but scattered over the large estate and concealed one from the other by groves or rows of trees. Space was no problem and every family enjoyed all the privacy it might seek.

The house which we were visiting could have been devised only by a people who must domicile themselves at little or no expense. In all my wanderings in "less civilized" countries, I had never seen a house so simple and yet so intricate, so practical and so picturesque, so secure and so cheap. Mud, timber, rice straw, reeds from nearby swamps, all close at hand, all cheap or free of cost (completely free, including the timber, in this village), were the materials that went into it. These materials were spliced and dovetailed, plaited and caked together without nails or even wire. Peasant architecture could not have been more ingeniously contrived or more skillfully executed. It bore further testimony to the Persian peasant's love of creative work and to his talent, despite his poverty and ignorance, for making the most of the tools and materials at his disposal.

Actually the house was a double dwelling, one part for summer, one for winter. The one was an enormous open shed, with a pointed thatched roof reaching to within a few feet of the ground. Inside and in the center of the shed, which hung umbrella-like over it, was the other house, a low square mud hut. The living space under the thatched shed was an immense veranda below and an equally immense balcony above, both outside the mud hut and connected with one another by a narrow ladder, hand-hewn from a log. Here in summer the family ate and slept, entertained and celebrated. Here it prayed. Nowhere was there a screen or a partition. Air and light flowed in from all sides, and so did insects, particularly the anopheles mosquito, which infested the surrounding swamps and streams and the drenched rice fields. Consequently, this was a malarial village, like all the villages in the Caspian region.

Nowhere did I see any furniture—no tables, no chairs, no beds, no benches—only handmade mats and hand-woven rugs on the floor. Nor was there a sign of a stove. None was needed. The cooking was done outdoors over an open fire. Here was a summer camp rather than a summer home.

When I walked inside the living room of the mud hut, or

winter house—the only other room in the hut was for storage of rice and other food—I looked up with a start. The mud ceiling and the walls immediately below it, as well as a cagelike platform made of sticks which was suspended from the ceiling, were so black and shiny they seemed as if freshly dyed with tar. But there was no smell of tar, there was only the smell of smoke.

"Where does the smoke come from?" I asked.

Pointing to an open stone grate by the door, my English-educated companion said, "Here in winter they build the fire, and the smoke"—pointing to the ceiling—"goes up there. That's why it is all so black."

"Why," I asked, "cannot they bore a hole through the wall and put in a pipe, so the smoke can blow outside?"

The man of the house, his hand ever over his heart, was interested in my question. He smiled with good-humored amusement. Of course he could have bored a hole in the wall and built a little chimney of mud bricks and rock, through which the smoke could blow outside. But the smoke was precious. Did I see the little cagelike platform? That was where the rice was cured. Without smoke, how could anyone cure rice?—A pertinent question from a man to whom rice is the staff of life for himself and his family, and who, generation after generation, century after century, follows the ways of his fathers, for he has learned no other, has heard of no other.

In such a mud hut, furniture would be neither useful nor decorative. If people sat on chairs or slept in beds, their heads would be in smoke, and the furniture might turn the color of the ceiling. Only because the custom is to squat and sleep on the floor is such a dwelling habitable.

The women—and not only those in this house—were among the most impressive I met in any Persian village. Here they were, the Ghilani women of whom I had heard so much. They had excellent white teeth, particularly the girls, and their eyes, oval and long-lashed, were shining with animation. The light-haired, blue-eyed woman was no exception, as in Shiraz. They seemed as openhearted as they were open-faced. They lacked neither in grace nor in decorum. They were personalities in their own right, and despite the Moslem faith, they were keenly aware of it. If they talked less than their men, it was because after all, even in Ghilan, the man was master of the household. He attended to all the business transactions with the landlord's agent. He visited nearby towns and bazaars more frequently than they. He picked up more news and gossip of the outside world than ever reached their ears. He might even be in a teahouse when some literate neighbor read aloud a newspaper. He himself might be able to read. Though less worldly than the men, the women were demonstrably aware of their dignity and self-respect.

And well they might be. The most arduous work on the land falls to them. Since rice is the chief source of food and of income, the amount and character of the work they accomplish in the rice fields confers on them both authority and prestige. How arduous the work is I learned on investigation. The mode of tillage and the implements used have not changed in at least a thousand years. The plow is a framework of flat sticks converging to a diminutive, round-edged shovel as a point. It is so light that I could lift it with one hand as easily as I could a campstool. Such a plow can dig up only a thin slice of earth. The field, therefore, is first flooded with water. After it is plowed, it is again flooded. With another implement, which looks like a scoop, the lumps of earth are ground up and churned until the field is deep mud.

With this preliminary cultivation over, the women appear on the scene and supersede the men. Earlier, sometime in April, they have seeded the rice, in a small separate plot of land, "as thick as hair on a dog's back," as an American missionary expressed himself. By the time the fields are prepared, the rice shoots have sprouted and are ready for transplanting. Wading more than ankle-deep in mud, the women set out the shoots about six inches apart. Barefooted and barelegged, there is no escape for them from the malarial mosquito. Often leeches are washed into the field from nearby ponds and ditches and they attach themselves and suck at the exposed legs. The women fight the leeches as they fight the mosquitoes, but the work never stops. No man can set out the rice shoots as deftly as the women. Rarely do they even try.

During the growing season the rice is weeded at least twice. Again the women go to the fields, and they stoop over each plant and pluck up by the root every sprig of alien growth. That is why the rice fields look so clean. When the stalks ripen, they go out with sickles and reap the rice and bundle it into sheaves. After the sheaves have dried in the sun, the women load them on their heads or shoulders and bring them home. Sometimes, if they have a horse, they carry the sheaves home on the horse's back. Neither wagons nor carts—nothing, in fact, on wheels—are known.

"Is there any polygamy in this village?" I asked the landlord's agent.

"Not much," was his answer. "But sometimes a man feels he needs another worker in the rice fields, and he will marry an additional woman."

"What does his first wife say when he brings another wife to the house?"

"Oh, she tries to stop it. She weeps and she screams, and sometimes she runs away to her parents. But she always comes back."

"Is there much divorce?"

"Hardly any. Our Ghilani women are such wonderful workers, men cherish them too much to divorce them, and they treat them very kindly."

"You won't find another village like it in all Ghilan," said my companion. "People are quite well off here—that is, in comparison with other villages."

"Even in comparison with your villages?" I asked.

"With *any* villages," he answered.

In confirmation of his words, he pointed to the road over

which he had driven to the village and which, several miles beyond, connected with the main highway. It was a dirt road, narrow and winding, and it cut through a dense and swampy jungle. "Now," he said, "neither spring showers nor winter rains completely isolate this village." In other villages all over Ghilan, roadlessness alone shuts off all association with other human beings for weeks and months. The abundant rains, which are a blessing for the fields, swell the streams so high that even where there are roads, bridges are never built, and the villagers are cut off from towns, hospitals, doctors, druggists, whose services they might desperately need in an emergency. Such villages are little islands of humanity, left to their own resources and their own helplessness. That was why the road to this particular rice village, though narrow and rutty, was so real an advantage to the people. "The landlord built it," my companion said. "He is a fine man, one of the most benevolent landlords in all Ghilan."

Outward signs of well-being were not wanting. Particularly striking was the dress of the peasantry. Few save the children were barefooted. None was in rags. Some wore low shoes, others low rubber slippers. Nowhere did I see the hand-woven *ghives* (sandals) of the South and only rarely the traditional tight-fitting felt caps. The men wore tailor-made caps with black cardboard visors; some of them paraded around in American business suits which they obviously had bought in town from merchants who specialized in secondhand American clothes. The women draped their heads in light-colored kerchiefs or wore *chadurs,* leaving their faces uncovered. The veiled face has never been a custom in Ghilan even as in villages everywhere.

Though the peasants received only half of the rice crop, they enjoyed privileges which substantially augmented their income. The garden plot—like all the land they farmed—was part of the landlord's estate, but the landlord claimed no share of the garden produce. The long, thick clusters of shiny onions and of garlic, favorites with Persians who prefer pungent foods to sweets, came from the garden. So did the tomatoes and the cucumbers, the beans and the eggplant. So did the honeydew melons and the pumpkins, each fitted into its own little net suspended from a rafter or a pole in the overhanging shed, where it would keep fresh during the winter months.

Wild berries and nuts grew plentifully all over the estate, and the peasant and his children might pick all they choose without offering a share to the landlord. Firewood from the landlord's forest was likewise free. Pasture was no problem—the untilled acreage was large and free, summer and winter, for the peasant's cow to forage in. Hardly a family but had its own cow.

There was wild game in the forest, and the game the peasant hunted and shot with his ancient long-barreled gun was his. Boars, which came down from the hills and mountains into the rice fields, were hunted with particular enthusiasm. Were it not that the Moslem faith bars the use of their meat, each family could provide itself with much of the fat it needed from the boars the men shot. Disdaining boar meat, the villagers left the carcasses for vultures and beasts to feed on. But there was partridge and pheasant and other wild fowl, and their meat provided a feast on special occasions.

I knew the landlord of this village. I had met him during the war years at a New Year's Eve party in Teheran. A cultivated gentleman with a fluent command of English and French, he talked at length of the improvements he had introduced in his villages. They were real enough in comparison with what other landlords had done. Nor was he completely an absentee owner. On the steep bank of a stream he had built a two-story brick house with a tin roof and spacious balconies. He made frequent visits to the village, alone or with friends to go hunting. He was not there during my stay. But on the bulletin board of the bazaar there was a handwritten announcement stating that he would soon arrive and would be glad to listen in person to any and all complaints.

As landlords go in Persia and all over the Middle East, he was one of the most understanding and benevolent I have known. He had built a school, a white-painted brick building, and some of the children, fifty in all, were now offered the opportunity to acquire a rudimentary education.

Yet even this village, with all the special advantages the peasants were granted, was symptomatic of the agricultural stagnation that lies like a hand of death over the Persian land. There was not a wagon or a cart, anything on wheels, nor the sight or the sound of a machine. All the work except the plowing was done by hand.

"How large an acreage of rice can the average family cultivate?" I asked the landlord's agent, a hard-faced, taciturn old man.

"One hectare," was the answer, or 2.47 acres. "Rice requires a lot of work." It does indeed, because of the utterly ancient methods of tillage.

Rice is the peasant's bread in this part of Iran. The reward of his year's labor he measures by the amount of rice he receives more than by any other income or produce. A bumper crop in this village, with its exceptionally lenient landlord, would yield as his share—a half of the harvest—between thirty and forty bushels. Some of it he sells to pay for kerosene, if he buys any at all, and for tea and sugar—or raisins—or to pay off an old debt to a shopkeeper or a moneylender. By early spring, especially if his family is large, he is likely to be without rice. He must borrow again or starve. Interest on loans in the countryside are the highest in the land, 100 per cent or much higher. Regardless of the favors granted him by his landlord, the peasant, even in this village, is rarely out of debt.

"Where do they get the money to buy the good clothes they wear?" I asked my companion, who, I wish to remind the reader, was himself a large landowner. He laughed.

"A most interesting question," he said. "They are American clothes and they are secondhand. They sell very cheap in Persia. You have no idea what secondhand American clothes have done to dress up our people." He laughed again. "That's something we never got from any other nation," he added. "Usually foreign nations squeeze things out of us."

Cheap castoff American clothes have been a blessing for the people, but not for tailors and seamstresses, nor the country's textile merchants and manufacturers. There have been demonstrations by tailors in protest against further imports, so they can again have customers—not demonstrations by the fashionable tailors in the Lelazar, whose customers order the finest clothes made anywhere, but of the tailors who must cater to earners of small incomes.

"So your peasants are always in debt?" I said.

"Always, in this village, in my village, all over Persia, most of them are always in debt," he replied. "I should say that roadlessness, debt, and malaria are the chief curses of our villages."

In this village over 90 per cent of the population suffered from malaria, and only a few could afford such a simple medicine as quinine.

There was such an abundance of wild berries in the vicinity of the village that I inquired if any of the women made jam. My question elicited amusement. "For jam you need sugar. Where would our peasants get money to buy sugar for jam when they haven't enough for their tea?"

There was such a charm about this village—the forests, the subtropical vegetation, the streams, the hills, the singularly impressive though utterly primitive houses with their huge overhanging thatch sheds; above all, the simplicity and the dignity of the people—that, some weeks later, in the company of a young man who had graduated from the Presbyterian college in Teheran, I paid it another visit. It was a bazaar day when we arrived. In an open field itinerant peddlers and shopkeepers had set up tents and stalls, teashops and little restaurants. Crowds, festively attired, the women in bright colors, surged to and fro among the alleys and pathways of the bazaar. Girls looked enviously at the gaudy displays of trinkets and necklaces, of textiles and leatherware. They walked around in twos and threes and in larger groups, without boys, or with boys following behind but refraining from talking to them, yet both eagerly exchanging furtive glances and covert smiles. Older women sat in little circles, sipping tea or just talking, loudly and with animation. Men, too, were grouped about, standing or squatting on the grass, talking and laughing, between sips of tea. There was nothing solemn about these people. Whatever their worries over debt, sickness, or other misfortunes, they did not bring these with them to the loud-voiced and garrulous bazaar. Here they seemed free from all anxiety. Though there were no side shows, as at an American county fair or a Russian market place, no musicians, no sorcerers, no puppet shows, no entertainment at all, the people were happy to be together, see one another, talk to one another. No books and no newspapers were on sale, and nobody missed them. More than 90 per cent of the crowd could neither read nor write. The Moslem faith bans alcoholic drinks, and these peasants scrupulously abstained, so that none were for sale. There was no drunkenness and no fights, no quarrels and no rowdiness, only the endless talk in which people with whom gregariousness is a virtue and a deliverance so joyfully indulge.

We walked around the village, and when we came to a grassy field in which a lone humpback cow was nibbling the grass, my companion asked:

"What do you suppose this is?"

"Pasture," I said.

"Look again."

I did. It was not a level field. It was studded with grass-grown mounds, and in a corner, in the shadow of a wild bush, I saw a freshly dug heap of earth.

"A cemetery," I said.

"Yes."

I surveyed it again. Save for an occasional stick over a mound, there were no mementos over the graves. The cow had kicked up several of the sticks. There were no flowers and no hedges, nothing but grass closely nibbled to the ground.

"How do people identify the graves of their dead?"

My companion smiled. He was born in an adjacent village and knew the people well. "Sometimes they know by the sticks, and if there are no sticks, they know anyway. They can smell out the graves of their dead."

Even as we were talking, a woman came to us, holding by the hand a pretty, dark-eyed girl, obviously her daughter. She wanted us to go and look at her house, which was falling to pieces. Sobbing, she told us that she was all alone with three little children. The landlord's agent had discharged her husband and he went to live with another wife in another village. He had propped up the overhanging shed with one pole, but the pole was sliding to one side. If it slid over all the way, the shed would crash down and she would have no house. "Come, please, and look at it," she pleaded. We followed her to the house, which was a few steps away. The roof was pressing hard against the pole. "If I had money I'd hire people to help me," she said, tears streaming down her face.

"Why don't you tell the landlord's agent?" said my companion.

"Ah, he!" She said no more, her silence more eloquent than words of her distrust and disdain for the agent.

"But maybe you will see the landlord," she resumed, with a flicker of hope. "He is a good man. He always means well by us. He is a gentleman and so kind. But he lives in Teheran, and how can I go to Teheran? Maybe you live there. Maybe you can see him. Maybe you can tell him." When my companion informed her he was not expecting to go to Teheran, she again broke into sobs. "What will I do, what will I do?" she repeated, shaken with grief and hopelessness. She felt consoled when we told her of the announcement in the village that the landlord would soon arrive and would listen to people's complaints and wants. "He is such a good man, he will listen to me, he will help me." We bade her good-by and left.

"They hate the agent here," my companion said. "He is an old man and people wish he would die, but he just doesn't."

We visited several of my companion's friends, and in the intimacy of their homes conversation was frank and surprisingly caustic. When I asked one of them if there had ever been a motion picture in the village, he said: "Yes, during the war the British consul showed a picture, only once, and from all over the countryside people came to see it. Three thousand people came, and they talked and talked and are still talking about what a beautiful thing it was."

"Wouldn't you like to see more pictures?" I asked.

"It would be nice, but——" He did not finish his thought.

"But what?"

"Some people mightn't like it. We might learn something."

"Who mightn't like it?"

He smiled and held his tongue.

"The agent?"

"Maybe."

"The landlord?"

"And maybe the landlord."

There was a neighbor in the house who had come to greet "the American," of whose presence he had heard from his little boy. When I asked what social diversions they had in the village, the neighbor quickly blurted out, "Our diseases." He was not bitter. He laughed as though he had told a jest, but there was no mistaking the implication of his words.

Yet another peasant, in answer to the question why there were no wagons or carts, nothing at all on wheels in so large a community, said, "You've been misinformed. There is one vehicle here, an automobile, for the landlord to run away in."

I did not expect to hear such sharp language about a landlord who was celebrated as one of the most benevolent in the province.

"They didn't talk like this," my companion remarked, "before the Tudeh party came here." The Tudeh movement[1] had col-

[1]The rise and fall of the Tudeh (People's) movement is explained in Chapter VI.

lapsed, but it was clear that it had stirred a deeper spirit of unrest than was perceptible to the casual visitor. No peasant would say he believed in the Tudeh party. After all, there was the "old man"—the agent—to think of. It was now dangerous even to whisper the word Tudeh. Even those peasants who spoke caustically of the landlord admitted they had no personal grievance against him. But he seldom came to the village, and the agent was always there and did as he pleased. If the landlord knew how rude the agent was, he might scold the old man—not discharge, only scold—because he was merciless in collecting the landlord's share of the crop. But who would voice a complaint against the agent to the landlord? Nobody would dare. The agent would always find a way of wreaking vengeance, and it was best to pretend friendship with him. He could shut off the water from the rice fields. Then what would they do? Of course, if the landlord was around all the time, he might not permit so pitiless a penalty on any of his peasants. But he was not around.

The Tudeh party had popularized slogans for a large increase of the rice crop, so that the peasant would be receiving three fourths of it. It had also advocated free medical service in the village, universal education, jobs for everybody so there would be no unemployment, and the expulsion of the hated gendarmes. Whoever the propagandists were, communists or non-communists, the language they spoke to the peasantry had evidently awakened thoughts and emotions that had formerly lain dormant. Nor did the Teheran Government remain indifferent to the promises and the commitments that Tudeh had loudly proclaimed. To allay unrest, it ordered landlords to increase the peasant's share of the crop by 15 per cent. Not all landlords have abided by the order.

When we left the village, my Persian companion said: "Ghilan is one of the richest of our provinces. We grow rice and tea and tobacco and jute and silk. We could and should grow more than we do, but we don't. We could grow excellent grapes, but we don't. Lots of land could be improved and cultivated, but the landlord does not care and the peasant has no incentive. We should work the rice fields with machinery as you do in America, but we don't. We should exterminate malaria, but we don't. The Government says it has no money, and the peasant is too poor, and the landlords would rather spend their income on good living in Teheran or in Europe or on the latest-model American automobile."

"What is the answer?" I asked.

"I don't know; I wish I did."

CHAPTER V

Shadows in the North

ARRIVING IN MIDSUMMER FROM TEHERAN AT Tabriz, Iran's second largest and second most important city, and the capital of Persian Azerbaijan, was a refreshing experience. The climate was more salubrious than Teheran's. The breeze at the airport was like a gift from heaven. The sun neither wilted nor scorched as in the capital. There was always a cooling stream of air from the mountains, and the nights were almost as chilly as in Montana.

I had never been in this northern city, and the people there struck me at once as being different from the Teheranis. They *are* different, not only in race but in physical make-up. More rugged, they are also more solemn than the citizens of the national capital. The Azerbaijanis, of the same blood as the people of Soviet Azerbaijan, speak not Persian but a dialect known as Turki. They are taller and larger-bodied than Persians, with broader faces, more massive shoulders, and a lighter complexion.

Their expression is more somber than that of Persians, their movements slower, and they gesture less profusely and excitedly. Thought diffident on first acquaintance, they are no less sociable and no less hospitable than Persians. They laugh easily and boisterously, as evidenced by their clamorous response to an ancient slapstick movie I attended in a stuffy and overcrowded theater. Again and again, as I was making the rounds of tea-houses, the audience would burst into spontaneous singing of a familiar tune which a local musician or orchestra might have started playing. Like Persians, they revel in poetry—in their own rich folk poetry and in the works of the celebrated Fozuli-Baghdadi and Haj Reza Sarraf, their most eminent poets. Beneath their somber exterior lurks a lively disposition, a love of talk and fun, which spills out of them when they get together in the city park or in the teahouses. They are also inordinately proud. Even beggars from Azerbaijan, when in Teheran or some other city away from their native province, will solicit alms chiefly among Azerbaijanis.

It was quite startling to walk along the streets of Tabriz and observe so many men, and sometimes women, wearing stylish or bright-colored American-made clothes.

"Where did you get them?" I asked a merchant of men's clothing.

"From America," was his cheerful answer.

Imagining himself face to face not with an idle curiosity seeker but an eager customer, he hastened to the racks and, unfolding coat after coat, pointed with pride to the labels on the inside and insisted I read them aloud. "American, yes?" he chanted every time I read the name of an American clothing manufacturer.

As in the rice village in Ghilan, all the suits were secondhand. American merchants in castoff clothes are evidently transacting a rushing business with Tabriz. As a lure to prospective custom-ers, dealers in women's secondhand American apparel displayed it outdoors on racks or on ropes tied to nearby trees. The splash of color in the midst of the dreary grayness of Tabriz was as cheering as the splash of verdure beside a flow of water in the blistering Persian desert.

The American Presbyterian Mission, which has been in Persia

since 1833, was another bright feature of the Tabriz social scene. A highly educated Persian woman in Teheran, who had studied in the American school in the capital, once said to the writer: "Your Presbyterians came to our country to save our souls, but they remained to save our bodies and liberate our minds." Neither the Presbyterian Mission in the North nor the British Anglican Mission in the South has achieved any significant triumphs in converting Mohammedans to the Christian faith. But the educational institutions of both missions, before they were outlawed in 1938 by the irascible and explosive Riza Shah, did not have their equal in Persia, according to graduates whom I met all over the country. In 1928 the New York Board of Regents had granted the American college in Teheran the right to confer the baccalaureate degree on its graduates, thus making them eligible for admission to American graduate schools. The closing of the American and British colleges has been a cultural loss which educated Persians are still lamenting.

The Presbyterian hospital of Tabriz is famous all over Azerbaijan. Dr. Charles Lamm, of El Paso, Illinois, is physician-in-charge and chief surgeon. He has been in Tabriz since 1913 and has acquired a fluent command of the native tongue. Patients come to him from all over Azerbaijan and the neighboring provinces of Ghilan and Kurdistan. One of the most distinguished surgeons in the Middle East, he was the first medical practitioner in Azerbaijan to realize the importance of a modern nurses' training school. He started one in the Tabriz hospital. Moslem parents at first would not permit their daughters to attend the school. The thought of their girls having to absent themselves from home all night disconcerted them, and the idea of close association with "infidels" was equally repugnant. But so remarkable has been Dr. Lamm's personal triumph with the population, and so implicit has become their faith in his personal and moral integrity, that now all the students are of the Moslem faith. The eighty graduates of the school are among the best professional nurses in the country. They are on duty in hospitals all over Persia, and they have attained special distinction as midwives.

In Search of a Future

In the thirty-four years Dr. Lamm has spent in Tabriz he has observed only slight improvement in the health conditions of the city. The water supply is still unsanitary. There is no chlorination plant. A sewage system is still only a dream. The public bathhouses, where many people bathe in the same tanks, are still a source of infection. The housing facilities of the poor are no better than they were a generation ago. Sickness—particularly eye diseases, smallpox, typhoid, and worms and other intestinal derangements—has not diminished.

Local citizens, including high government officials, concurred in Dr. Lamm's statements.

A native pharmacist with whom I became acquainted and who, like other businessmen in the city, spoke fluent Russian, related that often when sick people come to him for medicine he asks them whether they have worms. The reply invariably is, "Hasn't everybody got worms?" The unnatural condition is considered natural. "When I tell them they must wash the fruit and the vegetables they eat with potassium permanganate," the druggist said, "they say it would wash away the taste. They don't see microbes, therefore they don't believe in them."

No less industrious than Persians, the Azerbaijanis are famous for their skill in handicrafts, particularly the weaving of beautiful rugs and the manufacture of silverware and leatherware. Yet nowhere in Tabriz did I see such "Persian gardens" as in Teheran or Shiraz, with foaming fountains, murmuring waterfalls, tree-shaded swimming pools, and incomparably beautiful flower beds. Even the trees in the streets lacked the lushness of those in Teheran, not because of lack of water but because of neglect and apathy.

Compared to Teheran, Tabriz, which a generation ago was Persia's leading commercial city, is a heaving, sprawling village of nearly a quarter of a million, with not a tinge of beauty, not a glint of modernization, with only a beginning, tardy and diffused, of modern enlightenment. There is only one public library in the city. There are 843 telephones, and one daily newspaper of four American-tabloid-size pages, with a circulation of less than a thousand. There is one semiweekly journal of the same size, with an even smaller circulation, and there is one other publication which sees the light of day as irregularly as the caprice, the political passion, or the pocketbook of its editor-owner allows. Literacy and literateness are accomplishments which Tabriz, capital of Persia's most populous and richest agricultural province, is as yet in no mood to undertake and under no external pressure to emulate.

To me, fresh from Teheran and other Persian cities, Tabriz on first sight appeared an anachronism. Persian since the days of its origin, it bore a striking resemblance to a provincial Russian city of pre-Soviet days. The harsh and solid architecture on the main avenue, the clutter of slovenly shops that lined both sides, the leisurely manner of its unkempt shopkeepers, the rumble of droshkies—carriages for hire—in the streets, the style of the droshkies, the type of harness used, the scrawny horses were reminiscent of the provincial Russia of Chekhov's time. At the hotel where I stopped, guests might lug their own baggage to save expense, precisely as they do in certain provincial Russian towns to this day. The pastries in the bakeshops, the black or dark gray cap worn low as if pasted to the head, the gleam of samovars in the teahouses, the popularity of Russian dishes in the hotels were further reminders of Tabriz's Slav neighbor.

Like the shopkeepers, the droshky drivers spoke fluent Russian. Yet the Tabriz droshky driver is a breed all his own, with a pride and a dignity which the old-fashioned Russian *izvoshtshik* rarely manifested. He is too taciturn and too contemplative, or perhaps only too aware of his self-respect, to ask or answer questions, and he never bothers to drum up a multitude of excuses for coaxing out of a passenger a higher fare than he had agreed to accept. However long the drive, his charge within city limits is never more than the equivalent of forty cents in American money.

Nor are these aspects of Russification unnatural, in the light of Tabriz's geographical proximity to Russia and the booming trade it once transacted with Russian merchants and manufacturers. Solely because of this trade, a generation ago Tabriz was the nation's most prosperous city.

Closer observation disclosed that the Russian coloration is only skin-deep. The bazaar, with its enclosed alleys and labyrinthine passages, was as Persian as the artisans that clanged and clattered there with their tools. Away from the main avenue, the narrow and winding streets with their tall mud walls and the enclosed courtyards with their inevitable small, slimy pools, their spray of flowers, their scatter of shrubs and trees were equally Persian, as were the occasional flat roofs on which families gathered for the evening meal and for the night's repose.

What was even more startlingly indigenous was the Moslem piety of the women. The Tabriz women were once more embracing the old-fashioned *chadur*—the ungainly, loose garment which swathes not only a woman's body but her face, and which the late Riza Shah had ruthlessly ripped off women's backs. Not only older women but girls in their early teens draped themselves from head to foot in this shroudlike garb. Overwhelmingly the *chadur* was black, lending the city a funereal appearance, as though it were in perpetual mourning.

Tabriz has taken with a vengeance to other old practices that had been discarded. For the first time in a generation, and throughout Ramazan—the lunar month during which followers of Allah are forbidden to touch food and drink from sunrise to sundown—all restaurants, including those under Christian ownership, were ordered closed. Several Christian owners, faced with bankruptcy, went out of business. Others wondered what it might mean. They saw in it an evil omen, not only for themselves but for the Moslem population. It would drive business out of Tabriz, they lamented, and Tabriz did not have too much of it any more. There can be no doubt that the present administration of the city, in its battle against political recalcitrance, is seeking the support of the mullahs, whom Riza Shah had stripped of all political power.

Indeed, the mullah is stirring again all over Persia. Since the end of the war, while the national government has been tussling with international problems of immense magnitude and importance, the fanatical Moslems have feverishly been swinging Persia back to the Mohammedan austerities and the religious intolerance of the days before Riza Shah.

The campaign, at first secret, has become more open and more bold all over the country. It is prosecuted along two clear-cut lines: on one hand, the resumption of practices which the father of Mohammed Riza Pahlevi, the present Shah, had outlawed, particularly the *chadur* or the veil; on the other, the incitement of hostility toward "the unclean," "the infidels"—that is, Christians and Jews. Among educated Persians, who will have none of the old-fashioned repressions and discriminations, the campaign has elicited contempt and derision. It is known that the Shah frowns on it, and so do his two sisters, than whom there are no more urbane and westernized women in all Persia. But the movement backward has scored no small triumph among the uneducated masses who constitute 90 per cent of the population. It has been notably successful among the illiterate women of Azerbaijan and Isfahan, and oddly enough at times among factory workers.

During my visit in Isfahan the workers in one large textile factory had banded together and demanded the expulsion of the one converted Christian among them. The management was ready to accede to the demand, and only after the British Anglican Mission in the city, perceiving in the move a frontal attack on all religious minorities, appealed to the local authorities for action was the demand quashed.

More serious was an incident in a village outside the city of Shiraz, where there is a small Christian community of ten families. Instigated by fanatical mullahs, several busloads of Moslem men drove to the village. After working themselves up all night long by chants and ceremony into a state of emotional frenzy, they proceeded to round up the local Moslem peasantry and the mayor for a joint assault on "the infidels." Aflame with mystical ecstasy, the city Moslems were ready to burn the little church and the homes of the Christian communicants. Fortunately the mayor and the Moslem peasantry rose to the staunch defense of their Christian neighbors, and their resolute stand averted a pogrom.

At Rezayeh, the second largest city in Persian Azerbaijan, when the autonomous regime collapsed in December 1946, Moslem fanatics sacked four Christian villages and plundered a dozen more of the forty-three Christian villages in the district. When I visited Rezayeh, Catholic and Protestant leaders said their people were so frightened that they were ready to emigrate and were hoping some Christian country, in Europe or America, would grant them asylum. Even in Teheran's old section, which is inhabited largely by workers and petty traders, the dormant fanaticism is bursting into the open. During my stay there, posters appeared in the bazaar denouncing women who refused to veil their faces. In support of this campaign, some merchants refused to sell goods to "nude women," as they were called.

The situation grew so tense that women not clad in *chadurs* were barred from the bazaar mosque and were jostled off the sidewalks in the streets. Alarmed over these disturbances, an enlightened deputy prime minister summoned the police to halt the outburst of rudeness and intolerance. For the present all is quiet in the bazaar quarters. The disturbers have slunk into hiding. But the underground agitation for a return to old-fashioned Moslem orthodoxy continues unabated.

The educated Moslem clergy of Persia, the most progressive in the Mohammedan world, is as vigorously opposed to the obscurantist mullahs as is the secular intelligentsia. That the mullahs are receiving encouragement from high quarters is freely acknowledged by the more discerning foreign observers and by Persia's progressive intelligentsia. An army officer who had received a technical education in pre-Hitler Germany, after a mournful recital of Persia's social corruption and military weakness, said to me, "But we have one weapon we must cultivate. It is an unfailing weapon. It will save us a lot of trouble."

"What is it?" I asked.

"Religious fanaticism."

Maybe he was only speaking for himself, and maybe he was expressing an attitude that is being fashioned into an ironclad policy. Persian intellectuals whom I questioned on the subject laughed with scorn at efforts to whip up religious fanaticism. "That is one thing nobody can ever again resurrect in our country," a distinguished writer remarked. "But I must say," he added, "somebody is trying very hard to do it."

Yet nowhere else have the mullahs already achieved so enormous a following and so formidable a power as in Azerbaijan, particularly in Tabriz, where only eight months previous to my visit one of the most violent social eruptions in centuries had shaken the province.

A journey to the countryside of Azerbaijan offers a wealth of illuminating information on the nature and the meaning of that eruption. The largest and most populous province in the country, it spreads over an area of 35,000 square miles, and, including the Rezayeh territory in western Azerbaijan, embraces a population of about 4,500,000. The people are overwhelmingly peasants, of whom not more than one fifth own their own land. The province abounds in streams, and its great pride is Lake Urmia, four thousand feet above sea level, which is so saline that neither fish nor mollusks live in it. Studded with islands, the lake is over eighty miles long and between twenty and thirty miles wide, and is deep enough for motorboats and barges. Despite its muddy shore line, its swimming facilities and the picnic grounds near it are among the best in the province. Zoroaster is supposed to have been born in the vicinity of this extraordinary lake. The valley all around is perhaps the most fertile land in all Iran.

In Search of a Future

Unlike the arid South, water is no source of despair in Azerbaijan. The mountain streams and the rivers swell out of their banks during the spring floods, after the heavy snows have melted. More water than has ever been tapped lies underground at depths of from nine to thirty feet. The soil is rich and the province is Persia's largest granary. Without Aberbaijan's wheat and barley, Teheran could not feed itself. The wheat is excellent and the potatoes are the best in the country. A part of the Kurdish tribe, one of the largest in Persia, lives in the mountains. It is noted for its flocks of sheep. Sheep and not cows are the chief suppliers of milk and curds to the Persian population.

The grapes of Azerbaijan are famous. Nothing is more refreshing while traveling along the dusty highways than to stop at a vineyard and glut oneself with clusters of sweet green grapes. Peasants are friendly; the Christians especially, who are among the most skilled grape growers in the country, overwhelm the stranger with their hospitality.

The almonds in Azerbaijan are likewise famous. The apricots, when dried, constitute an important source of exports, particularly to Russia, and so do the raisins. Azerbaijan's tomatoes and melons—in fact, all its vegetables—are of superior quality and would be still better had the peasantry been made aware of the importance of select seed and been supplied with it. Though the province lacks forests, its orchards, especially on torrid summer days, are as refreshing as they are decorative. Nowhere else in Persia did I see such magnificent pears.

Yet what a dismal picture its agriculture and its rural life unfold. There is so little traffic on the highways that one travels for miles before encountering an automobile, a truck, or any vehicle. The dearth of wagons and carts is everywhere manifest. Nowhere did I hear the roar of a tractor, the whir of a threshing machine, the sound of any mechanical implement. Harvest was in full swing. Gathered outdoors in stacks, the grain was being threshed, and not even in biblical times could the process have been less ingenious or more wasteful. The most advanced method of threshing I observed used a spiked roller that a horse or an ox drew over the sheaves, the spikes tearing into the ears and shaking out the grain. Not even in Czarist Russia did the peasants of the Ukraine, Siberia, or the other grain regions thresh the wheat or barley so primitively.

Only around the town of Khoy were fanning mills in sight, not many and quite old-fashioned, with a difficult crank to operate them. They were probably of Russian origin and of ancient import. Usually the farmer scooped the threshings with a long-handled shovel and tossed them with all his strength as far and as high as he could, so the seed and the chaff and the particles of straw would drop in separate places. Such grain is never clean. Little pebbles, particles of dirt, and the seeds of weeds fall with the grain. When sown, the seeds of grain and weeds alike drop into the soil, and the crop is certain to be contaminated. It seemed unbelievable that a province so ideally suited to the cultivation of cereals, which are so badly needed in Iran, would be pursuing so arduous and so wasteful a mode of tillage.

The magnificent orchards were rarely pruned. Left to nature, the fruit, though of excellent size and quality, was at the mercy of insects and worms. The apples and the pears, shaken off the trees instead of being picked by hand, often get so bruised that rot starts by the time the fruit reaches the bazaars.

Because Azerbaijan is overwhelmingly a cereal province, it practices the same system of sharecropping that is pursued in other parts of Iran. It is known as the "five-fifths system": one fifth for the land, one fifth for water, one fifth for seed, one fifth for animal power, one fifth for labor. When the Azerbaijani peasant owns his work animals, he can count on receiving two fifths of the harvest. But since he is often obliged to eat up or sell his grain before planting time, the landlord supplies the seed, and as he also owns the land and the water, the landlord is in a position to exact three fifths of the crop. One of the most money-minded persons in the country, the Azerbaijani landlord lives off the income from his crops but far away from his land and his villages, usually in Teheran. The result is agricultural stagnation and a poverty-stricken peasantry in Iran's richest agricultural province, its most bountiful breadbasket. The ever-present moneylender adds to the peasant's woes. The crowds in the villages which I passed, always friendly to strangers, were often so ragged as to be indistinguishable from beggars.

During 1946, the year of the Azerbaijani autonomous government, only a few of the landlords dared to visit the province. Some of those who did openly supported the new regime, not out of sympathy for its program, but in the hope that they would be permitted for a few more years to collect their share of the crop. Now that the rebel regime is no more, the landlords have flocked back and assert their power over the peasant with a vengeful ruthlessness.

Though the Teheran Government has issued orders that arrears in grain deliveries are not subject to collection, the landlords persist in collecting them. Rare is the landlord who heeds this Teheran ordinance. The peasant is at his mercy. He has not the grain which the landlord demands of him, for during the rebel regime the landlord's share was taken from him by the autonomous government.

In the wake of the landlords, and often preceding them, have come the gendarmery or rural police, and like the landlords they seem to have learned nothing from the social tempest that rocked Azerbaijan and all Persia. Bribed by landlords, they unlawfully seek to enforce the collection of arrears in grain. In consequence, the burden of peasant indebtedness mounts higher and higher.

A young American diplomat who was making a journey through Azerbaijan by automobile had occasion to stop for the night with a peasant family. A short time earlier a gendarme had spent the night with the same family. Though the police officer, without cost to himself, had enjoyed the best foods the family had in its larder, on his departure he demanded two thousand rials (the equivalent of sixty dollars), a fabulous sum to any Persian peasant. There was no power the peasant could invoke against the gendarme, and the extortionate demand was somehow made good.

With the gendarmery and the landlords back in Azerbaijan, flouting not only the law but all sense of prudence, the peasantry is becoming increasingly restless, and the whisperings of underground rebels are certain to fan this restlessness.

"Our country," said a gifted Teheran writer, "is like a man who is sitting on a pot of gold and is starving."

Azerbaijan is a vivid demonstration of the meaning of these words. Once modern machinery and science were introduced, the farming lands of the province would bloom with harvests such as it never has witnessed. But the cash-minded landlords are preoccupied with immediate profits rather than with long-range benefits. More than ever they are disinclined to plow capital back into their holdings. Supposing a new rebel movement springs up, with or without Russuan instigation and Russian participation? The landlords would lose not only their lands but their investments in capital improvements. Why then should they squander ready funds on any improvements? So they forge on as they always have done, collecting their share of the crop, converting it into cash, and living their own good life in Teheran. As for tomorrow, have not their great poets exalted the good life of today? What has even the great and noble Hafiz chanted?

> *The house of hope is built on sand,*
> *And life's foundations rest on air;*
> *Then come, give wine into my hand,*
> *That we make an end of care.*

Or again:

> *Wake me not, I pray thee, friend,*
> *From my sleeping;*
> *Soon my little dream must end:*
> *Waking is weeping.*

CHAPTER VI

Storm Center in Asia

DURING 1946, TABRIZ WAS A STORM CENTER IN ASIA.
Drawn to it was the attention of the world, nowhere with such
alarming concern as in London and Washington or with such
hopeful anticipation as in Moscow.

The storm had been long in gathering. It started in the days of
the ironfisted Riza Shah who, side by side with his vigorous pro-
mulgation of the modernization of Persia, had throttled all freedom in the country. The building of new highways, a spectacular
railroad, and new factories had brought on the Persian scene a
new social force, the wage earner—or rather had increased his
numbers and his influence to a magnitude never before known.
So flagrant was the Shah's intolerance of labor organizations that
he forbade the use of the word "worker," which to him symbolized a person affiliated with an organization—a trade union—
that might challenge his undisputed absolutism. In its stead, he
approved only of the word "laborer." Violently anti-Russian and
anti-Bolshevik, his phobia against the word "worker" was also
a reaction against Moscow's insistence, particularly in the twen-
ties and early thirties, that the worker was the redeemer of mankind and the embodiment of the highest virtues ever attained by

85

man. The phobia was further intensified by his personal clash with the native Bolshevik leader in Ghilan, Mizra Kuchek Khan, who for several years, while in power in the North, had played up and dramatized the words "worker" and "proletarian."

With a relentless hand the Shah wiped out the few desultory labor organizations that had survived underground. As a reaction to this suppression, socialist and communist intellectuals, as well as laborers and liberals, formed a secret society to combat the Shah's absolutism. In 1937 fifty-three of them were apprehended and flung into jail, and others were exiled to remote communities in the southern provinces. The leader of the group, Dr. Tagli Erani, according to Teheran reports, was put to death by the injection of an air bubble into his veins in the Qasre-Qajar prison outside of the capital.

In August 1941, after the British and Russian troops moved into Iran, Riza Shah was deposed and exiled. The imprisoned conspirators were liberated. Among them was Sayed Ja'far Pishewari, who had been jailed earlier than the others, and who subsequently led the Azerbaijani rebellion. He had been imprisoned for ten years.

Anti-fascist and anti-German, the liberated political offenders, together with fresh recruits, formed in October 1941 the Tudeh (masses or people's) party. They founded a newspaper, *Mardom* (the *People*), and at first centered their fire on the pro-German groups that the deposed Shah had cultivated and encouraged. Tudeh drew into its ranks intellectuals, workers, peasants, and traders, and rigorously excluded the friends and supporters of the former monarch.

In October 1942, Tudeh started to organize trade unions. By the end of 1945, for the first time in its history, Iran had a solidly organized labor movement, under the leadership of the Federation of the Trade Unions of Iran. The federation embraced the workers of private and state-owned industries.

The compilation of statistics in any oriental country is a new science, and accuracy is not one of its virtues. Figures, therefore, only approximate the truth. After consulting all available sources, including the British and American labor attachés, I learned that the number of industrial workers in Iran is about 175,000, an insignificant proportion of the population, yet welded together by the Tudeh into the most powerful and most militant group in the country.

The federation frightened employers, landlords, and the government. The effective strikes in the Isfahan textile factories and in the Anglo-Iranian Company's oil fields convinced them that they were facing a power that might in time wrest from them political control of the country. They had never encountered anything like it. They therefore launched a counteroffensive. Because of the prominence of communists in the movement, they denounced it not only as communist but as Russian-inspired.

Had it not been for Pishevari, who, after the refusal of the Majlis to recognize his credentials as a deputy from Tabriz, returned to the capital of Azerbaijan and founded a party of his own—the Democratic party—an offshoot of Tudeh, the movement, according to the best-informed Iranian and foreign opinion in Teheran and in Tabriz, would still have been a powerful political organization. It had made striking progress. In 1943 it had elected its own deputies to the Majlis. A government crisis resulted in their being accorded three portfolios in the Cabinet—those of Education, Health, and Commerce and Industry.

The Minister of Commerce and Industry was Iraj Escandari, scion of an old and distinguished family. Even the most violent opponents of the Tudeh party would not accuse him, not even now that he is an exile in Europe, of dishonesty or of seeking to further the cause of a foreign power. A socialist, and a distinguished lawyer and orator, he was one of the fifty-three political offenders whom Riza Shah had imprisoned. One of the reforms he sought to promulgate was distribution of the land. He did not advocate outright confiscation. He proposed that landlords be remunerated for their lands in annual installments over a period of twenty years. With a landowning peasantry and an organized labor movement, Iran, he was convinced, could advance into the modern age and catch up with the civilization of the West by evolutionary methods, without dictatorship, without bloodshed, and with neither foreign guidance nor foreign intrusion.

Escandari's proposed land reform was cried down as revolution, equally harmful to peasants and to landlords. Spokesmen of the landlords insisted that the Iranian system of sharecropping, the "five-fifths system" explained in the preceding chapter, was one of the most equitable in the world and particularly beneficial to the peasantry. Escandari, according to his friends in Teheran, warned the Majlis, eloquently and passionately, of stern and ruinous consequences if the prevailing sharecropping system continued unchanged. His warnings were cried down as loudly as his proposed reform.

Having failed to achieve an agrarian reform, Tudeh was more successful in obtaining a momentous improvement in the conditions of factory workers. It was under Tudeh's pressure, and also with a view of winning labor away from Tudeh's influence, that the Council of Ministers, headed by the aged and most astute Ahmad Ghavam, passed on May 18, 1946, the new Labor Law, the most advanced labor legislation that any Mohammedan nation in the Middle East has enacted. It established the eight-hour labor day and 35-per-cent increase in pay for overtime work and for work during night shifts. It provided for a legal day of rest each week, on full pay, and for six legal holidays a year, on full pay. One of these holidays was May 1, the international labor day. It made annual vacations compulsory, on full pay—one week for six months of continuous employment in a factory, and longer periods for those who exceeded the minimum term of uninterrupted employment.

The new law banned the labor of children under thirteen, and the employment of girls under sixteen in restaurants and shops that did not provide special guardians for them.

Working women were accorded attention they never had

known. Factories were obliged to establish crèches for children. Mothers who nursed infants were to be allowed, every three hours during the workday, a half-hour leave, on full pay, for feeding them. Expectant mothers were to obtain a leave of six weeks before and six weeks after childbirth, on full pay, and half of the amount was to be granted by employers and the other half by the so-called Factory Aid Fund. No children under sixteen and no women were permitted to engage in heavy and hazardous occupations such as mining.

The right to belong to a union, to strike, and to engage in collective bargaining was a part of the new law, and a further provision banned the use of force or coercion in the recruitment of union membership and in the calling of strikes, though with not-too-severe penalties for violations.

The Aid Fund, which was derived from a one-per-cent levy on wages augmented by double the amount from management, was to provide for social insurance, health, unemployment, and old-age needs. The age of retirement was sixty (for workers in the mining and other hazardous occupations, fifty-five).

The Labor Law established factory councils made up of three members, representing labor, management, and government. The councils were to enforce the law and to settle disputes between labor and management.

The Tudeh unions had by their own efforts regularized and increased the daily allowances of free bread in factories and the annual allotments of free clothes—work uniforms as well as suits for everyday and holiday wear.

Mere proposal of the new law was a historic event in Persia. The Tudeh movement had become a power which inspired hope of a peaceful transition from Persia's age-old absolutism and feudalism to a modern progressive democracy. However anti-communist Persian intellectuals and foreign observers may be, those with whom this writer spoke in Teheran and in Tabriz emphasized that the Tudeh movement, despite all its failings, had aroused among the common people and a large part of the intelligentsia a spirit of hope and a sweep of energy such as Iran had not experienced since the golden days of Shah Abbas, 1587–1629. Of him the noted French traveler Chardin wrote: "When this prince ceased to live, Persia ceased to prosper."[1]

It was the events in Tabriz that ultimately led to the collapse of the movement not only in Azerbaijan but all over Persia. The complicated story of the rebel regime in Tabriz still awaits the impartial judgment of the historian. Both adherents and opponents of the regime, though they speak freely, are actuated by such violent passion that the foreign investigator feels lost in the tempest of emotion that spills over him from both sides. The events are still so recent that neither the pros nor the cons have sobered from their fierce partisanship. I have heard both sides in various parts of the country, but especially in Tabriz and Teheran. I have read documents in foreign embassies and have listened to stories and comments of foreigners who were eyewitnesses of the struggle. Out of this mass of conflicting testimony, often interlarded with sensational melodrama and hair-raising tales, the one conclusion from which neither diplomat nor historian can escape is that the Azerbaijani regime, examined in retrospect, must be viewed as the dress rehearsal of a real revolution. Though the movement is now shattered, the events of the dress rehearsal must continue to haunt leaders of the Iranian Government as well as the chancelleries of those foreign countries—particularly Russia, Great Britain, and the United States—that were particularly aroused over the battle between Tabriz and Teheran.

Forswearing any intent to separate from the Persian state, the Democratic regime which Ja'far Pishevari and his followers founded in Tabriz in December 1945 elected its own parliament, appointed its own cabinet, organized its own constabulary, collected its own taxes, issued its own laws, and maintained only a vindictively fictitious relationship with Teheran.

Russia supported the Azerbaijani regime, and the United

[1] J. Chardin, *Travels into Persia* (London, 1686).

States and Great Britain perceived in it a Russian-inspired attempt to rend Persia in twain and eventually perhaps to annex Persian Azerbaijan to Russian Azerbaijan, of which the oil city of Baku on the Caspian Sea is the captial.

Alarmed over the rise of the defiant regime in Tabriz, Teheran strove to effect a settlement. The intimate story of the negotiations between Pishevari and the leaders of Teheran has never been fully revealed. I spent a Sunday with the member of the Teheran Majlis in whose house Pishevari had stayed during his visit to Teheran for conferences with Ahmad Ghavam, then Prime Minister, and others. My host had no particular criticisms to make of Pishevari as a person. After all, Pishevari was a cultivated man, lacking neither in the cordialities nor the graces that are so distinguishing a feature of educated Persians.

But the negotiations collapsed. According to highly informed sources in Teheran, Pishevari had overplayed his hand. The chief bone of contention was his insistence that the army officers in Azerbaijan continue to hold the high ranks to which they had been promoted by the rebel regime. The young Shah was quoted to me as saying that he would rather lose his right arm than accede to this demand, which would lead to fierce jealousies between high-ranking Teheran and Tabriz officers and would only demoralize the national army. Had not Pishevari been adamant in this demand, an agreement could somehow have been reached. It might not have lasted. But it would have eased, at least temporarily, the conflict between Teheran and Tabriz and the international tension it had stirred. Such an agreement, I was further informed, would have been of immediate advantage to Russia, for it would have facilitated her drive for an oil concession in northeastern Persia. Tabriz, which favored the concession, would have been a power in Iranian diplomacy and would have used its influence to swing Teheran into an oil agreement with Moscow. How much truth there is in the report that Moscow was displeased with Pishevari for his failure to come to terms with Ahmad Ghavam the author has been unable to ascertain.

Since there was no reconciliation between Tabriz and Teheran, after a year's preparation Teheran dispatched an army to overthrow the Tabriz Government. On December 30, 1946, three days before the arrival of the Teheran forces in Tabriz, the Democratic regime fell to pieces. According to Teheran sources, Pishevari and other top-ranking leaders fled in trucks loaded with grain and goods to Russia, whose border is eighty miles away. According to Pishevari's friends, he is still somewhere in Azerbaijan. The truth probably is that he travels back and forth.

Leaders who failed to escape were seized by infuriated mobs and killed; others were court-martialed and hanged. Textbooks in Turki, which Pishevari had made the official language of Azerbaijan, were stacked and burned.

Thus an incident holding within it the tinder of a world explosion—for the United States, in this writer's judgment, was prepared to act had Moscow rushed military aid to the Tabriz regime—went up in smoke. Save for a few desultory skirmishes, Teheran triumphed over Tabriz without even a show of force.

Now not a shred was left of the Democratic coup d'état in Tabriz. The Teheran Government was in complete mastery of the city. As I wandered the streets I did not perceive any suggestion of brooding rebellion in the outward appearance of things. The disaffected part of the population was evidently biding its time. Tabriz was demure, perhaps sullen, and quiet. There was martial law in the city, but it did not obtrude into the sluggish course of daily events. There were not many soldiers in the streets, which attested to the government's confidence in its own authority and in its power of enforcing it.

Yet I could not help reflecting on the future of Tabriz and Azerbaijan, particularly as—according even to its most implacable enemies, including foreign observers—the Democratic regime had during one year of its existence enacted more reforms than the city had ever known. I heard harsh words, even from its friends, of the abuses of its power and of the terror it had fostered. It had frightened merchants away from the city, and business had slumped heavily. It was also accused of maintaining close relations with the Russian Consulate. But it had asphalted the four-mile stretch of road from the city to the railroad station. It had swept beggars from the streets and driven prostitutes from the city—nearly all of them. It had opened a maternity hospital and founded a university, the first Tabriz had known, with faculties in medicine, agriculture, and pedagogy. It had set up a radio station, and it had policed the city so efficiently that crime diminished and women could walk the streets alone after dark without fear of insult and molestation. It had started, though had not carried very far, a land reform. It had enforced the Teheran Labor Law as Teheran was no longer doing. It had effectively fought the opium traffic. It had simplified government administration by stripping it of inflated personnel.

Yet the swift collapse of the regime demonstrates that it failed to muster a sufficient fighting force to engage the Teheran army in combat. Only a short time previously the Kashgai tribesmen in the South met the Teheran army in battle and fought its garrisons into surrender. Eventually the Kashgais might have been defeated. But the audacity they displayed in challenging Teheran was significant.

Despite the smart uniforms of its officers, the Persian army, riddled with corruption, has no claim to any distinction of soldierly valor. Considering the superior physique and fighting qualities of the Azerbaijani people, who are of the same racial origin as the Kashgais and speak a similar dialect, had the rebel state won popular support, it might have won the fight or lost it with a display of dignity.

With all the help they originally obtained from the peasantry, the Democrats did not awaken their decisive or enthusiastic support. By collecting the landlord's share of the crop, they kept alive the suspicion that landlordism had not vanished. The Azerbaijani peasants drew no distinction between the landlord's agent and the representative of the Tabriz Government. While they were promised land, and in some parts of the province had actually received grants, they were still under obligation to pay tribute to outsiders. They could not count on the full crop for themselves. Like peasants the world over, they are excessively today-minded, and they judge a government by the failures of the moment rather than by the promises of tomorrow. Pledges of ultimate complete land reforms and of the importation of machinery and livestock with which to transform agriculture and enrich rural life had fallen on ears that were becoming increasingly deaf to eloquent rhetoric.

According to the testimony of some of the best friends of the rebel regime, it weakened itself still further by its failure to divest itself of the charge of Russian sponsorship and Russian support. The name Russia has evoked no warm sentiments among Persians any more than the name England. The memory of Czarist aggression has not died out, and the violent anti-Russian propaganda during the reign of Riza Shah had reinforced the historic antipathies and suspicions. Secret agents of the Teheran Government moved about in Azerbaijan and fed the flame of anti-Russian emotion and of the fear of Russian conquest. Russian radio broadcasts in support of Tabriz were of no help to Pishevari in combatting anti-Russian sentiment in the province. "People were worried too much about Russia," an Armenian shopkeeper in Tabriz testified.

The attempt of the autonomous regime to fan a separate national consciousness among the Azerbaijanis aroused no vigorous response among the mass of the population. Again and again invaded by outsiders, the province had always reverted to Persian sovereignty. Some of Persia's most eminent leaders and rulers had come from there. Had the rebel regime continued in power and succeeded in its economic and social program, it might have weakened or uprooted the traditional sense of Persian nationhood. But during the year of its power, it had utterly failed in this mission. The attempt to stir up a new national consciousness was like applying a torch to a water-soaked pyre—the flame failed to catch.

Tabriz was tranquil, but it was cheerless. Its economic distress was everywhere in sight. Beggars swarmed the streets. The unemployed wandered in search of work, of which there was none. A day laborer commanded a wage of three tomans (sixty cents), while a donkey earned from five to seven tomans. The scarcity of goods in the bazaar of this once-thriving city told its own sorrowful tale. Stalls and shelves were empty of the flashy brass, the gleaming silverware, the ornate textiles which once enlivened the very dimness of the enclosed alleys. Most of the traders seemed to specialize in secondhand ware—china, samovars, shoes, clothes, trinkets, toilet articles. In no other city had I seen so empty and desolate a bazaar.

Moneyed people refuse to make investments in new business enterprises. "Why?" I asked a merchant. "Because," was the reply, "Tabriz is only eighty miles from the Russian border and is linked with it by a Russian-built broad-gauge railway, and who knows what will happen tomorrow?"

Poverty and uncertainty haunt the Tabriz of today.

Ali Mansur, a former prime minister and one of Persia's most capable administrators, was governor general of the province when I was in Tabriz. Of medium height and slender build, with a lofty forehead, reflective, handsome eyes, and a mere sprig of a mustache over his broad, strong mouth, he admitted that the province which he administered was facing a severe ordeal. He was hopeful that the Seven-Year Plan, of which there was much eloquent talk in Teheran, would usher in a new day for Azerbaijan. Yes, its agriculture needed modernization. Its livestock had to be improved. But the people were the healthiest and sturdiest in all Persia, and with proper planning and encouragement, they could convert the province into a haven of prosperity. New industries would have to be developed—canning, textiles, sugar refining—to make use of local raw materials. The plans for

the regeneration of Azerbaijan were being drafted. Their fulfillment would require much capital. When it was made available,
presumably from America, the work would start in earnest.

Persians hailed the collapse of the Democratic regime as a
triumph of Persian patriotism. "Iran for Iranians!" became the
fervent slogan of the day and stirred a gush of national sentiment.
The visit of the young Shah to Azerbaijan was acclaimed up-
roariously. At last all threat of political and territorial cleavage
had disappeared. Foreign diplomats in the Persian capital were
happy. Here was a decisive victory of West over East, of America over Russia. Azerbaijan was not only free from Russian
troops but was liberated from an autonomous regime which was
an offshoot of the Russian Revolution and which, it was widely
declared, might, had it remained in power, eventually have de-
tached Persian Azerbaijan and annexed it to Soviet Azerbaijan
across the border.

But the happiness which foreign diplomats manifested is
rapidly waning. Neither British nor American representatives in
Teheran have reason to congratulate themselves on a lasting
triumph over Russia or over Soviet ideas. They know that, because of the default of the young Shah's government, the victory
is degenerating into defeat. Nor do they fail to inform London
and Washington of the grave actualities that are once more
sweeping over Azerbaijan. The indigenous causes which gave
rise to the rebel regime are, like the mountains of the province,
rooted in the land.

However vigilant the new administration may be against underground propaganda, the promises of full employment, of free
land, and of a happier life cannot but invite a sympathetic hearing in the dreary villages and the somnolent towns of the province. Deep in the mountains, squads and garrisons of the rebel
regime are yet active. Of the twenty-four thousand rifles that the
rebels were supposed to have had, only two or three thousand
have been recovered. The others presumably were hidden or carried off into the mountain fortresses which the rebels are holding.

Secret radio stations—two in Azerbaijan and one in neighboring Sanjan—are, according to the latest advices, broadcasting messages and propaganda to the people, in an effort to fan and inflame their spirit of restlessness and their rebellion against Teheran.

The Teheran Government hopes that foreign diplomacy and foreign—particularly American—military might will protect Azerbaijan from indirect and direct Russian encroachment, which to Teheran is synonymous with internal upheaval. But foreign military protection, highly implemented by the latest weapons of war, even by atomic bombs, may blow up cities and devastate farmlands. It cannot furnish work for the unemployed nor lift the burden of debt and impoverishment from the Azerbaijanis, Iran's most stalwart peasantry: only the Iranian Government can achieve that salutary end.

CHAPTER VII

The Unanswered Question

ON REACHING RAMSAR, DEEP IN THE HEART OF the northern province of Mazandiran, I had the illusion I was no longer in Persia. Nowhere did I perceive a glimpse of the civilization amidst which I had been living since my arrival. Nowhere was there a sight, a sound, a smell of the Orient. The Caspian resort, of whose glories Persians had told me with enthusiasm, appeared a strip of prewar Europe at its best, or present-day America at its best, as if bodily transplanted to the Persian soil.

The shining, white-painted hotel rose in splendor on a high knoll. The glare of glass in doors and windows, the immense, breeze-blown verandas, the broad and winding outdoor staircases, the riot of color in acres of flowers, the cyprus and the orange, the eucalyptus and the magnolia, the jasmine and the palm, all superbly tended, were as much a revelation as the up-to-date installations inside the hotel—rooms with gleaming tile baths, faultless plumbing, hot and cold water day and night, and, for once, drinking water from a mountain spring as cool and pure as anywhere in the world. The bright, often gaudy, and invariably expensive rugs from Kashan and Kerman in rooms, lobbies, and social halls enhanced the hotel's luxurious glow.

At the front door of this beautiful place loomed mountains so dense with primeval jungle that only during the rare hours when the sun was upon them could one glimpse a patch of bare rock, like a patch of skin through a rent in a resplendent garment. Here roamed the wildest of game—tigers, bears, boars, leopards, foxes, wolves, jackals; and birds of many kinds—eagles, wild pigeons, above all pheasants flitting about the age-old and ageless trees. Streams cool and clear, abounding in native trout, now murmured, now roared, down the mountain heights.

At the rear of the hotel, edging the glimmering sea, blue or brown or green or a fusion of all colors, sprawled an immense and sandy beach, still unkempt and still waiting to be cleared and embellished. Astride the boulevard that led to the sea towered the casino, no gambling den but a social hall with roof garden, outdoor verandas, and in its far-flung wings dressing chambers for bathers, furnished with every conceivable convenience.

Here was a sportsman's dream, a vacationist's paradise— mountain and sea, the peaks of the mountains dark with clouds, the sea aglow with sun, all on the threshold of a shiny hostelry with all the comforts one might seek, and, outside every door and window, the very earth hidden under blossoming bush and blooming flower. I had not imagined there was anything so modern and so wild, so inviting and so beautiful, anywhere in Iran, indeed anywhere in Asia.

Yet only seventeen years earlier, Ramsar was a village of dilapidated mud huts, with a caravansary for passing travelers —not in automobiles and busses, for the roads were impassable, but on foot or horseback—a rude place offering food and lodging and, despite the ban on its sale, opium.

It was Riza Shah, that monarch of ruthless will and energy, who demolished the caravansary, tore down the mud village, and converted the jungle-grown knoll and the brush-swept sand dunes on the shores of the ever-drying Caspian into one of the most attractive holiday resorts in the world. Having built it as his own private undertaking, nobody knows how much it cost. The king never gave anyone an accounting of the sums he squandered on his favorite projects. Nor is there any record of the toll in human life it entailed. Death from malaria and other fevers which struck the multitude of peasants who were engaged in the construction of Ramsar was more frequent than the Shah ever realized.

However much merchants and landlords hate the former king for the extortions he practiced on them, however deeply the socially minded intelligentsia is pained at the thought that, unlike Turkey's Kemal Pasha, who spurned a crown and foreswore personal aggrandizement, the Shah wantonly seized the one and by fair means and foul eagerly amassed the other, they readily admit that had it not been for him, there would have been no Ramsar. There would have been none of Iran's other handsome resorts and hotels. Nobody else would have built them.

Ramsar the fact is not nearly so significant as Ramsar the symbol of the drive and the speed with which, however capriciously and wastefully, the former monarch embarked on the modernization of the country. Nearly everything modern in Persia—railroads, most of the highways, the factories, the main avenues in the northern towns and cities, the transformation of the capital from a community of typically Asiatic mud streets, mud walls, and mud huts into a modern city—is a monument to Riza Shah's appreciation of the modern world.

He did all this because, whatever the historic circumstances and psychological causes, nobody before him had done it or thought of doing it, neither the state nor the most affluent private citizen. A Persian scientist with a French education, whom I met in Ramsar, said plaintively, "We are a rich country, richer than France, with greater agricultural resources than Germany, and since the expulsion of Riza Shah, we've been standing still, just marking time."

Why?

Essentially because the Persian man of wealth, the merchant

and the landlord, is the most anomalous capitalist in the world. He will not use his capital, or will use it only rarely and sparingly, for capital investment.

Nothing so clearly demonstrates the truth of this assertion as the rise of the privately owned textile industry in Isfahan, a city that has acquired a historic reputation for the astuteness and sagacity of its business community. In 1931, Riza Shah came there on a visit. In the home of the governor general he met thirty-six invited guests, all of them, except a newspaper editor, men of wealth. After shaking hands with them, the Shah delivered a brief, pointed speech.

"The world," he said, "is changing, and we must change with it. We have been accustomed to doing everything with our hands, but the world is doing everything with machines. You citizens of Isfahan ought to get together and build factories."

In an aside to the editor, who related the incident to me, the king said: "Write about it. Tell the people the world is changing and that we must change with it. Write and write and write."

The assembled citizens held their tongues and their breath. They wondered if the Shah was only offering a suggestion or proclaiming a command. A suggestion they might ignore, but not a command, not without peril to their possessions or their persons. The next day, after the Shah had departed, the governor general called them again to his house and said, "You must build factories." They knew what the word "must" signified. So with great reluctance and painful misgivings they proceeded to build factories and made Isfahan Persia's Manchester.

Since then the investment has yielded them greater profits than they have ever gathered from any enterprise. They have amassed millions of tomans. The gold treasure that had lain at their feet they never would have uncovered had they not, at the peril of their very lives, been pushed into reaching down for it. To a Westerner, such a capitalism makes no sense.

Nor can a Westerner appreciate the psychology of such capitalists who, even now, in the face of mounting competition with

British and Italian textiles that are already beginning to flow into the Persian bazaars, hold back from spending a small part of their inflated earnings on spare parts and on salaries for European engineers who would keep their plants in top working condition. The Teheran Department of Labor has had to argue and scold them and point to the disaster threatening their industry unless, like the British and Italian capitalists who are reaching out for the Persian market, they keep up the efficiency and productivity of their plants.

I was in Teheran in the autumn of 1947 when the Majlis, by a vote of 102 to 2, rejected Russia's demand for an oil concession in the northeastern part of the country. Teheran was in a mixed mood. The strain was over, but for how long? The Persian intelligentsia, who constitute the most public-spirited body of citizens in the country, was divided in its feelings. Those who had memories of the Tudeh movement and mourned its collapse were sad and bitter. But those who hailed the action of the Majlis as a national triumph, second only to the overthrow of the autonomous regime in Tabriz, did not disguise their elation. They were hoping that at last their own business community would finance, or help the government to finance, the development of the oil lands. They were encouraged in their hope by the reflection that the investment would prove a bonanza for the investors and would simultaneously brush out of the way the conflict with their powerful Slav neighbor.

Yet for a long time nothing happened. When I left Teheran in November 1947, the intelligentsia of both the right and the left were wondering what the future held in store for their country. They knew that no American oil company would risk a dollar in an oil concession on Russia's border, nor would such astute financiers as the Dutch, the Swiss, or the Swedes care to embark on so hazardous a venture. None of them would welcome a quarrel with Moscow, which would regard their presence in northern Iran as a foreign imperialist conspiracy to launch an attack on the Caucasian oil fields, from which Russia obtains at least half of her oil.

The intelligentsia knew that, in this day and age of mechanization, when engine power dominates not only industry and transport but military equipment and agriculture, oil is too precious a mineral to remain underground, unexplored and untapped. Since then, however, there has been an announcement that Persians will develop their own oil in the North. With the political insecurities that hover over the Persian North, one must guard against an optimistic response to the announcement.

The Persian is a merchant par excellence. He can drive as shrewd a bargain as any of his colleagues anywhere in the world. But he is no builder. He is no industrialist. He has neither the habit nor the urge for long-term projects. Addicted to commerce and to the quick turnover of cash, he is, as a Persian university professor once put it, primarily a money-changer, with neither the gambling spirit nor the creative ardor of the Westerner, particularly the American businessman. By their own default, Persian businessmen are driving their government into state ownership of the very institutions which American businessmen are vigorously fighting to hold in their own hands.

There are reasons, of course, rooted in Persia's tragic history. The foreign conquests and invasions, the foreign threats and conspiracies, the foreign squeezes and humiliations have shattered the businessman's confidence in the stability of his homeland. Persian shahs with their ruthless repressions, and the century-old rapacity of the Persian police and the Persian Army, have added to everybody's vexations and confusions. Such at least are the explanations Persian businessmen offer for their failure to exploit their country's resources with their own capital and their own energies. Yet to a Westerner there is something more than these external pressures of which businessmen speak. Oriental resignation, contentment with the today, love of ease have been the tradition and the habit, and nothing has happened —no internal social upsurge, no intellectual renaissance—to shatter the one or unbend the other. Riza Shah gave Persian history a powerful push, but his methods, instead of stirring the businessman into creative action, only stunned him with dismay.

Persia is clamoring for a foreign, particularly an American, loan. No doubt such a loan would stimulate development. But were Persian landlords men of energy and imagination they could immediately introduce measures in the villages for the amelioration of the cruel lot of the peasantry. Nor would they have to experiment with theories or abstractions. The Near East Foundation has shown the way, a tested and infallible way.

Dr. Lyle Hayden, from Pittsfield, Illinois, representing the foundation, has demonstrated in five villages in the fertile Veramine Valley, which the Ministry of Agriculture has assigned to him for experimentation, that even in the absence of an agrarian reform, instantaneous improvements can be achieved, and at small expense. It was an enlightening experience for this writer to visit the village of Mamazan, one of the five, and to find every mud hut, every chicken coop, cleansed of the flies, fleas, spiders, lice, scorpions, and other insects which the peasant has come to accept as a part of his daily ordeal as much as the blistering sun or the violent sandstorms. For once I was in a village in which nobody was scratching himself, not even the bony chickens and the growling dogs.

In one courtyard I saw a group of children, barefooted, unwashed, with disheveled hair, squatting on the ground and eating honeydew melon. Not one of them had to lift a hand to slap at a biting fly or mosquito. In hut after hut I saw babies lying on a rug on the floor, nude or with a flimsy cloth over the loins, peacefully asleep with not a welt or a fleck on the tender skin to mark the sting of an insect. Poor as the peasant sharecroppers were, strenuously as they might toil for an absurdly meager living, for once they were privileged to enjoy rest and repose without the torments which insects of one type or another had been inflicting on them. The cost of the chemicals that achieved this result was the equivalent of $1.75 per household, and one third of that was for customs and transportation.

The extermination of insects in the villages is Persia's primary problem. Were this accomplished, there would be very little malaria and eye disease would be under control. Fevers that now plague the peasantry would abate. A healthier and happier peasant would be a more industrious farmer. He would cultivate his lands more energetically, and his own and the landlord's share of the crop would be higher. No other cause is more worthy of the landlord's immediate attention.

Yet in 1948, the second year of his stay in Persia, so few landlords responded to Dr. Hayden's demonstration that he has been able to extend his work to only thirty villages—thirty out of forty-six thousand!

Dr. Hayden has told Persians that at the nominal expense of only five dollars a family, the country can within three years rid itself of the number-one scourge, malaria. There has been much talk but no practical effort, not even the beginning of an effort, to launch a nation-wide campaign for cleansing the country of the disease that is ravaging a vast majority of the peasantry.

The cultivation of courtyard gardens, an urgent need in the desert part of the country; the filtering of drinking water; the building of sanitary latrines; the introduction of new breeds of poultry, particularly well-laying hens; the introduction of new garden vegetables or of select seeds of the vegetables already known; the use of chemicals to kill ticks and other vermin on sheep (at an expense of only one and one half cents a head); the construction of inexpensive schoolhouses—these are some of the other improvements which the Near East Foundation has been successfully pioneering.

Yet there has been only vague and fleeting recognition of the importance of such achievements in villages in which thirteen million Persians live.

"In our country," said a university professor, "people make money out of land, out of commerce, and out of politics."

By politics he meant only one thing—graft and extortion. Persia has a model income-tax law. Yet a British banker with many years of experience in Persian finance told the writer that the business community of the country pays no more than 10 per cent of the amount the state should be receiving. The Teheran Government derives 23 per cent of the national revenue from the tobacco monopoly, 27 per cent from customs, and 12 per cent from fees and royalties on oil. It obtains only 6 per cent from income tax!

Nor do businessmen, when they are in a talkative mood, hesitate to acknowledge that they juggle their accounts so as to make it impossible for the Ministry of Finance to collect the full amount of the tax. It was a leading merchant in Teheran who told me: "Why should we pay high taxes to the state? Does the state use the money to build up the country? Not so as you can discover it with a microscope. The more we would pay, the more would slip into the pockets of the rascals in the government."

An eminent Teheran lawyer frankly admitted that the ordinary landowner or businessman keeps two sets of books, one for his private information, the other for the finance inspector. If the inspector starts asking embarrassing questions, a bribe silences him, and the amount of the bribe is sometimes larger than the tax. The "first-class" people talk openly and spiritedly of their tilts with the government and of the crafty schemes both have evolved in dealing with one another. "Sure," said a businessman, "we do cheat the government, but the government fleeces us even more, much more." He meant not the government as such, but state functionaries, high and low.

The American military mission which is helping to reorganize the Persian Army at one time insisted on the dismissal of six generals. These generals were more preoccupied with enriching themselves through graft than with the transformation of the army into a fighting organization. With rare exceptions, career officers enter the army poor, and when they retire with the rank of general they are among the richest men in the country. Needless to say, they do not accumulate their wealth merely from salaries or padded expense accounts.

So great is the businessman's distrust of the government that he rarely sells it merchandise on credit. Rice merchants sell to the army only for cash. Persia has no internal debt, for the simple reason that Persians would never subscribe to an internal loan.

That Persians do command the ingenuity and the skill to transact business on as high a level of efficiency and rectitude as any Western people is eloquently demonstrated by the remarkable record of the National Bank. Amir Khosrovi, its founder, a brigadier general who was high in the councils of the late Riza Shah, started the institution on the assumption, quite revolutionary for Persia, that corruption is no more natural to a Persian than murder. He would prevent it by offering so much incentive to executives and employees that they would not be tempted to indulge in the practice. His policy has been singularly successful. Abol Hassan Ebtehaj, the present governor, is perhaps, as a business executive, without a peer in all Persia. However sly and strenuous the attempts of his enemies to entangle him in political difficulties and to dishonor his reputation, no charge of personal corruption against him has ever been sustained. A worldly man, who was educated in France and subsequently at Beirut University, he would have attained eminence as a business or public figure anywhere in the world. The ample salaries the bank pays its four thousand employees and the social benefits it offers them—in vacations, health insurance, dowries to girls who marry, benefits to employees' wives who become mothers, and the sale of food, particularly tea and sugar, flour and rice, at cost price (and sometimes, to employees in the smaller-income groups who have large families, at half cost)—are only some of the measures Mr. Ebtehaj has installed or perfected to keep the curse of dishonesty and corruption away from the institution over which he is presiding.

"If the four thousand employees of the State Bank can work with supreme loyalty and honesty," he told the writer, "four hundred thousand employees can be made to do so, provided they are so well treated that graft does not tempt them." Often I heard university professors and schoolteachers and even businessmen say, "If we had a hundred Ebtehajes in the country, we could transform Persia into a land of plenty for all."

The report of the Morrison-Knudsen engineers of Boise, Idaho, is a monumental document. Over eight hundred pages long, its purpose was to present authorities in Washington with facts and figures for a loan on projects that would be self-liquidating and pay for themselves. This is not the place to analyze or even summarize the mass of authentic information which the American engineers have gathered. It would require a long chapter merely to catalogue the recommendations they make for the upbuilding of Persia.

To a layman like myself, one of the most impressive features of this report is the extravagant waste in Persia's agriculture. Because of damage to cotton, barley, wheat, sugar beets, and fruit, pests alone cause an annual loss of thirty million dollars. Preventable disease causes the death of sheep and cattle to the amount of another thirty million dollars a year. Thirty million doses of serum would reduce this loss by twenty-five million dollars.

One need not be either agricultural expert or economist to realize that, loan or no loan, Persian landlords and tribal chiefs could do much with their own funds to prevent these extraordinary wastes. By spending two and a half million dollars on serums, they could recover 22.5 million dollars now lost to them and their people.

Iran is one of the great tea-drinking nations in the world. The Persian word for samovar is *samavar;* for tea, *chai;* for tea glass, *stakhan*—all Russian words, attesting that indulgence in the beverage has come from or been stimulated by Russia. According to the Morrison-Knudsen report, Iran grows four thousand tons per year of its own tea. The rest must be imported at a cost of ten million dollars per year in foreign exchange. But in the

Caspian region there are twenty thousand acres of land suited to tea cultivation. What else but lack of business enterprise makes it necessary for Iran to squander ten million dollars each year on a product it could conveniently gather on its own lands? Not only would the cultivation of new tea plantations save millions in foreign exchange; it would, according to the American engineers, provide employment for thirty-five thousand workers, who are now without jobs.

The case of sugar is equally enlightening. Iran consumes one hundred and ten thousand tons a year. It refines only thirty thousand tons. The cultivation of the sugar beet is so faulty that the yield per acre is only one fourth of what it is in the United States. Iran could manufacture thirty-eight thousand more tons and save itself more millions of dollars in foreign exchange.

Equally revealing was the statement that Persia could increase the productivity of the lands now in cultivation by 50 per cent.

I have selected only a few instances of the prodigious waste which Persian enterprise could sharply reduce or wholly eliminate. But absentee landlords have little or no ambition to correct these sinister failings in their agriculture with their own funds and their own energies.

Written in simple, matter-of-fact language, the Morrison-Knudsen report, which the outside world has as yet neither heard of nor read a single word of, is one of the most exciting and illuminating studies of a nation in the Middle East that this writer has read.

Quite significantly, the report makes no mention of agrarian reform. Perhaps it was not within the province of the American engineers to concern themselves with so complex and explosive a subject. When I asked Ahmad Ghavam, then Prime Minister, if such a reform was contemplated, his reply was that there was much land in Persia which could be reclaimed, and that, when reclaimed, it would be distributed free to new settlers. To help these settlers in their new life, the government would exempt them from taxes for a period of from ten to fifteen years. The reclamation projects, he said, are contingent on Persia's ability to obtain an American loan.

Another minister in Ghavam's Cabinet felt that Persia should establish a *cordon sanitaire* against Russian propaganda in the border regions. He believed that the distribution of the land to a depth of one hundred and fifty kilometers (ninety-three miles) from the Russian border and the creation there of a landowning peasantry would dam up or beat back the infiltration of Soviet ideas. Such a reform, he said, might be acceptable to the landlords. Most significant is the recognition that a peasant with a homestead of his own is immune, or likely to become immune, to revolutionary propaganda.

Persia is a land of extraordinary beauty and fertility, and Persians, prince and peasant, are a people of extraordinary charm and gifts. Yet in the words of Isaiah: "From the sole of the foot even unto the head there is no soundness in it; but wounds, and bruises, and putrifying sores: they have not been closed, neither bound up, neither mollified with ointment."

At one stage in antiquity, Persia was the mightiest and most progressive nation in the world. In the museum of Persepolis, the capital which Darius built and Alexander the Great set afire, and which has only recently been disinterred from a mountain of earth and rock, I saw a remarkable exhibit. It was a large, rusty, triangular-shaped scrap of iron—a plow the Persians used twenty-five hundred years ago. It is superior to any plow I saw in any of the villages I visited.

The collapse of the old science of agriculture, particularly in irrigation, and of the old morals, the old devotion to creative effort and truthtelling, is a major and a catastrophic event in Persian history.

Whence will come the deliverance?

Will it be through "the strong hand" of which Persians and foreigners in Teheran are talking? If so, will it be a despot like Riza Shah or an autocrat with the wisdom of a Cyrus, a Darius, a Shah Abbas?

Will it be through an indigenous revolution or a communist dictatorship that must inevitably bind itself to the will and the power of Moscow?

Will it be through some brilliant idea, implemented by a gigantic financial appropriation out of London or Washington? A foreign resident in Teheran who has had a generation of business experience in Persia said: "A billion-dollar loan and one hundred American and European engineers could regenerate this country within ten years." The assertion is beyond dispute. But the project could be accomplished only under a progressive government that commanded the confidence of the people and that was firm in the execution of its policies and in the banning of international jealousies and intrigues.

Two things are certain: continued stagnation in an age of spectacular technological advance and fiery power politics is not the answer; and any program, however ingeniously contrived and enthusiastically exploited, must begin with the land.

CHAPTER VIII

Cairo

CAIRO IN THE SUMMER OF 1947 WAS NO MORE LIKE
the Cairo of the war years than a New England fog is like the
Egyptian sun. As always, its manner was languid, its people
loud-voiced, its turbaned dragomen stately, its beggars numerous,
its street vendors bumptious. But the flush of its wartime prosperity had ebbed as low as the pale green waters of the Nile in
early summer.

The leading hotels were half empty. There was no need now
for the newcomer to hunt out a friend or acquaintance who
would permit the management to intrude on his privacy with an
extra cot and an unexpected companion in his room. The
choicest rooms were available for travelers upon request of the
smiling, immaculately dressed room clerk. The famous bars at
Shepheard's and the Continental Hotel, once overflowing with
gay crowds, were now as quiet as hospital wards. Shopkeepers
on the main avenues were no longer out of breath and temper
tending the varied, oft-fantastic wants of khaki-clad young men
from all over the English-speaking world—New Zealand, Australia, Canada, Great Britain, the United States.

They had all the time in the world to relax and reminisce
nostalgically of the fabulous years that had brought to their very

doors the greatest flow of gold they had ever known. Eagerly they invited the stranger to pause for a cup of hot Turkish coffee and engaged him in leisurely discourse on the state of the world, with mournful accent on the subject of tourists, American tourists, the only ones in the shattered postwar world who could make the golden rain fall again.

Despite the lament of shopkeepers, the arrival in Cairo from Europe was a startling experience. It was like landing from the sky not only on a new continent but on a new planet with a new climate, a new people, a new civilization. The plethora of goods was as dazzling as the white-hot sun after the chill mists of Europe. Even in Switzerland, the one country where the dollar is neither king nor hero, passengers on the de luxe train which had taken me from Zurich to Geneva were served not sugar but saccharine with their coffee. But in dollar-starved Cairo nothing was lacking, nothing was rationed, nothing was inaccessible. Here it was not customers who cried for goods but shopkeepers who moaned for customers. Silks and satins, cottons and woolens, rayons and nylons, glass and leatherware, watches and jewelry, all were on brilliant display. In bazaars and grocery shops the choicest vegetables, the most luscious fruits, fresh from Egypt's rich, profusely irrigated gardens and orchards, greeted the eye at every turn. After Europe's leanness, the heaps and baskets of figs and dates, bananas and guavas, and shiny, yellow-fleshed mangoes were a delight and an exhilaration.

Outwardly the war had disarranged nothing. In Cairo the comforts and amenities of living, instead of decaying as in Europe, had gained fresh substance and fresh luster. The Egyptian capital was the one city where the newcomer did not have to squander time and energy finding living quarters, transport, soap, laundry, and cigarettes, or fretting over calories and vitamins. Not even Zurich and Geneva, with all their glut of dollars, offered the visitor such a surfeit of comforts and pleasures in food and shelter, drink and entertainment. The choicest British whiskies and French champagnes were there for the asking.

Coca-Cola, an inheritance from the American Army during the war years, was as plentiful as it is in Atlanta, Georgia. Night clubs, dance halls, bars, cinemas welcomed the foreigner with bursts of rapture. Outside the hotels, bearded dragomen in turbans, with flowing white and blue robes billowing over their paunches, procurers, and confidence men buttonholed him and pursued him for blocks. In clipped English and with increasing gusto, they sought to whip up his enthusiasm for excursions to bazaars and mosques, parks and pyramids, museums and slums, or to rouse his desire for any sort of carnal gratification he might care to indulge, with a black, a white, a brown girl, with girls of any age, any race, any shape or shapelessness, or with boys. Despite law and police, nothing was forbidden, nothing was unattainable.

If Cairo, despite its mass unemployment, overwhelms the newcomer from Europe with its abundance, it astounds him no less with its paradoxes. Side by side, mud hovels next to high-domed mosques, is some of the most pretentious architecture of our times. Situated on the edge of a vast and parched desert, with only two rainfalls a year, with winds whipping up clouds of dust that float over the outskirts of the city as high and dense as rain clouds, Cairo boasts some of the most luxurious gardens and boulevards to be found anywhere, with trees whose very names drip with melody—eucalyptus, casuarina, tamarisk, jacaranda, and of course the palm and the acacia.

The flashiest and most expensive American automobiles roll side by side with processions of donkeys, of camel packs, and of streetcars so thin and wobbly that they seem as if pasted together from kindling wood and barrel staves. Here are some of the gayest people in the world and some of the surliest, some of the most affluent, flaunting the latest fashions in clothes and as exquisitely mannered as any European gentleman, and some of the most bedraggled and poverty-stricken specimens of humanity to be encountered anywhere.

Here are women who piously cling to the *mala,* like the

Persian *chadur*—a black, loose-fitting gown that leaves the hands and feet uncovered, with mere slits for the eyes in the black veil that hangs like a mask over the face. And here are Moslem girls, among the most beautiful in the world, chiefly students and daughters of the upper and middle classes, who wear lipstick quite unstintedly, who polish their fingernails and toenails and flaunt their bobbed hair and shapely legs with the gay abandon of Western girls. Here are men and women who converse fluently in half a dozen languages, and others, the vast majority, who cannot sign their names in any language.

Cairo is a city of guile but of little sophistication, of spontaneity but no steadfastness, of extraordinary rhythm and ear-splitting brashness. One of the noisiest cities in the world, it is also one of the most leisurely, in fact so leisurely, with sidewalk cafés so crowded, that I often wondered when the citizens of Cairo did their work. A city of loud-voiced men, it is also a city of singularly soft-spoken women. Its beggars are the most insolent, its street vendors the most impertinent, yet its shopkeepers can hold their own in courtesy and refinement, if not always in efficiency, with any in Europe or America.

The contrasts between extravagant luxury and direst poverty are especially flagrant. Cairo's taxis are shinier than those of most European cities; the latest and swankiest American passenger cars are more brilliantly in evidence than in Zurich, Europe's citadel of dollar prosperity. Yet in five minutes' walk from Shepheard's Hotel, one stumbles on one of the world's dreariest slums. The streets are narrow and dingy and the stench and the squalor are appalling. Swarms of flies darken fruit stalls, blacken meat shops. Crowds of children hover around with eyes so diseased they drip with pus. Stupefied with fatigue and hunger, beggars crouch on sidewalks as silent and lifeless as mummies. Egypt's death rate is one of the highest in the world, 26 per thousand.[1] So is its infant mortality—255 per thousand in the Egyp-

---

[1]Charles Issawi, *Egypt, an Economic and Social Analysis* (Oxford University Press, 1947).

tion quarters of Alexandria in 1913; 224 in 1935. One child out of every four dies in its first year. The life expectancy of a boy who reaches the age of ten is thirty-eight, as against fifty-six for England and fifty-nine for New Zealand. Egypt also holds the world's record for blindness, the incidence of which is almost four times as high as in India.

A place of startling contrasts and sensational incongruities, Cairo is one of the oldest cities in the world. Founded presumably by Babylonian mercenaries in 525 B.C., it has witnessed a fabulous rise in the twentieth century. In 1907 its population was 654,476. By 1917 it had grown to 790,939. During the succeeding twenty years it almost doubled, and at the present time, according to government spokesmen, it is close to two million.

Visitors to the Egyptian capital cannot help marveling at the energy and imagination which have gone into building so magnificent a city on the edge of a dreary sand-blown desert. Here is the East, at its best and at its worst, and the West, too, at its best but mostly at its worst. The neon lights are as resplendent as those of any city in the world, yet the kerosene lamp, often empty because there is no money to buy the oil, is as cherished as the mud-brick oven. Hotels, night clubs, other gay resorts, are as bright with light as those in any Western city, but only one fourth of Cairo's population has electric lights at home. Thanks principally to British enterprise, Cairo, unlike other cities in the Moslem Middle East, has underground installations for water and sewage. Yet, except in the select hotels and restaurants, it is unsafe to eat raw fruits, vegetables, or salads, or to drink raw milk. "Gyppy tummy" and virulent fever of one kind or another may lie in ambush in the gleaming fruit and succulent leaves served the foreigner.

The largest and most tumultuous city in Africa, Cairo is also known and celebrated among the followers of the Prophet as "the city of a thousand Mosques." The richest and most cultivated Moslem city in the world, it is also the citadel of Mohammedan orthodoxy—the home of the far-famed University

Mosque of el-Azhar. Founded in 972, it now has an enrollment of over thirteen thousand, of whom six hundred are Moslem students from all over the world. By sheer magnitude of numbers and prestige, of tradition and Moslem scholarship, el-Azhar is "the throbbing heart of the Moslem world,"[2] as Mohammed Lhaled Hassanein Pasha, formerly Inspector of Science and Letters in the university, has expressed himself. Something of the political complexion of the university may be glimpsed from the same authority's testimony that "el-Azhar, which has never ceased to enjoy the favor of rulers and princes, owes its present revival to the late King Fuad I,"[3] father of the present King. The university is the staunchest and most brilliant defender of Mohammedan orthodoxy in the world.

Cairo is also headquarters of the Moslem Brotherhood, which never ceases to thunder imprecations and anathemas on anyone who counsels change in life and politics, in morals and manners. "Filthy" was the mildest of the string of epithets with which it branded the conduct of students, both men and women, and of professors of the Agricultural College who at a soiree wore evening clothes and danced and included alcoholic drinks in their refreshments. Its leading journal, during my stay in the city, called for the arrest of an Egyptian writer who had scoffed at the custom of bride and groom becoming acquainted not before but only after marriage. Hotly it demanded the ban of publications that dared print pictures of girls in bathing suits or other abbreviated costumes. Like el-Azhar, the league is fiercely intolerant of any encroachment on established Mohammedan usage.

Yet one evening an Egyptian student of Cairo University, whom I had met casually in the street, invited me to go with him to the Badia, a well-known outdoor café and restaurant. It is noted for its floor show, and its principal patrons now, unlike the war years, are Moslem Egyptians and Moslem visitors from other countries. In the light of the influence and the power of the

[2]*Egypt Today* (Cairo: Schindler Press, 1945–46).
[3]*Ibid.*

Moslem Brotherhood and of el-Azhar, the performance was a surprise and a revelation. A bevy of brown-faced, buxom girls, chiefly of Moslem origin, sang and danced and strutted and gallivanted about the immense, light-flooded stage with no more thought of concealing or disguising their feminine allurement than European or American performers might have had. The climax was the "belly dance," a performance so bawdy that the more sensitive-minded communities of Europe or the United States would find it more shocking than amusing. I had not imagined that so rank and lurid a display would be tolerated by any Moslem audience, particularly in the city of the University of el-Azhar. When I asked my companion, himself a Moslem, how he explained so audacious a defiance of Mohammedan usage and tradition in the presence of a tumultuous assemblage of followers of the Prophet, his crisp answer was, "This is Cairo." Neither the Moslem nor the Christian, the European nor the Oriental yardstick of manners and morals may be applied to the Egyptian capital. It truly is one of the most fantastic cities in the world.

Even the shopkeepers' clamor for tourists is expressive of Egypt's divided mind and soul. Since the end of the war the country's flaming nationalism has again and again burst into violent street demonstrations against foreigners. There have been riots, pillage, blood, death. Yet Egypt's dollar-starved economy cries for the closest possible ties with foreign nations. Tourism has always been a major source of foreign exchange. One of the many official tourist bulletins I was handed in Cairo reads: "It is with confidence based on the knowledge that they will enjoy their stay that Egypt looks forward to welcoming an ever-increasing number of visitors to her shores."

While both government and private agencies proclaim their joyful welcome to tourists, and shopkeepers yearn for visitors with dollar traveler's checks and letters of credit, Egyptian consulates are so wary of foreigners that, despite orders of the Ministry of Foreign Affairs, they encumber the issuance of visas with delays and irritations which discourage pleasure trips to their country.

The government woos the foreign investor, but seeks to fasten on him restrictions which frequently thwart the consummation of business deals. These particularly concern the employment of Moslem Egyptians. The need for highly trained technicians is desperate, but the racial minorities of Greek, Armenian, and Italian origin, who are among the most skilled technicians in the country, are beset with anxieties and harassed by fears of what is in store for them. Graft is so rampant that non-native business-men search the globe for countries that would open their doors to them and in which they could strike fresh roots for a life of peace and security. Since the Jews turn their eyes toward Israel, which Egypt hates, and the Armenians toward Russia, which Egypt distrusts more than it hates, these two minorities are harassed by special burdens and discriminations.

Positive and negative forces stride side by side, like a moving object and its shadow. At every step the contrasts in Cairo's civilization are as bold as they are bewildering.

Though linguistically Cairo is essentially Arab, racially and culturally it is an agglomeration of strains, ancient and modern, a fusion of old and new ideas, a clash of old and new ambitions. Here the Old World, one of the oldest we know, is engaged in a fierce, perhaps mortal, combat with the New World. That is what makes Cairo a spectacle and a drama, a reality of yesterday, a symbol of today, a question mark of tomorrow.

Nor is the city just one more cosmopolis in the Middle East or in the world. As goes Cairo, so goes Egypt and at least a part of the Arab world. Cairo's geography, history, wealth, massiveness, culture, social turbulence and intellectual ferment, both modern and traditional, make this inevitable. Yet despite its overwhelm-ing and grandiose antiquity, Cairo has something of the vanity and impetuosity of adolescence, of youth's boisterous disregard, indeed contempt, of its own derelictions and imperfections.

Cairo is so proud of its newly won wealth and importance in the twentieth century that, forgetting the poverty of its peasantry and its impotence, it is as impatient to flaunt its will and prestige before the world, particularly the Arab world, as a youth eager to show off his strength before a crowd of adult onlookers.

Cairo is fevered over a host of international issues, but most particularly over Palestine, the evacuation of British troops from the Suez Canal and the Anglo-Egyptian Sudan. It insists that the Sudan (that is, the section of it through which the Upper Nile flows, and which is at present a British-Egyptian condominium) is geographically, racially, culturally, historically an integral part of Egypt and should be completely under Egypt's will and sovereignty. At the Foreign Office, I was favored with an armful of publications setting forth, in English, Egypt's inviolate right to the Sudan. Perhaps the most telling and manifestly the most realistic argument favoring Egypt's case is expressed in the following passage:

"It may safely be asserted that nowhere in the world does a country so much depend for its future economic development on the extension of cultivable areas as does Egypt. The reclamation of barren lands is possible if an adequate supply of water for irrigation purposes is made available. This result can only be achieved by the execution of projects destined to control the water flow of the Nile and increase the volume of water stored during the flood season. The fact that the prosperity of Egypt as well as absolute and complete dependence of her economy rests on her control of the Upper Nile and the wise use of its waters has impressed itself on the minds of Egypt's rulers and statesmen with increasing force, more particularly since the early decades of the nineteenth century."[4]

With a foreign power—Great Britain—exercising a dominant voice in the Sudan's affairs, the flow of water to the Nile might be so seriously thwarted as to endanger not only Egypt's independence but its very survival.

[4]*The Unity of the Nile Valley* (Cairo: Government Press, 1947).

Yet the merest suggestion that the Sudanese be permitted to decide their own destiny by plebiscite makes Egyptian officials writhe. With the rare exception of those who believe that a more reasonable attitude on the part of Cairo might result in a compromise that would suit all the parties involved, including the British, Egyptians are as unanimous on the issue as they are in their antagonism to the intrusion of any foreign power in their internal affairs.

It so happens that the Sudanese in Cairo are among the city's most dignified and impressive residents. Their pursuits are humble. They are waiters in hotels and restaurants, and domestics in the homes of wealthy Egyptians and of foreigners. Some are taxi drivers. Tall, broad-framed, and sturdy, they have dusky, handsome faces which are branded with the inevitable tribal marks. Reserved and well-mannered, they are as uncommunicative as Egyptians are articulate. "You can always trust a Sudanese," foreigners and Egyptians agree. There may be Sudanese beggars in Cairo, though I never heard of or saw them. I never rode with a Sudanese taxi driver who failed to find the address to which he was directed or who attempted to falsify the fare registered on the meter. For all I know, the Sudanese in Cairo may be the pick of their race; but they are so healthy, physically and morally, that they have earned for themselves the universal respect and admiration of Cairo's residents. Yet when I suggested in the course of a discussion with an official in the Foreign Office that perhaps the bitter controversy between Egypt and Great Britain on the subject of the Sudan could best be solved by a plebiscite, he reacted as though I had leveled at him and all of Egypt the supreme insult.

In no other Mohammedan land in the Middle East is the educated woman so emancipated in thought and in usage as in Egypt or the illiterate woman so pious. Foreigners often speak of Cairo's "flappers" and "bobby-soxers." The terms may be misapplied but the implications are illuminating. More and more

Moslem girls are determined to challenge their elders and to assert their right to live their own lives in their own way, in defiance of convention, religious precept, and parental authority. Though the number of these rebels is small, their audacity is astonishing. They will have none of the old codes and pretenses. They scorn the veil and the *mala*. Their slogan is freedom and their passion is feminine self-expression. They wear make-up, gobs of it, and sometimes with questionable artistry. They bob their hair and affect the latest hairdo, wear knee-high dresses, and are as proud of their shapely figures as any Western girl. Though their elders denounce the form-fitting bathing suit as the invention of the devil, they glory in it and only regret the limited opportunities in Cairo to display it.

Avid film fans, they go to the cinema at least twice a week. They have dates with boys, though not at home. They attend parties and dances, and sometimes smoke cigarettes and sip cocktails, though—ever aware of their femininity—they do neither to excess. They know the Hollywood stars as any American girl does, nor do they mind telling foreigners which Hollywood idol they would choose as an especially desirable boy friend and the one they would prefer as an especially desirable husband. At a party of young people in a private home I heard one Moslem girl select Cary Grant for the first, Herbert Marshall for the second, and Clark Gable for both.

When I asked what her family would say, she replied: "My father is dead, my mother thinks I am a lost soul, and my grandmother says someday I'll see the light and drop my profane ways. But I tell them I don't want to be like them. I want to be a new woman and nothing else." After a pause, and with a flirtatious toss of her head, she added, "It's so much fun to be free, and, anyway, I earn my own living and they cannot stop me."

With all her lively defiance of Mohammedan usage and tradition, the emancipated Moslem girl is neither coarse nor brash. She is not aping man's ways. She will put on slacks but she will spurn dungarees. She will not dilute her femininity with tomboy manners or masculine affectation. Delicacy and decorum are as much a part of her as modern dress and modern make-up.

She is ebulliently a symptom and a result of the social ferment that has been seeping into this stronghold of Mohammedanism in the wake of the two world wars. The modern education which girls of the upper and middle classes have been receiving in recent years has abetted this ferment. There are already twenty-one girls' high schools in Cairo, ten run by the state, eleven by private organizations. In 1938, of the seventy-eight thousand students in foreign schools, chiefly French, the majority were girls. Here attendance of a foreign school implies divergence or break from established native tradition. In 1925 a college for girls of the upper stratum of society was opened in Cairo, and another in Alexandria in 1934. In these colleges girls study general culture, and if they choose, they may specialize in literary or in domestic subjects. Students and graduates of these schools are irretrievably lost to orthodox Mohammedanism. The unfolding of new ideas and the vision of a new life which the study of general culture implies make that inevitable.

Since 1928, in the face of violent opposition of men, women have likewise been admitted to Cairo University, with the result that out of five thousand physicians in the country, one hundred and fifty are women. This is a spectacular record for a country in which, at the beginning of the century, according to a local saying, women were seen in public only twice—when they were married and when they were buried.

More vigorously than the enlightened clergy of Iran, the educated Egyptian women deny that the Koran is responsible for the stultifications and inferiorities to which their sex has been subjected in Mohammedan countries. They absolve the Prophet from guilt for what they are persuaded is a complete perversion of his teachings. Asmah Fahdy, assistant dean of the Women's Institute of Education, writes:

"Islam, contrary to the prevailing idea among Europeans, encouraged the education of women. The Prophet himself was

eager that his wives should learn reading and writing and was
believed to have said that learning was a duty enjoined upon
every Moslem man and woman. Many references in Moslem
literature point to the fact that girls attended 'kuttabs,' or elementary schools, where they were taught the Koran, reading, and
writing, side by side with the boys, or were educated at home or
sent to 'kuttabs' of their own. Moreover, there are many references in Moslem biographies to women who distinguished themselves in literary and religious studies and to women scholars
who lectured to famous men."[5]

Who, then, according to this scholarly Egyptian woman educator, is to blame for the "decadence, intellectual and spiritual,"
as she expresses it, that has engulfed women in the Mohammedan
world? Her answer is as terse as it is unequivocal. "Reactionary
views," she writes, "which are never absent in any society,
triumphed; and while the European woman began to feel her
way in the path of learning and advancement, the Egyptian
woman lost many of her intellectual privileges, for Moslem men,
led by bigotry and ignorance, came to regard the confinement
and ignorance as the best safeguard for preserving their chas-
tity."[6] Though such a radical interpretation of the Prophet's
teachings arouses the wrath of the Moslem Brotherhood, it is
significant that these words appeared in a book dedicated to "His
Majesty Farouk, the First King of Egypt," and published in
Cairo.

In Mohammedan tradition and in Arab folklore, there is no
lack of support for Asmah Fahdy's argument. "Endeavor for
knowledge," reads a Mohammedan pronouncement, "is the duty
of every male and female Moslem."

The memorable love story of Leili and Majnun is of Arab
origin. Many a Persian poet has been enraptured by this story of
the beautiful Leili and the never-faltering Majnun and has composed his own poetic version of it. Nizami's is so brilliant and so

[5]*Egypt Today.*
[6]*Ibid.*

powerful that it is spoken of as Persia's *Romeo and Juliet*. It is one of the most beautiful and most moving poems this writer has read. But it begins in a *kuttab* where Leili and Majnun are pupils, in the same class, in the same room, under the same teacher.

In 1945 thirty-seven Egyptian women were admitted to the agricultural college of Cairo University and three girls had the courage to seek and to gain admission to the engineering college. In the school of journalism, women outnumber men, and several lively publications in Cairo are edited by young women who are graduates of this school.

Yet Egypt's feminism, like so much that is new and challenging and exciting on the Egyptian scene, is an accomplishment solely of the cities, chiefly Alexandria and Cairo. The villages are as untouched by it as they were in the days of Pharaoh.

An American university professor, a specialist in agriculture, while visiting the Agricultural College of Giza, expressed a desire to attend some of the classes. Regretfully the dean informed him that there were no classes that day—the students were on strike.

Student strikes are as much a part of the pattern of Egypt's social and intellectual ferment as its feminism. More boisterous, they are no less significant. Nowhere else in the Middle East are university youths so loudly and violently articulate. In November 1946 the medical students, after a demonstration they had planned was broken up, were so incensed at the police that in what they considered retaliation they burned medical textbooks and flung out of the windows irreplaceable laboratory equipment to the value of $100,000. Obviously they were not punishing the police. They were only hurting themselves. When they returned to the university upon its reopening sometime later, they were confronted with a new regulation which they could only resent. They were required to carry identification cards, so that, if they again indulged their fury at the expense of the university, they or their families would be held responsible for the full amount of the damage.

Nor are students alone in their spirit of rebelliousness. Since the end of the war no other Mohammedan city, not even Bagdad, has witnessed so many demonstrations and riots as Egypt's capital. Now it is aimed against the British, now against all foreigners, now for the Sudan, now against Palestine, and of late against their own government. There is always a national or international issue to cause an explosion. Paradoxically enough, one reason for the intermittent outbreaks of student rebellion is that, as a Cairo educator expressed himself, "there are too many of them" —too many students. An enlightened citizen, he did not advocate the curtailment of the number of youths who are clamoring for a higher education. He only said, "Our country is too undeveloped to provide suitable employment for all of them." That administrative offices which employ intellectuals are already inflated almost to bursting with personnel becomes manifest to anyone who has had experience with official agencies or institutions. An exit visa for which I once applied necessitated visits to about half a dozen different offices, in each of which some functionary placed his seal of approval on some paper my guide was carrying. One reason for the corruption that infests Egypt's administrative offices is the inordinate splintering of functions. It is always easy for some official to descend on a shopkeeper with the charge of violating some ordinance of which the shopkeeper may never have heard. Natives, not to speak of foreigners, who live in Cairo and do business there have learned that a sizable gratuity will absolve them of all guilt and rescue them from harassment by this or that functionary.

Because government offices are crowded and overcrowded with functionaries, salaries are usually inadequate. Bribe-taking and extortion provide a ready means of supplementing the inadequate income.

Unemployment of the educated youth swells the chorus of rebellion. Nor is any relief for them in sight. Quite to the contrary, the ranks of the white-collar unemployed are constantly augmented by fresh recruits. Egypt's system of education—unbalanced to a profligate point—makes that unavoidable. Though the Constitution provides for the universal education of children between the ages of seven and twelve, at present only one million children, or 40 per cent of all, are receiving an elementary education. But Egypt spends twice as much on higher education as it does on primary education. No wonder that Egypt is outgrowing itself. Its spirit is more mighty than its body. Its ambition is more lusty than its means of gratifying it.

For the youth with a secular modern education the burden of personal vexation is increased by a grim national frustration. The student or the young lawyer may be the son of a merchant, a manufacturer, a landlord, a high government official. He may even be the son of a fellah. He studies foreign languages, principally French and English. He attends classes in history, psychology, geography, and related subjects. He discovers a new world of ideas and movements. The shelves of the French and English bookshops are liberally stocked with the choicest literary and political writings of our times. Reading these books expands and fortifies his knowledge of the new world he has discovered. He admires and he hates this world. He wants it and he spurns it. It is the world from which have come the conquerors that lorded over Egypt, now with enlightened selfishness, now with cruel benevolence. He abhors and fears this world, yet knows he cannot escape it. Every plane that lands in the Cairo airfield only sharpens his awareness of personal and national frustration. He cannot shake off the new ideas he has gathered. They have become an inseparable part of his dreams of a new Egypt, the Egypt he loves, no less than of the dreams of his elders, yet with a passion for reform they neither share nor approve. The city slums, the glumness and sordidness of the villages pain and enrage him. He talks and he protests. He hates the foreigner, but he has no love for the pasha. He clamors for action. He does not always know quite what he wants, but he is quite certain of what he does not want. Sometimes he is a communist. More often he is a flaming patriot who wants his nation, as a nation, to stride forward and catch up with the civilization it has missed since the ancient days of its power and glory. Bottled up with discontent and anger, he explodes into deeds of desperation.

It is significant that in this citadel of Mohammedanism there are youths who do not hesitate to speak of their fathers as "thieves" or "reprobates." When the fathers hear their sons express themselves on the state of affairs in Egypt, they may gently dismiss the protests as the "ravings of immature youths" or take them to heart and worry over the "queer ideas" of their own begotten flesh and blood.

There are youths who break with their families and proclaim they will have none of the luxurious living which a father's wealth offers them. There are also youths who are captivated by such all-inclusive slogans as "away with landlords," "away with poverty," "away with inequality," "away with capitalism." They would welcome any upheaval which would give immediate reality to their dreams of a new Egypt. Though they are in a hopeless minority, their mere presence in a Mohammedan city is symbol and portent.

"Do you want to follow Russia or America?" I asked a group of students at a party.

"Neither," was the reply, and there was no dissent.

A law student said: "We want Egypt to preserve its independence, its absolute independence, but we don't want the pashas and their old lawyers who monopolize our Parliament and our Senate to shackle the gifts and the energies of our people."

The majority of the young intelligentsia are so fervently nationalistic, so jealous of Egypt's hard-won independence, so fearful of a situation which might offer a foreign power, Eastern or Western, an excuse or an opportunity to clap its authority over the country, that they shudder at the very word revolution.

Though the government had attempted to suppress *El Jamaheer* (*The People*), a weekly journal edited by young professors, lawyers, and students, somehow it managed to keep alive until Egypt began to war on Israel. It was the one publication that scoffed at and fulminated against Egypt's participation in this war. Students solicited subscriptions, and circulated it every way they could. Labor leaders helped along, though there is no labor movement in Egypt in the European sense of the word. The law of 1942, which permits trade unions, bans their federation into a central body. The 19,727 transport workers in the country are splintered into 67 unions. A total of 139,546 workers belong to 489 unions. One of the best-informed labor attachés of one of the most eminent embassies in Cairo said to me: "France on the eve of the Revolution was socially more advanced than is the Egypt of today."

A high official in one of the Egyptian ministries, himself only a few years out of college, said gloomily: "Had Hitler won the war, he would have captured the imagination of our educated youth."

Fascism once made a powerful appeal to Egyptian youth. In the thirties an organization known as "Young Egypt" mustered a large following and built up a powerful press. Allied victory split it to pieces—the organization, not the spirit that animated it and the fanaticism that actuated its practices. Quite recently, in a new disguise, it has again come to life, and Palestine is its fighting issue of the movement. Then there is the clamorous Moslem Brotherhood. Founded in Ismailia in 1928, it has since grown into a powerful political body of over one hundred thousand, with a union of militant crusaders of ten thousand. Thunderously anti-foreign and flamingly pro-Moslem, it looks to the past and not to the future. Or rather, it would clothe the future with the dogmas and traditions of the past. Though it accepts industrialization, this is the sole concession it yields to Western culture. It will have neither the intellectualism nor the social emancipation of the West. As violently anti-Bolshevik as it is anti-democratic, it frowns on any freedom for women. It seeks to bind all education and all life to the most orthodox Moslem formulas and to Moslem fanaticism. It is the most eloquent and most vociferous exponent of a united Arab world, presumably under the Egyptian crown.

Modern-minded and Moslem-minded youth are arrayed in battle against one another. But while modern-minded youth has little support from its elders, and battles for its ideas in its own fashion—now openly, now secretly, now by word of mouth, now by printed pamphlet or journal—Moslem-minded youth has the powerful support of the Moslem Brotherhood, of el-Azhar, and of functionaries of highest eminence in the government. Save that neither camp has the scholarship and the sweep of imagination of the Slavophiles and the Westerners in the Russia of the nineteenth century, they stem from sources not too dissimilar to those that animated the struggle of these mutually exclusive champions of Russian salvation. Though the Brotherhood accepts the modern machine while the Slavophiles repudiated it, both would have none of the culture of the West. What the word "Slav" was to the Slavophile, the word "Moslem" is to the Brotherhood.

Modern-minded Egyptian youth, like the Russian Westerners, though much vaguer in aims and purposes, welcomes the West—of which it is jealous, and of which, unlike Russian Westerners, it is afraid—for the contribution it can make to the salvation of Egypt. As fiercely anti-foreign as the Brotherhood, it yet wants to learn from Western ideas and Western experience. It is easily excited by Western slogans and Western symbols.

The parallel of the conflict in Russia and Egypt only emphasizes the sharpness of the clash between modern-minded youth and the ultra-fanatical Moslem Youth and Moslem Brotherhood.

One afternoon I watched a funeral procession pass by Shepheard's Hotel. The coffin in which the body lay was draped in a carrot-colored cloth, which rose and fell as the pallbearers marched slowly along. The front of the cloth made an inverted funnel, the peak of which was decked with a tasseled tarboosh, indicating that the dead person was a man of consequence.

A crowd of women, all in conventional loose-fitting black

dresses, followed the pallbearers, some of them wailing and screaming. Yet heading the procession was a brass band of ten pieces, the musicians in khaki uniforms and in lofty tarbooshes. This was something new for an Egyptian funeral, and even more startlingly new was the playing of Chopin's funeral march.

Here orthodoxy and modernism strode side by side. It was symbolic of Cairo, a city of gross fanaticism, yet a city bursting with challenge and revolt against everything orthodoxy symbolizes.

CHAPTER IX

Egypt's Agony

THE MOST PRECIOUS POSSESSION OF THE EGYPTIAN fellah, or peasant, is the buffalo cow. He prizes it so highly that to prevent its being stolen he shelters it in his own hut. The only exception to this practice I discovered was in the model village of Vahtim, which is a benevolent enterprise of the Royal Agricultural Society. Here are newly built huts, and the peasant and his family do not have to walk through the stable to reach their living quarters. The buffalo enjoys the privacy not only of a separate chamber but of a separate entrance.

The buffalo cow gives milk for the family, about one fifth the amount of the average North American cow, but of much higher butter content. It also does the draft work on the land. Besides, children love the beast. Lazy and good-natured, it exercises its passion for water at every opportunity. Children scream with glee as they watch it wallow and loll about in ponds and ditches, sometimes raising its head, as if begging to have it splashed with water.

While there are about three million peasant families in Egypt, there are only about one and a half million buffaloes. Were they distributed one to each family, which they are not, half of the peasantry would still have none. When peasants who do not own a buffalo cow want milk they must buy it, if they have the cash. A goat helps, but not all fellah families can afford a goat. The ordinary milch cow is still much of a stepchild and has not received the recognition it so abundantly merits. There has been a diminution in the number of cattle in the country. According to Armand Delpart, managing director of the Land Bank of Egypt, "since 1939 there is a marked regression oscillating from 15 per cent to 49 per cent."[1] It is "a serious crisis," and not so easy to overcome. That is why dairying, like meat production, is still woefully neglected. The consumption of milk in Egypt is about one twenty-eighth as much per person as it is in Denmark.[2] The bloated bellies of the nude and semi-nude children one observes in the Egyptian countryside attest to malnutrition, caused in part by lack of milk.

In the absence of milk, peasant mothers begin at an early age to accustom their children to strong black tea, boiled and steeped over and over. The addiction to tea is universal. The fellah will forego cloth for a new garment and encumber himself with debt to the local shopkeeper rather than do without the stimulation and the pleasure tea affords.

All Egypt, with a population of eighteen million, cultivates only five million five hundred thousand acres of land. But what land! There is none more fertile in the world. For thousands of years the Nile has been enriching it with the silt it brings down from the upper regions of Africa. Year after year its floodwaters have poured fresh nutriment into the Egyptian earth. "Nowhere in the world," states a government report, "do people depend for their existence on a river as the people of the Nile basin depend on the Nile; and no country in the world is so indebted for the fertility of its soil to a river as Egypt and the Sudan are indebted to the Nile. Egypt and the Sudan owe both their life and existence to this great river."[3]

[1]*Egypt Today.*
[2]Charles Issawi, *op. cit.*
[3]*The Unity of the Nile Valley* (Cairo: Government Press, 1947).

Without the Nile there would have been no ancient and no modern Egypt.

Egypt is not a "wet country" and receives but little rain. Every span of arable land is under irrigation—one fourth under so-called basin irrigation, the remainder under perennial irrigation. In basin irrigation, which has persisted since antiquity, flood-waters drench the land for about a month, then are diverted back to the Nile. Perennial irrigation is of comparatively recent origin. The redoubtable Mehemet Ali (1769–1849), "that barbarian genius,"[4] as Viscount Milner speaks of him, ambitious to enrich Egypt and to make the land yield both winter and summer crops, set about carving up the desert with perennial water canals. The British contribution to this stupendous revolution in Egyptian agriculture is of incalculable value. "While the basin system," writes Lord Lloyd, "continued to hold the field until the arrival of the British occupation . . . the raising of the Aswan Dam was the last act in the completion of a vast scheme of hydraulic engineering which created modern Egypt and made it one of the richest producing areas in the world."[5] However wroth Egyptians may still be over the British occupation of their country from 1882 to 1922 or over British diplomacy since the end of World War II, British constructive achievements, especially in the field of perennial irrigation, have given Egypt a measure of prosperity it had never before known or dreamed of.

Egypt's sun is another priceless boon to agriculture. Daily it warms the earth for ten or more hours. The combination of rich land, water, and sunlight preclude a crop failure. The Egyptian landowner, pasha or peasant, can always count on a harvest. That is what makes Egyptian farming, for the man who owns a substantial acreage of land, one of the most profitable pursuits in the world.

There is almost no limit to the variety of crops Egypt can grow. Cotton, of course, is Egypt's gold. Though about one fifth

[4]Viscount Milner, *England in Egypt* (London: Edward Arnold, 1926).
[5]Lord Lloyd, *Egypt Since Cromer* (London: Macmillan and Co., 1933).

of the land is planted with it, it accounts in terms of money for four fifths of the nation's exports. Only the West Indies and Persia (by virtue of its Filestani brand, developed some fifteen years ago by a landlord) may claim to grow a cotton of superior quality, but the acreage in both localities is quite small. A government advertisement in an English-language publication in Cairo reads: "Egyptian cotton excels all other varieties as regards length of staple, fineness, strength, evenness of fibres, and the insignificance of its waste. . . . [It is] especially superior as regards [its] silky touch and lustre."

The extraordinary quality of Egyptian cotton lends it to such a multitude of highly specialized uses, especially as a sewing thread, that it has earned for itself an enviable reputation in the cotton markets of the world.

Not only the quality but the yield of Egyptian cotton is phenomenal. With an average of 606 pounds an acre, it surpasses the yields in India, Russia, and the United States, the other large cotton-growing nations of the world.

Cereals do exceptionally well. Wheat is a staple crop and the harvests compare favorably with those of Great Britain. As the bread of the city proletariat and the most important food he eats, it constitutes the largest item in his budget.

Because it is the favorite food of the peasantry, maize, or Indian corn, is the leading cereal in the country. It is the chief source of calories in the peasant's daily diet. The yield is good, though not as good as in Iowa, averaging thirty-five as against Iowa's fifty bushels an acre. Millet, rice, and barley are other cereals that yield excellent harvests.

Vegetables in extravagant variety and profusion gleam out of garden plots, large and small, all over the Nile-watered earth. The same publication which carries the advertisement on cotton prints a full-page advertisement by the Ministry of Agriculture offering for export not only cotton seeds, rice, and barley, but nuts, lentils, and onions. Still another full-page advertisement opens with the flamboyant headline, "BUY CONCENTRATED SUN-

SHINE." It then proceeds to chant the virtues of Egyptian onions, carrots, peas, beans, potatoes, artichokes, and a host of other vegetables. Egyptian onions have already found favor in Great Britain, the Scandinavian countries, and Switzerland, and, in much smaller quantities, in Brazil and Canada.

Fruit grows as luxuriously as vegetables. The mangoes, according to foreign opinion in Cairo, have not their equal in the world. Dates, figs, oranges, lemons, bananas, and olives flourish, and would flourish even more bountifully had they been accorded as vigilant attention as cotton—Egypt's number-one moneymaker.

Despite its incomparable agriculture, the richest in the world, so rich that Egypt is spoken of as "the garden site of the world," the people who cultivate the land live as dreary a life as I have ever observed in any country, more dreary even than in Persia. I shall ever remember my first journey to the Egyptian countryside. During my stay in Cairo I had seen the Pyramids and the Sphinx; I had browsed in the Cairo Museum and thrilled as does every visitor to the exhibits of the glory of the Egypt of the Pharaohs. Yet once I reached the countryside, all was blotted out of my mind. I did not think of the pomp and splendor of court life in ancient Egypt, of the great science and the matchless art, especially in sculptured stone, that the old kingdoms have bequeathed to mankind. I might have come to a new and faraway land which had never known any art or any science, any comfort or any convenience. I was face to face with an Egypt which, despite its brilliant sun, was as bleak as it was poverty-stricken.

The mud huts were low and dingy, with nowhere a hint of comfort, a glint of decoration. Not that homes built of mud bricks are necessarily ugly. In the model village of Vahtim I saw mud huts that would be a boon to the fellah—cool in summer, warm in winter, with raised platforms for sleeping, with an ingeniously contrived heating system underneath the platforms, with solid roofs where one could go for relaxation or sleep, and with a separate part for the buffalo. But the cost of such a house on the basis of prewar prices was the equivalent of one hundred dollars, a fabulous sum for a fellah, and would be several times that amount on the basis of inflationary postwar building costs. The fellah must build a hut as cheaply as he can. Mud costs nothing, reeds and cornstalks and cotton stalks cost little or nothing, and these are his chief building materials. Rarely is there glass in the windows—glass is too expensive for a fellah. The entrance is through the stable, in which not only the buffalo but also the goat and the sheep and the poultry are housed. There is a separate chamber for the spacious mud-brick oven, and since the only outlet for the smoke is the door, the walls and ceiling are black with soot. Dung is the commonest fuel, camel dung and buffalo dung, gathered by the women and children from the fields and roads. The smells in the house are so unpleasant to Western nostrils that the odor of smoke, when there is a fire, is a relief. Flies infest the house, and there is no escape from them. There is no flypaper or insecticide. Luckily the climate is so balmy that the fellah and his family spend most of their time outdoors.

The water the peasant drinks comes from irrigation ditches. Children bathe in the ditches, goats and sheep drink from them, ducks and geese paddle in them, buffaloes wallow in them. The water swims with impurities, not only animal excretions but sometimes the carcasses of dead animals and birds.

In the village, shoes are a luxury. Rags are a common sight, especially among men and children, though women, in their black cotton garments with black kerchiefs on their heads, make a presentable appearance. Though exceptionally pious, the women wear no veils, which would hamper them in the arduous work on the land. With tall clay jars of water, or baskets of produce, or loads of freshly cut grass balanced on their heads, they make a picturesque sight and give an impression of vigor and sturdiness.

The fellahin, the women to a slightly less degree than the men, are perhaps the most diseased people in the world. Malaria is rampant; at least two thirds of the peasantry are afflicted with it. Trachoma and other infections of the eyes are widespread. Hookworm is a perpetual affliction. But the number-one scourge of the rural population is bilharziasis. It is caused by a parasite, *Bilharzia haematobia,* discovered by Dr. T. Bilharz in 1851 and named after him. The parasite that causes the disease has two hosts, snail and man. The eggs hatch in water and penetrate a type of snail, inside whose liver the parasites undergo a further process of growth. Then they once more escape into water and become a danger to man. Penetrating the skin, they enter the blood stream, settle in the liver, and there mature into worms. Since the Nile and the irrigation ditches abound in snails, the peasant who works in the ditches can hardly escape the floating parasites. Stout shoes might offer effective protection, but he is too poor to buy such shoes. Competent foreign and native physicians estimate that from 70 to 80 per cent of the peasantry suffer from hookworm and bilharziasis. An American writer concludes: "The general spread of the diseases of bilharziasis and ancylostoma [hookworm] . . . together with trachoma effects some 95 per cent of the population."[6] Perennial irrigation, which has been a source of immeasurable wealth to Egyptian landowners, has, ironically enough, brought in its train the most widespread bodily affliction the peasantry has ever known.

Perhaps the medical mission which the United States Navy maintains in Cairo for the study of parasitic diseases, may stumble on an effective cure of bilharziasis. If so, it will confer on the fellah the greatest gift with which man or nature has yet favored him.

During my first visit to Egypt in 1942, while walking along the bank of the Nile on a hot day with a British physician, I suggested a swim in the river. I had been in the country only a few days and had not yet heard of bilharziasis. "Don't ever bathe in the Nile," the Britisher warned earnestly. "Not even at Luxor or Aswan?" I asked. I was contemplating a journey to

[6] W. Cleland, *The Population Problem of Egypt* (Lancaster, Pa., 1936).

these well-known resorts, and swimming was one of the pleasures I looked forward to. "Nowhere," was the firm reply. The only safe bathing places in Cairo are the private swimming pools in the city.

Yet children in the villages are as sprightly and playful as anywhere in the world. Their loud shouts and ringing laughter are a joy to hear. During the month I spent in Aswan, in a hotel on a high rock overlooking the Nile, I often went walking in the surrounding countryside. The hills and caves outside the town in the immediate vicinity of the hotel made an excellent playground for children and attracted crowds of them from the town and from nearby villages. As I watched them play I observed that many of them, while romping and shouting, frequently flailed away at the flies around their faces. Sores and swellings attracted swarms of flies, which sometimes formed a black ring around the eyes. This is a common sight in Egyptian villages, and the fellah is too poor to buy, or too ignorant to use, disinfectants that might save a boy or girl from eventual blindness. Egypt, I wish to repeat, holds the world's record for blindness.

Thus, though blessed with one of the most magnificent climates in the world and a river that never ceases to fatten a large part of its soil, Egypt, the wealthiest and most spectacular nation in the Middle East, is also one of the most poverty-stricken and sickest nations on earth.

Once, in the company of a young Egyptian agricultural expert, I visited a large village some distance away from Cairo. While my companion stopped to talk to friends whom he had met in the street, I drifted away from him. Passing an open courtyard, I ventured inside. Instantly I heard an excited cry from my friend —"Come back!" Frightened, I hastened back into the street. Rushing over, my companion drew me away by the arm and, smiling to indicate that he did not mean to be angry or impolite, he said, "You must never go into a courtyard alone." When I asked why, he explained that it was dangerous. There was no telling what might happen to a stranger, especially a foreigner, who walks unescorted into a place where there are women. He might be suspected of seeking to make advances to a wife or a daughter; and, hot-tempered as Egyptian men are, someone might hurt or even kill him. When I protested that it was midday, that the courtyard I had entered was thronged with people, and that it would be absurd for anyone to assume that *I* could be motivated by dishonorable intentions, my companion shook his head and replied, "Sorry; but you must understand Egyptian psychology. An outsider must not take any chances." Subsequently I learned that most of the many murders which are committed in Egypt occur in villages, and that jealousy is one of their chief causes.

Jealousy is also a source of family quarrels and a frequent cause of divorce. Though polygamy in Egypt is insignificant, divorce is common. One out of three marriages in the villages breaks up. For a peasant people this is an astounding record, yet is not unrelated to the material misfortunes of the fellah.

Excessively sex-conscious, Egyptians, including the fellah, are continually apprehensive of their sex potency. Though the drug is banned by law, the use of hashish as a sex stimulant is more widespread than Cairo authorities would care to acknowledge. On a boat on the Upper Nile, I met a Nubian youth who was on his way to a village to be married. He was seventeen, his bride-to-be fifteen. To my interpreter, who was a university student, he confided that his parents had given him hashish to fortify him for "a powerful experience" with his virgin bride. Nor is this an uncommon practice in villages.

The defective diet of the fellah, insufficient proteins, and the diseases to which he is exposed and to which he succumbs may at an early age sap his sex vitality. In fear of becoming impotent, he will stimulate himself with large quantities of strong tea or with the inevitable hashish. Often he blames his wife for his waning powers and divorces her for a younger and more appealing woman. Since in Mohammedan countries divorce for a man is

141

essentially a matter of desire, the shift from one wife to another involves no legal or other complications. Social workers in Cairo speak with alarm of the high incidence of divorce in the villages. "It is bad for everybody," a woman social worker said, "but especially for the children. It is one of our greatest misfortunes."

Like peasants the world over, the Egyptian fellah, despite his failings, which no sane or thoughtful investigator would attribute to degeneracy, has his fund of virtues. Though suspicious of outsiders, and by no means as easy to approach as the Persian peasant, he is humble and kind. Despite the prevalence of divorce, he loves children and treats his wife with respect and affection. Industrious and neighborly, he is ever ready to help another fellah with the work on his land or with chores. Though overwhelmingly illiterate, once his aloofness passes he is fluent of speech and is eager to ask questions and hear news and stories of foreign peoples and foreign ways. He is as extraordinarily curious and inquisitive as any Slav peasant I have ever known. His anger is easy to arouse, yet in the presence of strangers with whom he has become acquainted he is extraordinarily correct and courteous. He loves nature and feels rooted in his village and in the land he cultivates. He abhors nothing more than to change abode from one village to another. Sentiment as well as habit keep him attached to his birthplace, and there is nothing he covets more than a parcel of land of his own. Land is the one source of livelihood and happiness he knows.

During the war years the Nazis shrewdly exploited the fellah's hunger for land. In the propaganda which they slanted toward the village they promised the fellah to rid him of the landlord, even as, in their appeal to the landlord and to the town population, they held out the promise of ridding Egypt of the foreigner. A member of the Ministry of Agriculture told the writer that in some villages the peasants were so beguiled by Nazi propaganda that they formed underground committees and mapped out plans for the seizure and distribution of the land after the Germans had ousted the landlords.

But Germany lost the war, and nothing, of course, has happened. Like a beast of burden, the fellah plods along from day to day, with little joy and little hope. He eats his maize, his green weeds, his vegetables. Rarely does he treat himself to milk, meat, eggs, fish, or other rich protein foods. He drinks his strong tea, countless glasses of it, with or without sugar. He buys what kerosene he can, what soap and textiles his meager income permits, and what sugar and tea—supreme luxuries—his budget or the shopkeeper's credit will allow. Neglected and abandoned, he is at the mercy of nature's cruelties—the malaria-carrying mosquito, the snail, the fly. Only the sun is his, the year-round sun, hot and white, offering respite from the gloom of his tomblike mud hut.

Egypt's glory, the man who with his hands whips the wealth out of the rich lands, the fellah, is also Egypt's supreme tragedy.

The King, socially minded intellectuals, and political leaders have launched a campaign under the slogan "War on Disease, Poverty, and Ignorance." Egypt resounds with this slogan. Everywhere I went I heard it recited and repeated with varying degrees of emotion, sometimes with smirks of contempt. Here and there a landlord will do something to give the idealistic slogan a semblance of reality. He will inaugurate a housing program, offer the fellah medical aid, dig a well to provide him with sanitary water. But such benevolence, however earnestly exercised, is still so meager that it barely reflects itself in the census figures on disease and poverty.

Volumes have been written on the subject of Egypt's overpopulation as the chief or sole cause of its poverty. Egypt is—in its populated areas—one of the most densely populated nations in the world. Though encompassing a territory of about 386,000 square miles, only 3½ per cent of it is arable. The remainder is desert. The Egypt of today, like the Egypt of six thousand years ago, draws its life from the Nile. In the course of the 960 miles the river traverses through the nation, it receives no water from tributary streams. The fact that only 5,500,000 acres of land are under cultivation and that at most only two million acres more can be brought under the plow tells its own eloquent tale of the overwhelming pressure of population on the land. According to Armand Delprat, the well-known Cairo banker, the density of population on the banks of the Nile is 533 to the square kilometer as against 266 in Belgium, the second most densely populated country in Europe.[7]

One proposed solution for this problem is migration to the Sudan. Here the fellah would live in the Nile Valley, in an environment akin to his old one. This fact might help to overcome his reluctance to pull up roots in the village of his birth and seek his destiny elsewhere. Yet nothing is happening, nothing is likely to happen in the immediate future, particularly as the fate of the Sudan is still undecided. Nor is birth control under prevailing circumstances a promising alleviation. Even in Europe only the more educated peasantries limit the number of their offspring. The illiterate or semiliterate peasant lets nature take its own course. In a Mohammedan land like Egypt, religion is a further bar and a strong one. Poverty, as in European peasant countries, does not curtail but stimulates childbirth. There is always the hope and expectation that a new worker in the family will contribute to its income and will provide sustenance for an aging father or mother. It would require a gigantic social and intellectual revolution in Egypt to sway the fellah into the practice of birth control. His resistance would be all the more stubborn because, in the absence of fun and entertainment in the village, sex is the one pleasure he is free to indulge in.

Egyptian authorities are of one mind that the average family, even with the ancient implements at its disposal, can easily cultivate four acres. This is another way of saying that less than half of the people who now live in villages would suffice to till the area in use. The other half could migrate to another country and Egypt's agriculture would suffer no drop in production. It is

[7] *Egypt Today.*

therefore often suggested that arrangements should be made with Iraq, which like Egypt is Mohammedan, for a mass migration of Egyptian peasants to its still unsettled lands. Of course these lands would first have to be improved. An extensive and expensive system of irrigation would need to be installed. This would require a gigantic outlay of capital, and who would supply it? There is no doubt that were such a migration feasible, and someday it may be, it would in some measure lift the burden of poverty which now enshrouds the Egyptian village.

There is much talk in Cairo of the possibilities of industrialization, which would absorb idle hands from both city and village. No doubt it would; and though Egypt is not rich enough in raw materials to enable it to build up a large steel and machine-building civilization, its potentialities in industrial development have not been vigorously exploited. Industry represents only 4 per cent of the entire wealth of the country.[8] But industrial output requires a market, and in a nation so overwhelmingly agricultural as Egypt the big market is the village. Yet if the highest daily wage for an adult is forty cents a day—*when* he works— and if such income is insufficient for the average family to buy the health-giving foods it needs, where would the fellah obtain his purchasing power? The increased output of hardware, leatherware, textiles, and canned foods, were the village shopkeeper persuaded to stock up with them, would remain on the shelves. Without a constant source of income from the land, the fellah would be only slightly less helpless than he is now.

Though the slogan "War on Disease, Poverty, and Ignorance" is loudly proclaimed, the one circumstance that holds the greatest promise of immediate relief—an agrarian reform—is rarely mentioned by those, including the King, who are most vociferous in the propagation of this slogan.

In Egypt, as in Persia, in Iraq, in Syria, in other Mohammedan lands in the Middle East, the one chief source of the woes that beset the rural population is landlordism. The figures on land

[8]*Ibid.*

ownership which the writer obtained from Cairo's Ministry of Social Welfare—the one ministry that concerns itself with the misfortunes of the fellah and with measures for helping him— make such a conclusion indisputable. Whereas 1,750,000 peasant families hold 700,000 acres of land, averaging two fifths of an acre per family, 12,200 landowners hold 2,500,000 acres. Less than one half of one per cent of the landowners hold almost three and one half times as much land as half of the entire peasant population. This grim fact is the cloud of darkness that hovers over Egypt's economy and Egypt's social life.

What is particularly striking is that while the acreage of the landlords has remained virtually unchanged through a generation, the holdings of the peasantry have been divided and subdivided among the inheritors of farm lands so that there are almost twice as many "pauper holdings" in the villages now as in 1913. Endless fragmentation of the land has made the peasant poorer and poorer, and the continuous integration of landlord holdings has made landlords richer and richer.

With the exception of the King and a few favored pashas, Egypt knows no such great estates as do certain South American countries or as does Persia. Only eighty-four estates embrace an acreage of from one thousand to fifteen hundred acres; only forty-nine landlords hold areas between fifteen hundred and two thousand acres; and only fifty-four possess land in excess of two thousand acres. But the land is so rich, the harvest is so dependable, that a man with a holding of one hundred acres cannot fail to be prosperous. Even when he lives up to the feudal code of a gentleman and refrains from the responsibility of operating or managing his estate in person, he can lease it to a tenant at a rental of one hundred dollars an acre. There are more such tenants crying for land than there is land to be leased. In Aswan, where the land is largely under the ownership of companies or corporations, I was informed that rentals have soared to one hundred and twenty-five dollars an acre. There are instances, though not many, of tenants paying one hundred and sixty dollars an acre and even one hundred and eighty dollars. A man with an estate of one hundred acres is thus assured an income of ten thousand dollars a year and he need waste no more energy than what is necessary to sign a paper document with a tenant.

For a landlord, Egypt is the most wondrous paradise in the Mohammedan Middle East. For the fellah, it is an inferno of "Disease, Poverty, and Ignorance."

CHAPTER X

Land Reform or Perish

DURING THE WAR YEARS, WHILE I WAS VISITING
the ancient city of Luxor far up the Nile, a local physician who
was a Coptic Christian introduced me to a celebrated pasha. The
man's scarlet tarboosh with its dangling silk tassel, the gleam of
his diamond stickpin, the still larger diamond on his finger, his
superbly tailored European business suit, his effusive hospitality,
the fluency of his French and English, the grace and gallantry of
his manner, all bespoke a man of wealth and culture.

He had studied in France and England and had traveled in
America. He had been in New York, in Boston, in Chicago, in
San Francisco. He spoke ecstatically about the California metropolis. There was no city anywhere like San Francisco, except
Paris. With nostalgic fervor, he reminisced at length of experiences in both cities. A man of cosmopolitan tastes, he said, need
never feel bored or lonely in Paris or San Francisco.

As an impassioned patriot, he blamed the British for Egypt's
troubles. It was they, he averred with some emotion, who had
been throttling Egypt's economy, Egypt's culture, Egypt's genius.
If they would leave not only Egypt but the Sudan, he repeated,
as though he were reciting the refrain of a song, Egypt would be

free to pursue its own destiny in its own way and would lift itself by its own genius and energies to new greatness and new glory. The outside world would then thrill to the new Egypt as it had to the Egypt of old.

Eloquent as he was, he was only reiterating words and sentiments I had often heard in Cairo—if the British would leave, Egypt could reorder its national life and solve its problems to suit its own people. The fierce nationalism which has swept Egypt has inflamed so much emotion that "the foreigner," particularly the Britisher, has been singled out as the chief cause of the evils that afflict the nation. Yet when I asked the pasha whether the British had ever banned or thwarted an agrarian reform, he admitted they had not. When I further asked why there was no such reform, he dismissed it with the bland remark that "it is a matter of higher politics." The contribution of British brains, British capital, British guidance, British enterprise to the development of Egypt, particularly to the enrichment of the pashas in the last half century, received but scanty acknowledgment from him. "They got paid for it, didn't they?" was his rejoinder.

The loud outcries against the foreigner, Egypt's preoccupation with the fight for the annexation of the Sudan, the war on Israel, these have fanned higher than ever the fires of nationalist emotion. Whatever else these campaigns may or may not have achieved, they have diverted public attention from the nation's internal vexations. They have yielded no succor to the fellah. The British are now gone; only the Suez Canal is still under their military control. Yet the poverty of the fellah is no less bitter; the snails in the Nile and in the irrigation ditches are no less multitudinous and no more merciful to the men and women who step shoeless into their waters or to the children who swim in them; the college graduate in Cairo who finds no place for himself in Egyptian society is no more assured of employment.

When we left the Winter Palace, Luxor's leading hotel, in which the pasha was spending his vacation, the Coptic physician asked whether I had heard of the recent malaria epidemic in

Egypt, which had taken a toll of over one hundred thousand lives. The malaria-carrying mosquito from West Africa, he explained, had found its way by airplane to Egypt, and during the years 1941–43 the epidemic raged fearfully. "Last year," he said, "you couldn't have come to Luxor, it was too dangerous. Hundreds of people died here, and there was nothing I as a physician could do. People were so undernourished their resistance was low or nil. Yes," he said gloomily, "undernourishment is Egypt's greatest calamity."

We discussed the causes of undernourishment. "There are so many——" and he stopped.

"What are they?"

"It is a long story. You have been in villages; you ought to know something about it."

"Tell me," I insisted.

"You might think I am prejudiced because I am a Christian."

"But you are an Egyptian."

"Yes, the purest of Egyptians." And suddenly, apparently changing the subject, he said, "Isn't my friend a charming man?"

"Most charming," I said. Charm and generosity, especially shown to foreigners they befriend, are as deeply ingrained in the pashas as their love of luxury.

"You see," he finally said, "men like my friend, who is a Moslem, are holding up the development of our country. That is why there is so much undernourishment in Egypt." And after a pause, as if to disabuse me of any suspicion that he cherished a religious bias, he hastened to add, "If he were a Coptic I would say the same. The pashas are rich and—well, they have a good time."

In his hesitant manner the Coptic physician was echoing sentiments which Moslem intellectuals in Cairo express freely. Not only students and young lawyers but public functionaries, and now and then an enlightened pasha, are more than worried over the plight of the fellah. However frenziedly a certain section of the press may fulminate against the villainies of foreigners to the exclusion of any comment on Egypt's internal adversities, the progressive intelligentsia, though passionately anti-foreign, is keenly aware that nationalist intoxication is no substitute for social reform. To them, Egyptian nationalism begins but does not end with anti-foreignism. Their number may be small but their sober appraisal of Egypt's problems and troubles is in sharp contrast to the exalted self-satisfaction of the pashas.

Some of these Moslem intellectuals, particularly those who have studied agriculture in Europe, deplore Egypt's overwhelming dependence on cotton. Times, they know, are changing. No longer is the world as dependent on cotton from the United States, India, and Egypt as in former years. To save or to gain foreign exchange and to render themselves independent of foreign imports, other nations have begun to cultivate the crop on an ever-expanding scale. Brazil and Russia are among the most energetic newcomers. Egypt can no longer count on a monopoly even of the long-staple cotton. Egyptians know also that as long as the absentee landowner persists in his quest of fortune solely or chiefly through cotton or wheat, which is heavily subsidized by the government, he will do little or nothing to help the country solve the food problem by modernizing its agriculture. He will energize it neither with new science nor with new machines. Cotton is still his deity, the cotton which once was Egypt's blessing, and threatens to become—indeed, is already becoming—Egypt's blight.

An American agricultural expert who has made an intensive study of Egyptian agriculture predicted the direst consequences for Egypt unless it diverts several hundred thousand acres from wheat and cotton to fruits and vegetables. "Egypt," he told the writer, "should reach out with its fruits and vegetables for the European market. It should become Europe's California." Egypt, he explained, has all the requisites—soil, climate, geographic position—for so salutary an accomplishment. During the winter months, when Europe's earth is locked in frost, Egypt's is aglow with sun and abloom with fruits. Egyptian artichokes, for example, are of matchless quality and would be a boon to Europeans. They are easy to handle and to ship. During the months of April, May, and June, Egypt could supply Europe with shiploads of artichokes.

Egypt harvests potatoes in January, and Europe would welcome new potatoes during the winter months. Egyptian oranges ripen two months earlier than Italian or Spanish oranges. In fact, the American continued, there are favorable conditions in land and climate in Egypt for growing almost any vegetable in winter —radishes, cucumbers, tomatoes, peas, okra, eggplant, sweet corn, and many others. Egypt's ports are closer to Europe than California is to the Atlantic seaboard. The problem of transportation should not be difficult to solve. A fleet of fast refrigerator ships would be needed and, with its enormous sterling balances, Egypt has the capital to acquire such a fleet. Nor, he continued, is the question of packing or of pest control beyond Egypt's power to solve. Already Egyptian shippers have acquired substantial experience in handling and packing of agricultural produce for the foreign market. "Egyptians are a keen-minded people," he said. "They quickly learn new methods of working and new methods of doing business." He concluded that, were Egypt to apply itself to developing a European market for the fresh fruit and vegetables it can grow so plentifully, it would achieve a double purpose: it would provide employment for idle or partially busy hands in the village, and it would tap a fresh source of riches for itself.

"Do you think Egypt will do it?" I asked.

"That is for the Egyptians to decide," was the diplomatic answer, and as an afterthought he added, "It won't be easy under their present system of land tenure. They must do something to change it."

The idea of Egypt's becoming a California for Europe holds out a fresh hope for the fellah, though he himself is as helpless to achieve it as he is to fight bilharziasis. Nor is this the only promise

153

of relief that foreign and Egyptian agricultural scientists perceive for a nation which, more than any other in the Middle East, is experiencing the burden of pressure of population against limited arable lands. There are many others. Dairying, for instance, is still only a toddling infant. There is one milk-producing animal to every five persons in the United States; there is only one to every ten or twelve—nobody knew the precise figure—in Egypt. Besides, the American cow is infinitely more productive than the Egyptian buffalo or the Egyptian milch cow. There are only a few scientifically managed dairy farms in the country which sell pasteurized milk, and none other is fit for human consumption. Egypt's *berseem* (clover) enriches the soil with the nitrogen it draws from the air and makes excellent fodder for cattle.

In a land that glows with blossoms on shrub and tree and plant, bee culture has been dismally neglected. Only in Persia did I see beehives that were more ancient, so badly contrived that they hampered instead of helping the worker bee take off for the field and re-enter the hive upon returning with its little cargo of nectar. Yet were someone to arouse the enthusiasm of the fellah for bee culture and demonstrate to him the ease and the pleasure of tending bees, much of the sweet he craves, and for which he often saddles himself with debt, he could furnish for himself. The utter absence of such guidance and stimulation only enhances the apathy that comes over a man without land of his own or with so little of it that, like a bird with clipped wings, he cannot rise to a new vision of the world about him.

Poultry is another source of much-needed food and income which Egypt has only halfheartedly exploited. Actually, Egypt does much better with poultry, in one respect, than does Persia or Iraq. It exports eggs, though its own population would improve its health were it to use for itself this excellent protein food. But Egypt has barely begun to realize the potentialities of poultry.

Because of the abundant waterways—the river, the canals, the ditches—ducks and geese thrive, and for some inexplicable reason seem nearly immune to parasitic diseases, though chickens and turkeys readily succumb to them. Goose and duck fat would be a precious boon to the fat-starved rural population.

Though Egypt has imported from America many varieties of grapes, the cultivation of vineyards is anything but American. Still, despite faulty cultivation, Egypt's table grapes lend themselves to export. Great Britain has already had occasion to sample them, shipped by air. Dates which grow on about a million rather neglected trees, as well as figs, bananas, and guavas, offer still further opportunities for both home consumption and export. Flowers, too, especially roses, could be supplied by air to foreign markets. Roses grow outdoors in Egypt as lush and beautiful as they do in European and American hothouses. Though not sprayed, they are apparently immune from most pests. They would be especially cheap to cultivate for export. In small amounts, shipments of Egyptian roses have already been made.

I am presenting here a summary of projects and of opinion regarding them, which I gathered from leading Egyptian and foreign experts, including agricultural attachés in various embassies. Yet all my informants were of one opinion—that as long as the fellah has no land or only a "pauper's holding," there is little hope of achieving the much-needed transformation in Egyptian agriculture. Because labor is abundant, the landlords have no inducement to shift their agriculture to a more rational basis. Cotton may contain within it the seed of future calamity, but for the present it is still a lush and ready money-maker. So is wheat, though at the expense of the bread-eating city poor, to whom the government passes on the heavy subsidies it pays the landowner for growing it. Besides, since the landowners are mostly absentee, they are neither future-minded nor agriculture-minded. They are only money-minded; and money to them is not a source of capital investment to create goods and new capital for their own and their nation's enrichment, but the means for immediate and riotous enjoyment. There are, of course, exceptions, but too few to merit special recognition.

I had heard so much of the youthful Dr. Ahmed Hussein, chief of the Fellah Bureau, which the Ministry of Social Welfare founded in 1940, that I went to see him. A man with a European agricultural education, Dr. Hussein is dedicating all his time to village life and village problems. In his knowledge of both he probably has not his equal in all Egypt. Tall and sturdy and handsome, wearing a red tarboosh, he is as calm as he is judicious, as frank as he is constructive. One of the busiest men in Cairo, he talks as fearlessly as he thinks and acts as energetically as he talks. A stern realist, he is given neither to flamboyant language nor to romantic self-deception. He understands not only the peasant but the rebellious intellectual, and perceives the relationship between the misery of the one and the revolt of the other.

"We cannot afford to leave our people in ill health and in economic slavery," he said, "and we can and should become Europe's California. That alone will not banish poverty from our over-populated villages, but it will give us a magnificent start." Yet to convert Egypt into Europe's winter truck farm and orchard, he continued soberly, two reforms were indispensable: in agriculture and in land ownership. Without these reforms little could be achieved. At least two hundred thousand acres now in cotton and in wheat should be diverted to truck farming and fruit growing. The intensive cultivation which these crops require would offer labor to a multitude of now idle hands in the villages and the income for the landowner would be higher. It was a question, not easy to solve, of breaking up an established pattern of Egyptian farming and of the landlords' addiction to crops that are easy to sell and that yield immediate cash.

The agrarian reform, Dr. Hussein continued, will be most difficult to achieve, yet if Egypt is to be saved from disaster and internal strife, it must be pushed through, regardless of all opposition. The two million acres of desert that are to be irrigated should be distributed solely among landless and land-starved fellahin. A half million families—between two million and two and a half million village folk—would be automatically settled on land of their own, with a sufficient acreage for each family to attain a comfortable standard of living. Nor should any landowner be permitted to hold more than one hundred acres. An income tax of 100 per cent on the revenue derived from lands above this acreage should be levied. Such a tax would automatically deprive the landlord of any inducement to hold more than one hundred acres. He could still enjoy an affluent living in a country like Egypt, where the soil is rich, water and sun plentiful and where rentals are extraordinarily high. On the acreage salvaged from such a reform fellahin would be settled, each on a small farm of his own.

"Would you confiscate the lands?" I asked.

He laughed and shook his head.

"No, I don't believe in confiscation. The landlords should be paid for the lands they find it under the proposed tax system unprofitable to hold. The state should assume the responsibility for these lands, their purchase and their disposal. The fellah should pay a part of his annual produce for the indemnification of the landlord. I know of no other way to solve the desperate village problem."

Continuing, Dr. Hussein emphasized that the money the landlords would receive for their lands should be used by them to build up industries, particularly those that would produce for the home market goods on which Egypt now spends precious foreign exchange. If the peasant had land of his own, he would have purchasing power with which to buy the commodities the new factories would put on the home market. He is no asset to industry now because there is so little he can buy. "Nothing does our fellah love more than land," said Dr. Hussein, almost as though he were reciting a peroration. "It is his work, his life, his joy. He would be so proud of it, so happy with it, he would do all he could to build it up. He would save it from the wastes and spoliations to which it is now subject. Of course he would need to be instructed how to do it, and this Bureau and other agencies would give him the proper instruction. He is so hungry for a better life, he would as a matter of self-interest follow our counsel."

An associate happened to come in with a handful of papers for Dr. Hussein, and he overheard the last words. As Dr. Hussein turned to glance at the papers, the other man said: "Why should any man own a thousand acres? If he has only a hundred, he still is rich. He still has an income for a pleasant life. On the other nine hundred acres we could settle more than two hundred families. If New Zealand could limit a man's acreage, why cannot we?" Bold language, I thought, in a land where pashas are so powerful. It was obvious that neither Dr. Hussein nor his associates were politically or in other ways hampered from speaking their minds openly and frankly.

"Do the pashas approve of agrarian reform?" I asked Dr. Hussein.

"They don't like it. But some of them are beginning to realize it would be dangerous not to have it."

"If the reform you propose were made into a law, would you not still face the problem of overpopulation in the village?"

"Yes, but we cannot do everything at once. I do not believe in totalitarianism; I believe in orderly processes of government. It is of no use rushing things in a revolutionary manner, though some of our young people are impatient of evolutionary change. When I tell them some reforms will take ten years to carry out, they become impatient and cry out, 'Such a long time!' But we mustn't do everything at once.

"Then, of course, we should help the fellahin in other ways. We should enforce the law of compulsory education for children between the ages of seven and twelve. At present, eighty per cent of our people in the villages are illiterate. When the fellah is educated it is easier to instruct him in new methods of farming and in new ways of life. We could print bulletins for him and he could study them in his leisure hours, even as your farmers in America are doing."

"There is much, very much, we can do," the associate interposed.

"Quite true," Dr. Hussein resumed. "We should teach the fellah how to build new homes. We are already doing it on a small scale. We should strenuously combat malaria and bilharziasis and the other diseases that infest our villages. We should give boys and girls who are already in school one good meal a day free. We are already doing it, and about half of the pupils in the primary school, a half million in all, get a midday luncheon free. The community pays the expense. The other half should not be neglected. Our children should grow up healthier than their fathers and mothers. We should also enliven the social life in the village, and we are beginning to do it through clubs and social centers for meetings and entertainments. We should encourage home industries, rug weaving, more gardening, more beekeeping. We must do everything we can to improve the food and increase the income of the fellahin. We must also do what, for example, Denmark has so brilliantly accomplished—organize co-operatives. We started to do this in 1928. There are already sixteen thousand of them in our country. We should strengthen the ones now in existence and organize more, many more. In Denmark the farmers buy seeds and machinery together, yet each farmer maintains his absolute independence. I am a great believer in the small individual farm. Though some people say it would decrease the productivity of the land, I disagree with them. I believe it would, on the contrary, increase productivity in the types of agriculture that are specially suited to Egypt. No, there is nothing like the small individual farm for our fellahin."

"What chance is there of realizing your program?" I asked.

"We have already drafted it into laws which have received the approval of the Ministry of Social Welfare. Anyway, the opponents of reform no longer cry that we have no right to interfere in their relations with the peasantry, which they claim have always been happy. They no longer call our program bolshevism."

Thereupon Dr. Hussein's associate added: "Either the landlords sell their surplus lands (over a hundred acres) and get paid for them and go on living their happy lives, or they run the risk of ultimately losing not only their lands but also their heads."

These were the most momentous words I heard in Egypt.

CHAPTER XI

Iraq—the Old Splendor and the New Ordeal

"AND TERAH TOOK ABRAM HIS SON, AND LOT THE son of Haran his son's son, and Sarai his daughter in law, his son Abram's wife; and they went forth with them from Ur of the Chaldees, to go into the land of Canaan; and they came unto Haran, and dwelt there."[1]

Abram must have been a tribal sheikh who, guided by divine inspiration, forsook his old home in ancient Iraq and went in quest of new pasture lands and a new destiny for himself and his offspring. However legendary the biblical tale may seem to the modern man, the town of Ur, uncovered and identified in 1852, symbolizes the stupendous decline of one of the most flourishing civilizations in the ancient world. Thanks to the efforts of the British Museum and the University of Pennsylvania, significant relics have been disinterred from the ruins of Father Abraham's native town. The accomplishments of this city of the Chaldees had for millenniums been buried deep in the earth.

Some three thousand years ago Ur was a seaport on the Persian Gulf. Now the site is one hundred and fifty miles inland. The

[1]Genesis 11:31.

161

desert has been driving the waters farther and farther away. "Century after century," Gottschalk writes, "the sediment brought down by the Tigris and the Euphrates rivers from the overgrazed highlands of Turkey, Syria, Iran, and Iraq has pushed back the headwaters."[2]

This is only one of a multitude of incidents that the student of Iraq's history might select to highlight nature's ruthless encroachment on man's world.

According to Walter Lowdermilk, eleven civilizations were born and have perished in Iraq during the past seven thousand years.[3] Though now vanished, these civilizations have embellished man's history with exciting legend and reinforced it with enduring achievement. Tradition has it that the Valley of the Twin Rivers—the Tigris and the Euphrates—is the cradle of civilization, the scene of the Great Flood, the seat of the Garden of Eden. According to an American historian,[4] the concept of the synagogue, the church, the mosque came out of ancient Babylon, in what is now Iraq, not from the Babylonians, but from the Jews whom the Babylonian King Nebuchadnezzar had driven as captives to his capital. The gatherings of the Jews for worship and religious discussion were the origin of communal worship as we know it today in the Jewish, Christian, and Moslem religions.

On the soil of Iraq, the once mighty and lustrous Arab Empire rose to its highest attainments. Here was fabulous Bagdad, the city of the Abassid caliphs, capital of Harun-al-Rashid, most powerful ruler of his day, well known to every reader of the *Arabian Nights.*

The agriculture of ancient Iraq was unrivaled anywhere in Asia or Europe. The soil was so fertile that, according to a say-

[2]L. Gottschalk, "Effects of Soil Erosion on Navigation in Upper Chesapeake Bay," *Geographical Review,* April 1945.

[3]Walter Lowdermilk, *Palestine, Land of Promise* (New York: Harper's, 1944).

[4]H. A. Foster, *The Making of Modern Iraq* (Norman: University of Oklahoma Press, 1935).

ing, when tickled it smiled a crop. Herodotus testifies that "of all the countries we know there is none so fruitful in grain. It will yield commonly two hundred fold or . . . even three hundred fold. The blade of the wheat plant and the barley plant is often four fingers in breadth. As for the millet and sesame, I shall not mention the height to which they grew lest it seem incredible."

With all the exaggeration that may have crept into Herodotus' writing, there is ample confirmation of the fact that old Iraq gleamed with irrigation canals and swelled with granaries. Its grains and fruits and grasses supported a population at least three times as large as the land has today. Bagdad in the days of Harun-al-Rashid—A.D. 786–809—was a city of two million. No other city could vie with it in prosperity or culture. In writing of that once mighty Arab Empire, Sir Mark Sykes presents a vivid portrait of the extraordinary quality of its civilization:

"The Imperial Court was polished, luxurious, and unlimitedly wealthy: the capital Baghdad, a gigantic mercantile city surrounding a huge administrative fortress, wherein every department of state had a properly regulated and well-ordered public office; where schools and colleges abounded; whither philosophers, students, doctors, poets, and theologians flocked from all parts of the civilized globe. . . . The provincial capitals were embellished with vast public buildings, and linked together by an effective and rapid service of posts and caravans; the frontiers were secure and well-garrisoned, the army loyal, efficient, and brave; the governors and ministers honest and forbearing. The empire stretched with equal strength and unimpaired control from the Cilician gates to Aden, and from Egypt to Central Asia. Christians, pagans, Jews as well as Moslems were employed in the government service. Usurpers, rebellious generals, and false prophets seemed to have vanished from the Moslem dominions. Traffic and wealth had taken the place of revolution and famine. . . . Pestilence and disease were met by imperial hospitals and government physicians. . . ."[5]

[5]Sir Mark Sykes, *The Caliph's Last Heritage* (London: Macmillan Company, 1915).

Science and art, religion and philosophy, flowered there and then as nowhere else in the world. "If the Greek was the father," writes H. G. Wells, "the Arab was the foster father of the scientific method. Through Arabs it was, and not by the Latin route, that the Modern world received the gift of light and power."[6] The Arabs had absorbed the culture of others—especially of the Persians, the Greeks, the Jews—and had added their stirring contributions to man's knowledge of himself and his surroundings. Eager and alert, the Arab mind, jolted by Mohammedanism, from century-old torpor, was the most creative in the world. Arab mathematicians gave us the zero and algebra. They added significantly to the science of trigonometry. They lifted astronomy to the level of a great science. They were great physicians and great surgeons. The *materia medica* they assembled has not been invalidated by the centuries. Presumably from the Chinese, they learned the process of manufacturing paper, which gave science and letters a fresh impetus. From the Arabs, in turn, Europeans learned how to manufacture paper. While Europe was steeped in ignorance and riven with disorder, the Arabs for a period of four centuries were the intellectual leaders of the world.

"It was Arabs and Mohammedans who started the European Renaissance," I was told by an Iraqi educator whom I met while flying to Bagdad. "We it was who brought back Plato and Aristotle and Euclid to Europe, and we gave Europe our own great contribution in mathematics, medicine, astronomy, and other sciences. Out of it all blossomed the Renaissance and Europe became a civilized continent." He was repeating, though with overemphasis, what every textbook on history gratefully acknowledges as Europe's indebtedness to Arab culture, and what educated Iraqis more than any other Arabs I have met are particularly eloquent in proclaiming. Proud of the extraordinary achievements of the once masterful Arab Empire, they are hoping and dreaming of the revival of its onetime glories.

[6]H. G. Wells, *The Outline of History* (New York: Triangle Books, 1940–41 edition).

Nor is there any reason, historical or biological, against the fulfillment of the dream, once the Arab world stabilizes itself and shakes off, as it did in the days of Mohammed, the lethargy of centuries. The supreme intellectual virility it once displayed could not have died out in the Arab individual. Dormant, the Arab world is waiting for someone or something to freshen it with a new fertility and inflame it, as Mohammed did, with a fresh inspiration.

As for architecture, one has only to visit Cairo and Isfahan to appreciate the exquisite beauty of the mosques, temples, and palaces which were built in the wake of the Moslem stimulation of the human mind.

With the passing of Harun-al-Rashid, internal jealousies and intrigues, rife among Moslem and Arab leaders in old times as today, weakened and degraded but did not destroy the power and the achievements of the Arab Empire. It remained for outside invaders, and first the utterly barbarous and uncreative Mongols, to strike the fatal blow. In 1258, Hulagu Khan, grandson of Genghis Khan and brother of Kublai Khan, laid siege to Bagdad. With true Mongol ferocity, he sacked the city and put to death eight hundred thousand noncombatants. The Arab Empire fell to pieces. An end came to the Abassid dynasty. Darkness enshrouded the once glowing land.

Weakened and disintegrating, Bagdad subsequently fell prey to the Turks. For nearly four centuries, from 1538 to 1918, Turkey ruled Iraq, and all creativeness was snuffed out. Man and nature deteriorated. Irrigation collapsed. The well-kept canals became choked with silt. The desert marched over the soil. The people lapsed into sullen submission. The Mohammedan faith to which they clung had lost its power to stimulate their intellectual vigor and their physical energies. They had no more inspiring teachers to guide them, no more valiant warriors to protect them. They were stagnating, withering in sterility.

The old splendors have vanished and have been buried deep underground. Archaeologists, notably from the British Museum, the Field Museum at Chicago, and the universities of Oxford, London, California, Harvard, Yale, Pennsylvania, and Chicago, are having literally a field day in Iraq disinterring and bringing to light ever-mounting piles of relics of the monumental achievements of ancient Iraq.

In 1918 a British army liberated Iraq from Turkish rule, and in 1920, Great Britain was given a League of Nations mandate over the country. After several violent clashes with the British, Iraq, in 1932, attained sovereignty. Its fighting spirit testifies to its passion for independence. It will not be officially beholden to any foreign power, even to the one whose armies liberated it from nearly four centuries of cruel subjection. But it is still a nation in process of being born. It is in more desperate search of a destiny than any other Moslem nation in the Middle East. It is striving hard to shake off the accumulated lethargies and sterilities of centuries. It is a crucible of ancient dogma and tradition and of modern knowledge and aspiration. With one foot in the ancient world, as symbolized by the wandering Bedouin, and the other in the modern world, as exemplified by the alert, English-speaking college student, Iraq belongs neither to the one nor to the other. It is as much at the crossroads of the world intellectually as it is geographically.

In outward charm neither the educated Iraqui nor the migrating Bedouin is lacking. Iraquis are the most restless and impetuous people in the Middle East. None other is so quick and loud in active resentment of internal grievances or external injustices, real or fancied. In the last twenty-six years Iraq has had fifty-two changes of government. During World War II, Arab pro-Naziism was more fiercely defiant in Iraq than in any other Arab country. In April 1941, Rashid Al Gailania, a former prime minister, staged a successful rebellion against the British. He occupied the British Royal Air Force airfield at Habanija, west of the Euphrates, and isolated the British Embassy in Bagdad. It required reinforcements from India and Trans-Jordan to quell the rebellion.

Quite recently there was a further outburst of rebellion, which was as much anti-British as it was anti-government. After the Selah Jabr Government had concluded a treaty with Great Britain on February 15, 1948, Bagdad rocked with protest which re-echoed around the world. The tumultuous demonstrations in the streets brought out the police. Bloody clashes ensued. Thirty-six civilians were killed. How many of the police lost their lives has never been disclosed.

The Jabr Government fell, but the latent forces of discontent have been neither subdued nor eradicated. Beneath the surface there surges a violent unrest. The domestic situation is whipping up waves of bitterness. The manipulations in the sale of grain have pushed up the cost of living sevenfold since the pre-war years, but earnings have lagged far behind. Obtaining the bread and the dates, the few vegetables, and the tea, sweetened or unsweetened, that constitute the daily fare of the poor and the laboring population has become a sordid problem for the mass of the citizenry, especially in the towns. The Bagdad airport, one of the most magnificent in the world, is an oasis of luxury, offering the weary traveler the coolness and the comfort he craves in the hot desert. But the airport is a little island of elegance and extravagance, a splendid achievement of which Iraqis are justly proud, but which is no source of gratification to the man or woman who must struggle for the bread and dates from which they derive their much-needed calories.

Whatever the immediate causes of unrest, the tangled land problem and the emergence since 1918, rather suddenly, of a powerful landlordism is one of the most unsettling forces in the country. The undernourishment of the fellahin—as the Iraqi peasants also are called—and the protests against the ever-mounting cost of food are as inextricably linked with Iraq's new landlordism as political immaturity is with the constant changes in government. Yet agriculturally Iraq is the richest land in the Middle East.

Despite centuries of stagnation, no other land has such brilliant prospects of revival, if only it would set its heart on accomplishing it. While Egypt has only one river to sustain its agriculture, Iraq has the Tigris and the Euphrates—two Niles, as an Iraqi once expressed himself. Like the Nile, these rivers have for centuries been bringing fresh nutriment to the valley they traverse. The silt they have been carrying from northwest to southeast has been enriching the fertility of the land. In the north, Iraq has appreciable rainfall, at times so heavy that it churns the alluvial soil into mud.

Besides, unlike Egypt, which is experiencing ever-increasing pressure of population on the land, Iraq is sparsely populated. While Egypt, with a population about three and a half times as large, must sweat out a living from an area which when fully rehabilitated comprises only 7,500,000 acres, Iraq can put under plow thirty million acres, or four times this area. In addition to rich lands, Iraq has vast stores of oil. It is seventh among the oil-producing countries of the world.

The climate is rather hot, reaching in summer a temperature of from 100° to 120° F. in the shade. While the sun scorches the European or the American, Iraqis have become hardened to it. Lean, and, when they are well fed, also hardy, they acquit themselves of a day's labor with no particular strain. One often hears foreigners deride Iraqis as being shiftless and lazy. The charge is no more worthy of credence when applied to Iraqis as when directed against Egyptians and Persians. I have seen peasants and laborers in Iraq, and in Egypt and in Persia, toil away in a broiling sun with a steadiness that no European farmer or laborer could match. It is not laziness but poor health, undernourishment, and lack of incentive that so often impairs the industriousness of the working people in the countries of the Middle East.

Cereals, as in olden times, are Iraq's most important crops, especially barley and wheat. Rice, corn, millet, sorghum, and sesame also do well, and cotton and tobacco hold forth much promise. Then there are the world-famed Iraqi date-palm plantations. Nowhere in the world do dates grow more luxuriously and more abundantly. Among the most beautiful sights in the Middle East, as one approaches Bagdad by plane from the east or the west, are the avenues and groves of date palms. After one has flown over immense wastes, the trees loom out of the brown earth like messengers of hope and cheer. There are thirty million date palms in Iraq, growing three hundred and fifty varieties of the fruit, though only five of an especially high quality yield the large tonnage for the foreign market—185,000 tons in 1938, the year before World War II had shattered international shipping.

Since liberation from Turkey, Iraq has made striking advances in agriculture. Irrigated lands have multiplied fourfold. Gravity canals and pumping stations are-the two common methods of irrigation. In 1921 there were 143 pumps in the country; in 1941 there were 2,778; and at present the number exceeds 3,000. There has been some introduction of agricultural machinery, and the nation has had the guidance of some of Great Britain's noted scientists and financial experts, most eminently of Sir Ernest Dowson.

Iraq is the one country in the Middle East which might have led the Arab world and Iran into an era of land reform. From Turkey it had inherited a land rich in agricultural resources which awaited only the application of modern science and the modern machine; and, which was even more striking historically, there was no landlord class. Had Bagdad taken to heart the policies Sir Ernest Dowson proposed, it would have built a solid —indeed an impregnable—foundation for its agricultural economy, and saved itself much of the unrest that is now shaking the country and is certain to shake it even more in the future.

In his penetrating and scholarly report on land tenure and land policy in Iraq, Sir Ernest perceived the dangers of the process of land-grabbing that was worming its way into the countryside. "Outside of the towns and certain garden reaches," he wrote, "the private ownership of land is rare in the country. With the relatively minor exceptions mentioned, the whole land surface in the country in cultivated land, pastures, wastes, forests, mountain, desert, steppe, marsh, is in law State Domain."[7] This was precisely the condition in America which invited the Homestead Act of 1862. With the land all State Domain, the state, in Sir Ernest's judgment, should set up "a sound system of settlement and of the registration of rights to the land as an essential preliminary to agricultural development."

Had Iraq taken a leaf out of American history and combined it with Sir Ernest Dowson's proposals, it would have insured itself, despite all the vicissitudes that new nationhood brought in its train, against the economic evils and the social hazards that its Mohammedan neighbors were facing. It is now beginning to encounter the same evils and hazards in its own land on an ever-mounting scale and amidst loud tumult and violent emotion. Iraq could have marched forward instead of pushing itself backward, with respect to its system of land ownership or land use. Sir Ernest had foreseen trouble. That was why he urged that the land under cultivation be granted by the state in leasehold. The state would then remain in an undisputed position to promote the development Iraq needed to obtain maximum bounty out of its immense and priceless acres.

The historic opportunity which, save for Jewish Palestine, no other nation in the Middle East was vouchsafed, Iraq—or it would be more correct to say Bagdad—coolly and bluntly forfeited. The tribal sheikhs, who had discovered, while still under Ottoman rule, the quickness with which gold could be gotten through the export of cereals, hastened to lay claims to tribally held lands, to which as individuals they had no legal right. Moneyed people from the city as well as sheikhs, by burdening the fellah with debt for the installation of irrigation pumps, acquired further large tracts of land. The fellah was dispossessed.

While there are individually established homesteaders in Iraq, the overwhelming area of the cultivated land has slipped into

[7]Sir Ernest Dowson, *An Inquiry into Land Tenure and Related Questions* (Letchfield, England: Garden City Press, Ltd., 1932).

the possession of the new landlords. About a thousand sheikhs now hold some two thirds of the acreage in use. Rich and powerful, they are a formidable political force closely allied with the Regent. They spurn and block all land reform.

Rarely is the sheikh or the city landlord an agriculturist. Neither has he any special interest in building up the land or in investing appreciable funds in science and machinery. Usually the sheikh is a man of no education and with no particular ambition other than to amass wealth. He is head of a society of his own tribesmen, and they must submit to his will—in his role of landowner more than ever. In consequence, the tribesmen are now worse off than they were when there was tribal ownership of land. Formerly they could count on a larger share of the crop than they now receive. Nor did they need to squander any of it on special fees to agents and sub-agents or to underchiefs and their hirelings.

"So long as tribal and other communal divisions remain strong," wrote Sir Ernest Dowson, "unrestricted individual freedom to dispose of the land would be dangerous to public peace and contentment." Yet without such freedom there can be but little progress, and "the small peasant and tenant remains a chattel in the hands of the landed proprietor."[8]

Because landlords have no special interest in maintaining the fertility of the land, the fellahin move from one area to another as soon as salinity sets into the soil, which, in the absence of proper drainage, it invariably does after several years of tillage. Moving is no arduous chore for the fellah, because his personal possessions in clothes, furniture, tools, and livestock are scant or nonexistent. Nor is a new home much of a problem—there are always reeds to make a shack, or home-woven cloth for a tent—for himself and his family.

Because of so shiftless a system of land ownership, the share-cropping fellah in the mountain districts obtains only from 30 to

[8] A. Bonnet, *The Economic Development of the Middle East* (New York: Oxford University Press, 1945).

40 per cent of the crop. Out of this share he must help defray the cost of maintaining the canals and sometimes pay a fee to Bedouins for protection against possible raids by themselves or by other Bedouins.

In cash terms, the yearly earnings of the Iraqi fellah during the prewar period were from twenty-four to forty dollars in the northern region and half again or even twice this much in the central and southern regions.[9]

The imprint of poverty lies bold and heavy on the Iraqi population. Like Egypt, it has one of the highest death rates in the world, 27 per thousand between the years 1930 and 1936. Its infant mortality in the years 1938–41 was 227 per thousand, higher than Egypt's. The six species of malaria-carrying mosquitoes infect from seven hundred thousand to eight hundred thousand people a year.[10] One third of the population, according to the same source, is afflicted with hookworm. Trachoma and bilharziasis are widespread, and in Bagdad alone there is a little army of the blind—seventy-five hundred men, women, and children. The life expectancy of the Iraqi in 1930–36 was twenty-six years for men, twenty-seven for women.

As long as poverty and disease on this scale continue, there can be no hope for stability in Iraq, regardless of how heavily Great Britain and the United States invest in new agricultural projects. Of the four and a half million population, three and a half million are fellahin of one type or another—settled farmers, Bedouins, and semi-nomads, some of whom have not yet emerged from the primitiveness of Father Abraham's days. They have neither conquered a new world nor discovered a new way of life. With no personal stake in the land, they are rootless, really homeless. They are on this earth because they are nowhere else. It is not their earth, and their sole interest is their immediate share of the crop. No one could stimulate them—and no one

[9]*Ibid.*

[10]"A Committee of Officials," *Kingdom of Iraq* (Baltimore: The Lord Baltimore Press, 1946).

is trying to—into a battle for the reclamation and rehabilitation of the land. Even if they were interested in or wanted modern machinery and modern methods of tillage, they could not, with the best will in the world, do anything about it. They have not the means to acquire implements or to initiate improvements. They cannot be drawn into a co-operative movement that would help them. They will crawl along, much as does the Persian or the Egyptian peasant, much as do their sheep that graze and over-graze the lands, but with even less assurance of adequate physical subsistence.

With the Iraqi fellah still landless or without a guarantee of adequate protection against dispossession and disinheritance, the sheikhs and the city landlords will have their way. With only rare exceptions they will pursue their own destructive methods of farming. They will move their fellahin from one area to another as soon as fertility is exhausted and salinity sets in. Proper drainage, when instituted, will prevent salinity, and fertility can be restored through scientific crop rotation, with a fine balance between grains, grasses, and leguminous crops, and through the ample use of manure. No other country in the Middle East has so much land for pasture and for forage crops with which to build up herds of sturdy livestock. Yet as of the present, according to the semi-official Baltimore publication to which I have already referred, Iraq is exceptionally poor in livestock: approximately 6,000,000 sheep, 2,000,000 goats, 600,000 cattle, 118,-000 buffalo, 100,000 horses, 140,000 donkeys, 30,000 mules, and 70,000 camels. Livestock would not only provide the manure for the land but the meats and the dairy foods for the enrichment of the daily diet of the fellah. A family cow, of a breed that yields an adequate supply of milk, and some well-managed poultry would rejuvenate the health of the peasant family.

Potentially the richest agricultural country in the Middle East, Iraq is actually the poorest. The most fiercely nationalistic, it is politically the least stable of the newly born Arab nations. Its young intelligentsia is second only to the Lebanese in intellectual earnestness and maturity, yet its sheikhs are the most backward of landlords.

Arab and Mohammedan, Iraq seems to have forgotten the words of Allah as uttered by the Prophet, which a Persian Moslem once quoted to me: "I gave you the earth as a blessing; eat and drink *and do not waste*" [my italics].

CHAPTER XII

Tel Aviv

"EVER BEEN IN TEL AVIV?" ASKED THE AMERICAN pilot who gave me a ride in his car from the airport at Lydda, Palestine, to the nearby Jewish city.

"Never," I said.

"Well, sir," came the answer, in a crisp and twangy Midwestern accent, "here is one city that's like home to Americans. We all like to spend our vacations here."

Though these words, and the other accounts of the city I had heard from various pilots and fellow journalists, had prepared me for a surprise, the actuality of Tel Aviv surpassed all anticipation.

It was early evening when we drove into the city, and as our automobile rolled slowly along the broad, well-lighted streets I had the sudden illusion of being bodily and spiritually lifted out of the Orient into a new and miraculous world. The city teemed with life and action. Traffic jammed the streets—columns of automobiles nosed and poked into one another. Crowds swarmed the sidewalks. Gay with window displays, shops were doing a rushing business. The city was obviously too small for the surge and swell of life within its boundaries. It was like a youth wearing the clothes of his childhood.

In Search of a Future

I had observed nothing like it since I left Switzerland. After Cairo and Teheran, Tel Aviv was a breath-taking spectacle. The very sounds were different, the very smells were new. Here were brightness and abundance, with no hint of the extremes of riches and poverty, luxury and want, grandeur and squalor so luridly conspicuous in the Persian and Egyptian capitals. Here were no processions of beggars, no throngs of street urchins, no turbaned dragomen and no long-haired dervishes, no pariah dogs and no homeless cats such as slink along the highways and pathways of any Persian city.

Here were no stately camels, their backs laden with rocks and grain, with timber and cut straw, pacing the pavements with the dignified and leisurely unconcern of creatures who fear nothing and nobody. Here were no caravans of donkeys bringing to the bazaars baskets of cucumbers and melons, blood-dripping carcasses of freshly slaughtered sheep, or goatskin pouches of fresh water. Here the horse and the truck superseded the donkey and the camel, and the roar and sputter of the motor signalized a lifting of drudgery from human shoulders. Only the swirls of sand which the Mediterranean winds blew up reminded the visitor, as in Cairo, of the desert. Only the wailing melodies of Hebrew songs pouring from the loud-speakers made one aware that one was neither in Europe nor in America.

For over half a year I had wandered in the Mohammedan world, villages and cities. Vigilantly I had observed the injunctions of British and American physicians, chiefly missionaries, never to let a drop of unboiled water or milk pass my lips, never to bite into a raw fruit or vegetable, never to be tempted into buttering my bread. They had treated too many Europeans and Americans, they said, who had paid a dire penalty for their dietetic trespasses. Only once had I blithely disregarded medical counsel. On a journey to Isfahan on a blistering day and over sand-swept road, the bus on which I traveled stopped at a village bazaar, where I saw a stall agleam with freshly picked grapes. In spite of the flies, the wasps, and the yellow jackets that swarmed

176

over the fruit, I bought a bagful, and following the example of my Persian companions, I sat down on the steep bank of a limpid, swift-flowing mountain stream, rinsed the grapes, and ate them. The unease I subsequently felt was too painful a penalty to pay for my reckless indulgence.

Now, at last, I was in a city in which I could drink water straight from the tap. I could take a bath without scrupulously checking with maid and room clerk in the hotel, as in Teheran, to learn whether the water had been boiled. "Eat and drink anything and everything as you would at home," the pilot had said. The words were cheering, and I copiously drank the fresh water. I drank and drank the fresh milk, which I had not tasted in over half a year. As I sauntered along the streets I strayed into a market place. The world over, market places are alike in brilliance and noise and bustle. This one was like the others. Here were wagons and trucks, stalls and shops. Here were stacks of vegetables and barrels of fruit, meats, and fish, and all the dairy foods in the world. Here were crowds of shoppers, chiefly women. As I watched them I pondered a thought which I felt certain had occurred to none of them: they had no notion of apprehension lest fever and plague lurk in the lettuce and the cabbage, the apples and the plums, the milk and the butter they were taking home to their families. I had not realized how disease-minded I had become. Instead of thinking of drink and food as sources of health, I had come to associate them with the most malignant sicknesses that afflict mankind. One gets that way in the East, where side by side with a charm and hospitality that exalt there is a sordidness and degradation that appall.

The sight of fresh fruit roused such a hunger in me that I bought a bagful of apples and pears. I wiped them only with my hands, which I had not washed since I left the hotel. While strolling along the busy market place, I munched the fruit as shamelessly as an urchin. I knew I was defying fate no longer, I was only pleasing myself.

I walked and walked the streets so effulgent with electric light that neither moon nor stars mattered. A white city, though not as white as Miami Beach, nor anywhere nearly as resplendent. No tall building, nothing like the skyscrapers in the Florida city or on the main avenues of Cairo. They are not permitted in Tel Aviv, where the height of a building is commensurate with the width of the street it faces. The skyline, therefore, is as low and unimpressive as that of a suburban American community.

As in Cairo, cafés line the main avenues, and here also the seashore. Though lacking their plush elegance and their urbane formalities, they are reminiscent more of pre-Nazi Berlin and Old Vienna than of the Egyptian capital. The tea is excellent, the coffee more to European than American taste, the pastry as rich and oversweet as in prewar Warsaw or Prague, baked perhaps by specialists from those Slav capitals. The service is prompt and correct and unflavored with the bows and genuflections that were as much a part of the Berlin and Viennese waiters as their black ties and their swallowtails. The open-necked shirt is as much in evidence as the collar and tie, and shorts are no more out of place than neatly creased trousers. Strangers talked readily to one another without formal introductions as they might in America's Midwest.

Tel Aviv is not only white, it is also green. Though built on sand dunes, it is a city of trees—grayish-needled desert pine, sycamores, acacias. Its seashore, four miles long, edged by a thin strip of park, would enhance the aspect of any city. In the residential quarters, shrubs and flowers brighten green lawns, though nowhere did I see anything as lush and brilliant as the Persian gardens still vivid in my mind. But then Persian gardens, with their geometrically spaced flower beds, their tinkling fountains, their sparkling pools, their dense groves, their twittering birds, are a peculiar Persian gift and are the supreme luxury of an elite which can afford the expense of so painstaking and beautiful an an accomplishment.

Yet Tel Aviv's appreciation of ornamental nature, individual and communal, reveals something of the transformation that comes over the Jews in Palestine, particularly those from East European countries. During the middle thirties I made several journeys to the newly founded Jewish villages in Russia's Crimea. Here, in some of Russia's choicest lands and most salubrious climate, Jews who had lived in ghetto towns away from blooming fields had learned to grow grain and fruit as competently as their neighboring German settlers, who had lived in the Crimea since the days of Catherine the Great. Their chickens were as sturdy, their pigs as fat as those of non-Jewish farmers. Yet the shade trees which they were ordered to set out in front of their homes withered from neglect. Rarely did anyone prune or water them, and sheep and heifers chewed the saplings to pieces. No blossoming poppies or other flowers enlivened their courtyards. New to the land, trees and flowers held little or no appeal for them.

But in Tel Aviv, Jews from similar environments displayed a remarkable appreciation of nature. The growing tree and flowering plant blossomed like symbols of deliverance from ghetto mentality. The very battle with the sands inculcated an appreciation of growing things whose roots held down the desert and averted sandstorms.

A modern city, there is nothing grandiose or arresting about the architecture of Tel Aviv. Some of it is as clean-lined as pre-war Berlin or the newest parts of Prague. Utility rather than art is the governing motive. The pioneering effort is superevident. Save for the Herzlia Hebrew College, with its looming white tower, modeled supposedly after the inner building in the courtyard of Solomon's Temple, there is scarcely a reminder of antiquity. Even the synagogues are in the modern style. There has been no visible effort to re-create the fashions of biblical times. Unlike Cairo or Persia's Isfahan, which, despite their dreary slums, overwhelm the visitor with the beauty and loftiness of their ancient architecture, Tel Aviv is no more a reminder of antiquity than is Des Moines, Iowa.

The names of the leading streets and boulevards signify a

fusion of ancient sentiment and modern achievement. They are named in remembrance of biblical ideas and heroes, of friends of Palestine, and of advocates of a Jewish homeland. There is *Geula* (Redemption) Street; Jeremiah Street, after the prophet from whose utterances comes the city's motto, "I will build thee and thou shalt be built"; Joan Hanavi Street, after the prophet Jonah who set sail from the port of Jaffa (then Joppa) and was swallowed up by the great fish; Herzl Boulevard and Nordau Boulevard, the one after the Austrian journalist who first conceived the Zionist idea, the other after the French journalist who was Herzl's most devoted disciple in his struggle for the acceptance of the Zionist idea by Jew and non-Jew; Achad Ha'am Street, after the Odessa Jew, whom Zionists credit with the creation of the philosophy of Zionism; Jehudah Halevi Boulevard, after the Spanish Jew of the Middle Ages who wrote distinguished Hebrew poetry; Rothschild Boulevard, after the wealthy Jewish philanthropist who aided the earliest Zionist settlers in Palestine.

The display of British names—at the time I was there—was enlightening: Allenby Road, Balfour Street, Sir Herbert Samuel Square, King George the Fifth Street, Lord Plummer Square. In the light of the flaming feud between London and Tel Aviv, the honoring of these men, including a British king, seemed an anomaly. "Not at all," explained a Jewish editor. "Field Marshal Allenby drove the Turks out of Palestine; Lord Balfour, with his Declaration for a Jewish National Home in Palestine, gave reality to the two-thousand-year-old Jewish prayer, 'next year in Jerusalem'; Lord Plummer, the second High Commissioner of Palestine—ah, there was a man! We shall ever cherish his memory." It is not, then, all hate and fury between Tel Aviv and London. The warm sentiment for the men of yesterday may yet be the balm with which the men of tomorrow will heal the wound which the men of today have inflicted.

Tel Aviv is the only exclusively Jewish city in the world. It was built by Jews; it is inhabited by Jews; it is governed by Jews; it has been enriched and elevated by Jews. Hebrew is the official language. English seems like a second mother tongue—everybody I met seemed to speak it, children and adults, taxi drivers and policemen. Street signs and signs over shops are in both languages. Some Jews, especially Jewish children, speak Arabic, which is compulsory in the schools. The young generation does not particularly care to learn the languages of the countries from which they or their parents have come. They are through with the old world and want nothing, not even language, to remind them of the spectral ghettos—or, as one Jewish teacher expressed himself, "of the pogrom-makers"—of East and West.

"What books do you read?" I asked a Jewish girl who was helping her father in a restaurant where I stopped for a cup of coffee. She had been only four when her father fled from Hitler's Germany.

"Hebrew and English," was her reply.

"Don't you speak German?"

"I never want to speak that language," was her sullen answer. Yet her father was reading a German newspaper published by emigrants from Germany. He did not share his young daughter's contempt for the language of the country which under Hitler had set out to annihilate the Jewish people. And the quest of learning, rife in Tel Aviv, will not seal the mind of the studious youth against the languages that are associated with Western civilization.

Yet the restaurateur's young daughter exemplified the spirit of militancy of the Jewish youth. It is infinitely more unforgiving and combative than are its fathers and mothers.

It is a tough youth, forged in strife and in hate, in hope and in determination. Sun-tanned and muscular, as sturdy as any youth in the world, it is as cheerful as it is tough. It loves song and dance but will not shrink from battle. It honors the plow as much as the book, and on the least awareness of danger, whether from internal foe or external enemy, will drop both for the gun. As alert as it is fearless, it sentimentalizes neither the Jewish past nor its own present. Given to sports and outdoor life, to open-necked shirts and shorts, it has not cultivated nor does it care to cultivate the excessive refinements and the ceremonious delicacies of "the gentleman," whether of the East or the West. It is obsessed neither by doubt nor by vexation, and will suffer neither insult nor humiliation. Its faith in itself is as boundless as the sky above Tel Aviv.

"We are through with tears and with pleas for mercy," said a youth, a born Palestinian, whom I drew into conversation while we were both sunning ourselves on the beach. "None of the tactics of our fathers and mothers for us! Either we live or we die. We have no other choice. We want no other choice, and none other can be forced on us whether by Hitler or Bevin." He was not angry or excited. Playfully he was tossing little pebbles into the sea. He talked as calmly as though he were discussing a soccer game or a swimming meet. Though he was only nineteen, there was no misunderstanding his spirit of resolve and desperation.

The girls share the tough-mindedness of the boys. They too wear shorts, or sometimes slacks. They bob their hair and wear make-up, though never as prodigally as the emancipated Moslem girls of Persia or Egypt.

Fresh from the veil and from the segregation which men had imposed on her, the Moslem miss of those lands is so enthralled with her personal freedom that she has made a cult of femininity. To her, Hollywood stars are modern womanhood in its supreme state. She is so intoxicated with the idea of feminine allurement that her transcendent ambition is to model herself after a favorite Hollywood queen. There are, of course, exceptions, in Egypt far more than in Iran, where among the Cairo college youth, social purpose vies with personal allurement. But the Jewish girl of Palestine, hardy and buxom, will have none of so self-indulgent a personal life. A child of the twentieth century, she is conscious of no social gulf or intellectual inequality between herself and her blood brother or any other man. She, too, has only scorn for morbid self-analysis, for sighs and tears. She will neither weep nor moan over the misfortune of the moment. For her, too, there is no choice but a new life or an early death. "No enslavement again," said the daughter of a fugitive Jewish physician, whose acquaintance I made in the lobby of the hotel in which I was staying. "Do you approve of girls joining the underground terrorist movement?" I asked. "I approve of anything that will make us free in our own land." I glanced at the father. He smiled and was silent. Whether he approved of his daughter's view he would not say. But it was quite manifest that nothing he would say would make her falter in her convictions.

While the Old Testament speaks of Joppa, now the nearby city of Jaffa, it makes no mention of Tel Aviv—literally the Hill of Spring. There was no such city in ancient times, or even in very recent modern times. Only a generation ago, the land over which the streets and boulevards of Tel Aviv wind was desert, where Mediterranean gales blew over the hot white sands, piling up miles of shapeless dunes. It was wasteland with barely a glimmer of verdure.

Founded in 1908 by sixty Jews from Jaffa, Tel Aviv began more as dream than reality. Inspired by the Old Testament, these Jews sought to restore some of the idyllic pleasures of their biblical ancestors. "The fig tree putteth forth her green figs, and the vines with the tender grape give a good smell." These words in the Song of Solomon enchanted them. They dreamed of living in their own little cottages under their own fig trees, smelling their own vines.

Without bulldozers or steam shovels, with only the hand tools they found in the Arab city in which they lived, they proceeded with the arduous labor of building a Jewish suburb of Jaffa. The battle with the sands was an endless ordeal. But their enthusiasm never waned. The original community was small, only three hundred souls.

Then the dream came to an abrupt end. World War I burst on

Palestine as on Europe. In 1916 the Turks, who were the rulers of the country, evacuated the Jews from Tel Aviv and from Jaffa and forbade them to return. Trees that had been planted, vineyards that had begun to flourish, were unspared by the Turkish soldiers in search of wood for their fires. Only in 1918, after Field Marshal Allenby's conquest of the Holy Land, did the original settlers return, and the community again stirred with life.

In that year the population swelled to eighteen hundred. The boom began. The Jewish persecution in Poland, Rumania, and other European countries, the Bolshevik Revolution in Russia, drove Jews from their homelands. Many of them sought refuge in Palestine. Subsequent persecutions by the Nazis in Germany and Austria stirred fresh waves of immigration, and the city grew. The population rose from twelve thousand in 1925 to forty thousand in 1929, to one hundred and thirty thousand in 1936, to over two hundred thousand at the present time.

Flourishing orange groves on the outskirts of the city have been uprooted and are in process of being leveled to provide space for new homes. Squads of Jewish engineers and technicians, hod carriers and masons, plumbers and carpenters are feverishly busy with new construction projects. An American architect, a native of Brooklyn, whom I met while visiting the new building areas, had the highest praise for former teachers and shopkeepers, peddlers and scholars who had taken up the building trades. "They learn fast," he said, "very fast."

His family was with him, and when I asked whether they were happy in Tel Aviv, he said, "Well, my wife misses the conveniences of her Brooklyn kitchen. She is always talking about it. But I tell her that in the pioneering days even America did not have what we have." Yet for the refugee from Poland, Rumania, or Hungary, the new homes, with their faultless plumbing, their electrical equipment, are more than they expected. The apartments are small, one or two rooms exclusive of kitchen and bathroom. But there is security here and no thought of eviction. In the houses it owns, the municipality applies the monthly payments against eventual ownership. "Our aim," said Mr. Nadivi, the town clerk, "is to make it possible for families to own their homes."

Since the immigrants to Tel Aviv, particularly those from the Germanic and the more advanced Slav countries, include some of the most highly educated men and women of prewar Europe, the cultural upsurge of Tel Aviv, enthusiastically supported by the laboring population, is matched only by its physical growth. Save among the older folk, particularly women, who had no schooling in the old world, there is no illiteracy. In 1947, out of the annual budget of ten million dollars, the city spent three million on education. It derives its revenues from its own system of taxation. The well-to-do send their children to private kindergartens, but in its own kindergartens the city provides accommodations for all other children between the ages of four and six. There is a special solicitude for children, and not only the kindergartens, but the schools, the parks, the playgrounds, and above all the far-flung beach and the adjacent park offer children opportunities for healthy growth and recreation of which their parents never dreamed. Americans and Europeans who visit the city are as astounded by the physical sturdiness of the young generation of Jews as by their cheerful demeanor.

As children grow up, the world of sports is theirs for the asking. Soccer, track, basketball, swimming, boxing, volleyball, boating, yachting, water polo—these have been popularized and have their special enthusiasts. The Maccabee Stadium, with a seating capacity of fifteen thousand, has, like nearly everything else in the city, already been outgrown by the population. The most exciting athletic event is the annual swimming meet in the Sea of Galilee, not far away from Tel Aviv.

Publishing flourishes as perhaps in no other city in the world of the size of Tel Aviv. There are seven morning, one afternoon, and two evening newspapers in Hebrew, and two more in German for refugees from Germany and Austria who are still struggling with Hebrew. During 1945 and 1946, 947 books were published in Hebrew. The most distinguished literary talent of the country is engaged in the monumental task of rendering into Hebrew the great classics of the world. These include not only fiction but philosophy, with Aristotle, Spinoza, Descartes, Leibnitz, Fichte, Kant, Bergson, and Einstein particularly favored. Writers of fiction and poetry already published include the foremost authors of Europe and America. From the Russian the chief novels of Tolstoy, Dostoevski, Turgenev, and Scholokhov, and Pushkin's poetry have already found their way into the Hebrew tongue. While I was in the city, Gogol's *Dead Souls* made its appearance.

Translations from English literature include *Hamlet, Macbeth,* and *The Merchant of Venice,* all rendered into Hebrew verse; of Shaw plays, novels of Dickens, Galsworthy, Wells, Priestley. From French literature have come the writings of Balzac, Zola, Anatole France, de Maupassant. The chief Italian work translated into Hebrew is Dante's *Divine Comedy.* From American literature have come the writings of Mark Twain, Jack London, Theodore Dreiser, Upton Sinclair, Sinclair Lewis; of Louis Bromfield, Fannie Hurst, and of Steinbeck, Hemingway, Saroyan, and Betty Smith. And of course *Gone with the Wind* can be read in Hebrew. Nevins and Commager's *America: the Story of a Free People* is the most widely read book on American history.

From German literature come Goethe, Schiller, Lessing, Heine, Thomas Mann, Jacob Wasserman, Stefan Zweig. The love of poetry is attested by the two separate translations that have been made each of Shakespeare's *Hamlet,* Pushkin's *Eugen Onegin,* Goethe's *Faust,* Poe's *The Raven,* Longfellow's *Song of Hiawatha.* For 1946 the prize of one hundred pounds ($400), which the municipality annually awards for the most distinguished literary accomplishment of the year, was conferred on the writer who prepared a new translation of *Faust.*

Yet the Bible is a perennial best seller. The beauty of its

prose, the story it tells of the Holy Land in olden times, lend it its own appeal to young and old. For the young it is not only a literary work but an invaluable textbook in history and geography, in morals and manners known to their own people in ancient times.

For a city of only a little over two hundred thousand, Tel Aviv fairly bulges with bookshops. There is nothing like it anywhere in the Middle East, not even in Cairo. While twenty bookshops deal exclusively in books in Hebrew, a hundred others have on display books in other languages, principally English. British and American best sellers woo the eyes on every side. The city spends annually half a million dollars on foreign books, of which the lion's share, twenty thousand dollars a month, goes to the United States and eight thousand dollars a month goes to Great Britain. Newspapers and periodicals, again chiefly from the United States and Great Britain, absorb annually three hundred thousand dollars more in foreign exchange. On every hand I heard complaints that the monetary restrictions the Mandatory Government had felt necessary to impose on Palestine kept Tel Aviv from spending more lavishly on foreign books and foreign journals. One third of all the books sold in Tel Aviv are of foreign import, chiefly from the United States and Great Britain.

There are several book clubs in the city, of which the largest, "Hassadah," has enrolled ten thousand subscribers. Tel Aviv is the one city in the Middle East in which the publisher sends salesmen to canvass homes for the sale of books in the same manner in which publishers of popular books or sets of books still do in the United States. There are five libraries in Tel Aviv, of which the largest, Schaare Zion, operated by the municipality, has a quarter of a million volumes, and there are forty private lending libraries. What a contrast Tel Aviv is to Isfahan, which, with a like population, has two public libraries—one, the municipality's, with three thousand volumes, the other the Board of Education's, with four hundred volumes, and with no privileges for anyone to take any volume home from either library.

In Search of a Future

Music holds an especially high place in Tel Aviv. With funds collected largely in the United States, the late Bonislaw Huberman, the Polish-born violinist, founded in 1937 the Tel Aviv Symphony Orchestra. It is still the only musical organization of its kind in the Middle East. Arturo Toscanini, Sir Malcolm Sargent, Bernardino Molinari, and Leonard Bernstein are among the foreign conductors who have wielded the baton in Tel Aviv. So large is the number of permanent subscribers that each concert has to be repeated four times to accommodate them.

The theater flourishes. There is the famous Habima, known as the National Theater. Its repertoire includes not only leading Jewish dramatists but Shakespeare, Shaw, Schiller, Molière, Chekhov, Ibsen, Dostoevski, Galsworthy, Maugham, Čapek, Romain Rolland, Gogol, and the young American, Irwin Shaw. There is the Ohel, the Labor Theater, which does not even pretend to preach a special proletarian message to its audiences. There is the Chamber Theater of Young Actors, the liveliest and most spirited of all. An American play, *Pick-up Girl,* was the rage of the city during my stay in Tel Aviv. There is the Matate —"The Broom"—which devotes itself exclusively to satire and neither neglects nor disdains to make merry over the foibles of Jewish as well as foreign dignitaries. Fun-loving and irreverent, it levels its barbs at anyone and anything that strikes its fancy and evokes its amusement. The latest comer is *Bamaten,* a children's theater, whose actors and audiences are children.

The Tel Aviv Press Association has inaugurated a form of literary entertainment the like of which, to the best of my knowledge, is unknown anywhere in the world. Once every two weeks authors, editors, journalists, poets present a program of original compositions—news stories, fiction, editorials, poems, essays, satirical and humorous sketches. No other entertainment has proved so popular. Though presented in an auditorium that seats two thousand, it is always a sellout. The association's editorial board makes certain the offerings are entertaining and of high literary quality, and the variety of the programs as well as the names of the participants make it a literary event of extraordinary popularity.

The literary and artistic tastes of Tel Aviv are perhaps more varied and cosmopolitan than in any city in the world, because the inhabitants have come from many countries and have brought with them a knowledge and appreciation of the best cultural attainments of the lands of their birth. There are neither ideological nor nationalistic pressures to fit art into a specific mold or a prescribed formula. The critical sense of the audience would tolerate neither. The only "holy of holies" in the cultural life of Tel Aviv is the Hebrew tongue. Save out of courtesy to guests, there is no by-passing this universally accepted mode of expression. Otherwise, intellectually and artistically, Tel Aviv is a prodigious melting pot.

It is no less so ethnologically. As one walks the streets or the spacious beach which is the city's favorite playground, one rarely observes what may be termed specifically racial types. The bearded religious Jew with curls over his ears is not enamored of Tel Aviv. It is too worldly and too profane for him. The hotel in which I stopped had no compunction in mixing dairy and meat foods. There was nothing kosher about its kitchen or dining room. Nor is it an exception in this exclusive Jewish city. For the religious Jew, Jerusalem is the chief city.

There are as many blonds in Tel Aviv as in Zurich or in Prague. Where do they come from? When I put the question to an eminent author his reply was, "That's the way the Lord wants it to be, I suppose." Once while I was walking along the beach with a pilot from Texas we saw so many red-haired girls that he was impelled to exclaim, "You'd think this was Ireland!"

The Arab in the adjoining city of Jaffa, also a Semite, seems to be of a race apart, not only in language and in manner but in physical make-up. Jews from fifty countries live in Tel Aviv—from all over Europe, the Americas, Africa, the Middle and Near East. For some mysterious reason the Palestinian-born Jew is often as un-Semitic as the proverbial Nordic, with light hair and blue or gray eyes. Yet the Jew from Yemen is so dark that he betrays no external mark of identity with the European Jew. Whether intermarriage or change of climate or some other social or natural circumstance changed the physiognomy of the Jews, especially of those born in Palestine, is a question for ethnologists and anthropologists to wrangle over. The incontrovertible fact is that Tel Aviv is a gigantic melting pot, and the new generation bears no more resemblance to the ghetto Jew of Warsaw than the physical environment of Tel Aviv bears to that doomed community.

Strange and significant things are happening to the Jew in Tel Aviv, as all over Palestine, to his physical appearance as well as to his mental make-up and his social attitudes.

In Tel Aviv the style of dress is modern—more American than European. The people I saw were so well dressed (or perhaps it only seemed so to me after a prolonged sojourn in other countries of the Middle East) that I asked a local editor if there were any really poor people in the city. "Oh yes, of course," he said. "We are quite civilized," he added, with good-humored irony. "We even have pickpockets and holdup men."

A British civil officer with whom I was riding in a taxi from Jerusalem to Tel Aviv told me, "Tel Aviv has a population of about two hundred thousand, but when you get there you think it is a city of half a million. That's how busy it is. Everyone works. Nobody seems at leisure."

Tel Aviv *is* one of the busiest cities in the world. Commerce and industry, the press and publishing, literature and art, music and dancing, all are centered here. It is the only manufacturing metropolis in the Middle East that rigidly enforces an anti-child-labor law respecting boys and girls under fourteen. It is now one of the diamond-cutting centers of the world. Driven by Hitler from Holland, Belgium, Germany, diamond cutters and settlers fled to Tel Aviv. They set up shop there and trained new artisans. Since the end of the war some of them have gone back to the lands from which they came, particularly to Belgium and Holland, whose governments encouraged their return. Many others, about four thousand, have remained in Tel Aviv. In 1946 the export of diamonds amounted to twenty-two million dollars, 84 per cent of which was sent to the United States.

Because it is a city of working people, with no aristocracy, and, save among the very aged, no leisure class, Tel Aviv is singularly free from the extravagances and ostentations that are so conspicuous a feature of Cairo and Teheran. There is no "Society," in the sense of an exclusive social class that dominates the manners or the culture of the city. In the more expensive hotels and cafés people may dress formally but neither with a desire to outshine their neighbors nor with a show of self-importance. They indulge in wines and brandies, in pastries and ice creams, but there is no splurging. Food and drink are gestures of sociability and stimulants to conversation as much as indulgence of appetite. There is neither miserliness nor opulence. There are no hovels and no palaces. Middle-class standards and tastes, good and not so good, with rarely a flash of extravagance to invite a second glance, predominate. There is rarely the gallantry or the chic that one observes in the Mohammedan cities.

If Tel Aviv works it also plays. The sun, the sea, the beach, make it an inviting pleasure resort. During the war it was host to over two million Allied soldiers on leave. Tel Avivans, despite their preoccupation with their booming trade and their booming industry and their feud with the Arabs, are convinced that in time their city will become one of the great tourist centers of the world, for Jews and non-Jews. The Holy Land, they say, is more inviting than it ever has been. With malaria practically exterminated and other diseases under firm control, with Tel Aviv's bathing beach, its superb sanitation and good water, its fruits and vegetables, its dairy foods and meats, its comfortable though unluxurious hotels, it is in a position to offer the religious pilgrim, the historical-minded person, and the adventurous tourist an enlightening and pleasurable experience. Over good roads he may make his way in his own car or in serviceable busses to holy shrines in Bethlehem, Nazareth, Jerusalem. He may spend his days recapturing for himself something of the story and spirit of the Old and the New Testaments. Evenings, he may return to Tel Aviv to a room with a bath, bars and cafés, cinemas and concerts, theater and sports. The tourist, be he so inclined, may lose himself in a spiritual dreamworld of mystical contemplation, yet not lack for material comforts or the social diversions to which he may be accustomed.

One evening I engaged in conversation the owner of the seashore hotel in which I was stopping. He was a tall, robust man with dark hair, dark eyes, an easy manner, and a serious expression. He was particularly popular with foreign journalists and world-flight pilots. He told me he had come from Germany soon after Hitler rose to power. He had had a flourishing mercantile business in Breslau. He had been wondering whether Hitler would actually dare enact all the terrors he had threatened to visit on Jews. A conversation he had overheard one evening between a neighbor and the neighbor's ten-year-old son dispelled all doubt as to what was in store for a man like himself.

"Is that man a Jew?" asked the boy, pointing to a pedestrian across the street.

"Yes," said the father.

"Then may I spit at him?" asked the boy once more.

"Yes," said the father.

The hotel owner rushed home and told his wife there was no use dallying any further. "We loved Germany," he went on quietly and soberly. "We hated to leave it. My wife wept and pleaded that we wait a while longer—perhaps Hitler and the Nazis did not mean all they were saying about Jews and 'inferior' races. But the words of the boy and the father's answer rang in my ears. I had never heard words like that before, and I did not care to hear them again. So we packed up and left."

Yet as he talked, holding the hand of his pretty and attractive seventeen-year-old daughter, he evinced no show of anger and no spirit of gloom. The past was behind him, and while he could not forget it, neither would he permit it to perturb him. He did not curse the Germans and he had no quarrel with destiny. He had found a new home and had built up a new business and was at peace with himself and the outside world. Hearty and cheerful, he brimmed over with optimism. He knew of troubles ahead for Jews in Palestine. But there was trouble the world over—such was the history of the times. "If we have succeeded in taming the sand and the dust storms," he said, "and in clothing the Palestinian desert with orange groves, we shall not fail in coming to terms with the Arabs—some day."

This about sums up the spirit of Tel Aviv, a city without swank and without pretensions. There is neither doubt nor dejection among the people. There is only the sturdy faith that comes from triumphant toil and from pioneering for a new life.

CHAPTER XIII

A New Society

THE DAY AFTER MY ARRIVAL IN PALESTINE, THE rainy season started with a slashing downpour. Though it rained intermittently for several days, the good roads prevented any delay in my journey into the countryside. After the feverish creativeness of Tel Aviv, as contrasted with the boisterous stagnation of Teheran and Cairo, the Palestinian countryside held an irresistible allure, and I hastened there at the earliest opportunity.

I went first to the village of Givat Brenner, of which I had heard much talk in Tel Aviv. It was, I was told, not only an exemplary farming community, one of the most scientifically managed in all Palestine, but one of the world's most impressive laboratories for a new type of social order. It was a completely co-operative agricultural settlement based on the principle of democratic self-government, the like of which had rarely prospered in other lands. Whatever its future, I was informed, its present was a highlight of Jewish pioneering, not only for its advanced methods of farming but for its way of life, in which production and consumption were shared alike by the member-inhabitants.

I was all the more eager to visit this village because, in my travels about the world, I had lived in communal agricultural settlements in other lands. Some years ago I had spent several weeks among the Dukhobors in Canada. Actuated by a religious fervor, these people—originally Russian peasants—had forsworn private ownership of land and of everything else. With the help of Leo Tolstoy and *The Times* of London, they fled from Czarist Russia and emigrated to western Canada. Hardy and toil-loving, they made an astounding success of farming. But because of their scorn for education and for all culture not of their own primitive origin, they easily fell victims to their leadership. At the time I visited them in Saskatchewan and British Columbia, their leader, Peter Verigin, once an intimate friend of Tolstoy, was something of a czar. He ruled the Dukhobors with a tough hand and a caustic though eloquent tongue. They knew no other authority but his. They cowered in his presence and catered to his whims. Two of the comeliest girls always accompanied him in his travels. However high their agricultural achievements, the social degradation that Peter Verigin brought them to would have made Tolstoy cry out in rage.

In Russia, in the pre-collectivization days, I had visited two communal settlements, the Lenin Commune in the province of Tambov and the Seattle Commune (named after Seattle, Washington) in the North Caucasus. The first was founded by Russians, the second by Finns, both of which groups had been immigrants in America. In the early years of the Revolution they had pulled up stakes in America, pooled their savings, equipped themselves with the finest American implements their money could buy, and sailed for the old country. They were determined to live their own lives in a new way, without benefit of private ownership. Because of their American technical training, their American implements, and their personal zeal, they built villages that were the show places of Russia. Their standard of living, material and cultural, was incomparably higher than those of the surrounding villages or of any other villages I had known in Russia. But with the sweep of collectivization, they were forcibly scrapped. The Russian Communist party would have no exception of so marked a nature.

Yet in Palestine such agricultural settlements thrive. Parts of grass-roots movements, unencumbered with political theory or political ideology, they have won for themselves an enviable place in Jewish colonization. At the end of 1947 there were 166 of them. More are in process of formation.

That the reader may fully appreciate the magnitude of the Jewish agricultural pioneering achievement in Palestine, it is well to explain here that there is no prescribed or dictated form of land ownership or tillage. The most profitable plantations, the citrus groves, are for the most part privately owned. Anyone with capital of his own may acquire land and work it privately to suit his own purpose, secure against intrusion of state or social agency.

During the early years of the century there was danger that Jewish farmers in Palestine would only swell the number of feudal lords in the country. They worked their lands with hired labor, largely Arab, because it was the cheapest. Their personal efforts were limited to riding around on a donkey and inspecting the fields. Had this type of land ownership prevailed among Jewish immigrants, there would have been no state of Israel now. Instead there would have been a new class of effendis—"masters"—no doubt more enterprising and more progressive than the Arab effendis, but with little personal inducement to push on with beaverlike assiduity for the transformation of Palestine into a normal, healthy, self-sustaining Jewish homeland. It was largely out of the struggle between Jewish workers and plantation owners over wages and conditions of labor that the movement of Jewish settlements came into being. Tired of fruitless tussles with Jewish landowners, the workers and the intellectuals, including Zionist leaders, who shared their sentiments, turned to the idea of the co-operative settlement. "We do not seek idyllic peace in agriculture," wrote Joseph Bunsell, one of the founders of Dagania, the original settlement. "Our eyes were opened when we worked as hired laborers."

Invariably the co-operative settlements obtain land from the Jewish National Fund. They do not pay for it, for the Fund is no real-estate brokerage, neither is it landlord. Its sole function is to enable Jews to return to the pursuits of their ancestors—"cultivating their own vineyards and tending their own flocks." The Fund attaches two conditions to the land it grants: that the farmers work it with their own labor and that they pay an annual rental of 2 per cent of the cost of the land. Hired labor is barred, and were a colonizer to make use of it other than in an emergency, he would forfeit his land. If crops fail and the farmer, be he individual or community, finds it beyond his means to meet the annual payment, it is deferred, sometimes canceled. Anyone accepting these two conditions obtains a lease on the land for forty-nine years. On the expiration of the term, the lease is renewable for another long period. So long as he works it with his own labor, the farmer is never in danger of losing the land; and since it is renewable unto perpetuity, he has every incentive to improve it and to think of it as his possession which his children will inherit. No special fee and no exchange of documents accompanies the act of inheritance.

Eminently practical for the achievement of its main purpose—to make farmers out of Jews who have for centuries been alienated from the land—the system of land control which the Jewish National Fund exercises is also vested with the spirit of biblical authority and biblical ethics.

Speaking of the Promised Land from Mount Nebo, Moses said: "For the Lord thy God bringeth thee into a good land, a land of brooks of water, of fountains and depths that spring out of valleys and hills; a land of wheat, and barley, and vines, and fig trees, and pomegranates; a land of oil olive, and honey; a land wherein thou shalt eat bread without scarceness, thou shalt not lack any thing in it. . . ." (Deuteronomy 8:7–9)

But it was not to be a land of landowners who would become

feudal barons. "The land shall not be sold for ever: for the land is mine [saith Jehovah]; for ye are strangers and sojourners with me." (Leviticus 25:23)

"Woe unto them that join house to house, that lay field to field, till there be no place, that they may be placed alone in the midst of the earth!" (Isaiah 5:8)

"The earth is the Lord's, and the fulness thereof; the world, and they that dwell therein." (Psalms 24:1)

"So shall ye divide this land unto you according to the tribes of Israel. And it shall come to pass, that ye shall divide it by lot for an inheritance unto you, and to the strangers that sojourn among you, which shall beget children among you: and they shall be unto you as born in the country among the children of Israel; they shall have inheritance with you among the tribes of Israel. And it shall come to pass, that in what tribe the stranger sojourneth, there shall ye give him his inheritance, saith the Lord God." (Ezekiel 47:21–23)

The tiller of the land, therefore, even when he is a stranger, a non-Jew, shall have his right of inheritance.

Fully realizing that the co-operative settlement is not suited to all immigrants, because it requires a special type of person with special gifts of individual and social flexibility to fit into the pattern of so highly socialized a scheme of living, Jewish colonists and their leaders have evolved several other types of village. Next to the co-operative settlement the so-called small farmers' village—a village made up of small landholders—has won the widest following. To this type of village the Jewish National Fund grants land on the basis of individual allotment, from five to seven acres when it is irrigated and from twelve to fifteen and even more when it is unirrigated. When scientifically cultivated, such a holding is deemed ample to keep a family busy and to provide it with a comfortable living. In this village, too, the farmer subscribes to the two conditions of the Fund: no hired labor and an annual payment of 2 per cent of the cost of the land.

The small farmers' village is rooted in the individual family organization. The mother does the cooking and cares for the house and the children. She helps in the fields, too, though not in the same measure as in the co-operative village. First and foremost she is a homemaker; only secondarily is she a field hand. But because of the limitations and disadvantages that a small farmer faces in his business dealings with the outside world, the small farmers' village has its co-operative features. Heavy machinery is purchased and exploited jointly. All trade, both sale and purchase, is delegated to co-operatives. In times of illness, neighbors feel obliged to help out with the field work and with chores. All mutual affairs are settled by the Town Meeting. By the end of 1947 there were eighty-three such villages in Palestine.

Of late, still another type of rural community with a yet higher appeal to the individualistic-minded colonist has been founded, the so-called middle-class farmers' village. It is precisely what the qualifying term implies—middle class—and the chief applicants have been middle-class Jews from central Europe, notably from Germany and Czechoslovakia. They buy their land, as much as their capital permits, or acquire it from an agency. They work the land themselves, with or without hired labor. They too avail themselves of co-operative organizations, which aid them in the purchase of machinery or in the disposal of their produce. By the end of 1945 there were thirty-five such villages.

It is significant that the intellectual, with a more keenly developed social consciousness, takes more readily to the co-operative settlement than the peasant or small-town man from Europe. The richer social and intellectual life the settlement affords outweighs for the intellectual his propensities toward individual ownership. But the Jewish peasant has grown up to associate tillage of land with ownership, and, unless re-educated, he looks askance at the co-operative settlement.

As we drove to Givat Brenner, the downpour had turned into bluish drizzle. The fresh moisture which the earth had soaked up brightened the hills and the valleys. The countryside was beautiful to see.

We passed village after village and at last climbed a steep hill and reached Givat Brenner.

The population is 1,250—650 children and 600 workers, men and women. The make-up of the population is a story in itself. It is a melting pot on a more diminutive scale than Tel Aviv. Though all are Jews, they have come from environments as unlike one another as the lands of their birth. Half of them lived in Germany, one fifth in prewar Lithuania, one eighth in prewar Poland, about one fourteenth in Italy. The others, about one tenth, came from the English-speaking world—South Africa, England, the United States.

What is especially striking is the high education of a majority of the colonists. Nearly three fourths of those who arrived from Europe have graduated from gymnasiums, whose courses of study parallel roughly those of a junior college in the United States. Few have had any previous agricultural experience or had imagined they would ever be farmers. They were educated for careers from which physical labor as a source of livelihood was excluded. They cherished other ambitions. Some of them— among the Italians—never thought of themselves as Jews. They were just Italians of the Jewish faith, even as their neighbors were Italians of the Catholic faith. They experienced no anti-Semitism until Mussolini, at Hitler's behest, had of a sudden sprung it on the Italian people. Outcasts in their own land, they had no choice but to seek a home elsewhere. They made their difficult way to Palestine.

Though educated for professional and business careers, here they were, dirt farmers, speaking among themselves the Hebrew tongue, which most of them had never learned as children and which some of them were still struggling to master.

The village was started in 1928. When the first group of colonists arrived, there was no village. There were no homes. There were no buildings. I was shown a photograph of the tent colony in which the original settlers lived. Immediately after they had put up their tents they went to work.

They started modestly with only twenty-five acres. It was not their land, of course, but a grant from the Jewish National Fund. As the community grew, the Fund granted them more land. Much of it was barren and desolate. From hills and swamps they reclaimed 375 acres. Now they are cultivating 875 acres, of which only 250 are irrigated. "Not enough land, nowhere nearly enough," said the secretary. He was a former German Jew in his middle thirties. Tall, broad-shouldered, with a weather-beaten face and a furrowed forehead, he was slow and deliberate of speech, and his loping gait denoted a man more accustomed to working than to talking.

As he and I trudged over muddy footpaths from field to field and building to building, I marveled at the care with which the land was cultivated and the buildings were kept. Nowhere did I see any slovenliness, except perhaps that here and there, quickened by the fresh rains, weeds peeped out of vegetable rows. The citrus groves of forty-five acres—shamouti oranges, Clementine grapefruit, lemons, tangerines—would compare favorably with the best in California. The clover meadows and alfalfa fields were thick and green with growth. Both are harvested four times a year.

On some of the unirrigated lands Givat Brenner grows cereals —wheat, barley, oats, bakia. Palestine should never have been a cereal country—the yield is too low, twenty-five bushels an acre at best. But cereals spell bread, which is the staff of life in Givat Brenner, even as, in one form or another, in all farming communities of the world. Since unirrigated land in Palestine does not lend itself to as wide a choice of crops as watered land, cereals, for the present, though not the main crop in Givat Brenner as well as in many other Jewish villages, are yet indispensable for the livelihood of the community.

The irrigated lands are of the greatest benefit to the community. On seventy-five acres it grows forage crops, corn and sunflower, the oil of which is pressed out and used in the kitchen.

On thirty more acres it cultivates garden produce, as many as three crops a year, for its own use and for the Tel Aviv market—potatoes, tomatoes, cucumbers, lettuce, green peppers, eggplants, summer squash, beets, cauliflower, beans, spring onions, spinach, cabbage. Because of the proximity to Tel Aviv, floriculture has become profitable, especially of gladioli and roses. A small plot of five acres is devoted to medicinal herbs, one of the most profitable crops on the farm. Fruits besides citrus are becoming of increasing importance. The village has a large orchard of apples, plums, and pears, as well as olives, figs, avocados, and other subtropical fruits. There is, of course, a large vineyard, for the grape, like the fig and the olive, has since biblical times been a traditional fruit of Palestine.

The growing crops showed such expert tillage that I asked the secretary how these farmers had managed to become so skilled within so brief a period of time. Picking a leaf off a tree and crumbling it in his lumpy fingers, he said, "I suppose we had to." And after a meditative pause he added significantly, "We are educated people here—we can learn fast."

I pondered these words. They held so much meaning. To these persecuted fugitives from Europe, farming in the ancient land spelled immediate salvation and ultimate promise. Being men of higher education, they realized at the very outset that they must avail themselves of all that scientific Western agriculture has achieved. Not for them the primitive monoculture and the exclusive manual labor of the Arab peasant. The farmers of Givat Brenner would make use of the latest methods and the newest inventions. As the years rolled by and they prospered, they acquired nine tractors, two combines, two steel rollers with which to smooth down the seeded fields, two mechanized sprinklers, two potato-planting machines, and a variety of other implements imported from the United States—grain drills, mowing machines, threshing machines, trucks, gang plows. While machines do the work on the land, twenty-one mules and horses in addition to trucks do hauling and transporting.

My greatest surprise was the dairy. Save for one farm in Persia and only a few in Egypt, I had despaired of seeing real milch cows in the Middle East, with clean and shiny skins and broad, low-hanging, milk-filled bags. Here was such a dairy—eighty-three milch cows, seventy-seven heifers, and a barn as modern as any I had seen in the United States, with revolving steel stanchions, individual drinking cups for the cows, brilliant light, and proper equipment for the prompt removal of excretions. From their large frames and black-and-white coats, I took the cows for Holsteins. "No," said the secretary, "they are our own Palestinian breed. We call them Damascene-Friesian." The average yield of milk a year was ninety-nine hundred pounds, which compares favorably with the best breeds in the United States, the Netherlands, and Denmark. They are using milking machines and have built their own plant for the manufacture of ice. Sanitation and refrigeration are no problem, as they still are in the Mohammedan Middle East.

Givat Brenner pioneering has gone beyond a scientifically managed co-operative farm. It has demonstrated that the farm can also be the source of much-needed and much-valued industrial production. There were times when a machine broke and neither spare part nor mechanic was available to set it in motion. Obtaining the spare part from Tel Aviv or sending there for a mechanic proved an inconvenience and an expense. The blacksmith shop in the village could not cope with complicated mechanical problems. It was therefore supplemented with a modest machine shop, which grew and grew until it manufactured not only spare parts but even certain machines.

Out of such beginnings, Givat Brenner has acquired a striking assemblage of busy cottage industries. Now there is a foundry in the village, on a small scale, employing ten workers. There is a machine shop, which fabricates pipes for irrigation and manufactures automatic sprinklers. There has been no slackening in the demand for these products. There is a small plant of four workers manufacturing insecticides. There is an elaborate, completely mechanized carpenter shop, which turns out furniture for the community and for the trade-union hospitals and sanitariums. There is a mechanized laundry, a bakery, a tailor shop, a shoe-repair shop. There is a building organization which includes masons, hod carriers, plumbers, and electricians. High on a hill there is a vegetarian hotel and health resort which accommodates one hundred and twenty guests in summer and about half that many in winter.

The most ambitious community enterprise is the canning factory, which employs sixty-five workers. Fruit juices, citrus concentrates, essential oils, marmalades, jams, all largely for export chiefly to England, are the foods in which it specializes. "What is this machine for?" I asked a mechanic at work over a red-painted piece of mechanism. "For the pressing of essential oils," he answered. "Yes," the secretary explained, "we make the machine ourselves. There is great demand for it all over the Middle East."

With flourishing cottage industries, there is no longer any slack season for the workers in the fields. There is always work for them somewhere in the shops. What is even more gratifying to the community, which is what today might be called Israel-minded, they have uncovered a fresh source of employment for new arrivals, and the end is not yet.

"What was your gross income last year?" I asked.

"In 1946 our gross income was 400,000 pounds ($1,600,000)," replied the secretary, "one fourth from our land and three fourths from the cottage industries." The average per working adult was twenty-six hundred dollars, a fabulous sum for any country in the Middle East.

"And how much cash is a member allowed?" I asked.

"None." He laughed. The question had evidently been asked him many times and he had expected it from me. "Hardly any," he corrected himself.

"Supposing," I said, "a member wants to buy a book, where does he get the cash?"

"Well," was the reply, "he asks the librarian to buy it, and when he finishes it he returns it to the library and others have a chance to read it."

"Suppose," I again asked, "an unmarried boy has a girl outside the village and wants to take her out for a bit of fun?"

"He goes to the treasurer and gets a reasonable sum for entertainment." And after a pause, and quite soberly, he added, "If it were his sister he wanted to take out, he would not get as much."

Much has been written about the Jewish co-operative agricultural settlements in Palestine, and much more will be written in the years to come. Whatever the process of transformation will make them, they are today the most remarkable rural communities in the world, agriculturally and sociologically. Though the philosophy of Tolstoy and Rousseau and Peter Kropotkin, with which the original intellectual immigrants were imbued, may have given the idea an impetus, the decisive circumstance was irrepressible necessity. Russian collectivization, with which the co-operatives are sometimes wrongly linked, could have been neither a model nor a guide. They antedated Russian collectivization by many years. The Dagania, the mother settlement in the Jordan Valley, was founded in 1909, long before the world had heard of Lenin, Trotsky, Stalin.

Whatever the idealism and the romance that went into their creation, the chief stimulus came from irresistible necessity. Had the land in Givat Brenner been divided on the basis of individual holdings, each member tilling his own proportionate allotment of less than one and a half acres, the village never would have attained its present development. It could not have acquired the tractors, the combines, the other implements. It could not have built the modern cow barn nor stocked it with a pure-blooded herd of cows. It never could have carried the expansion of the highly profitable cottage industries to so eminent a place in the community's economy. It could not have so easily cleared and reclaimed and built up the acreage it has rescued from disuse.

Nor could it have operated a profitable hotel and health resort. Each family would have had to grub in the earth for a living. Individually no member, unless possessed of substantial personal capital, could have accumulated or borrowed the required sums for the purchase of machinery and livestock. The idea of cooperation was a driving necessity for the advance of mechanized scientific agriculture even as it was for the reclamation of neglected and abandoned lands and for the training of skilled farmers.

Because Givat Brenner is one of the most advanced and most prosperous settlements in the country, I delved into its socialized scheme of living. Each family has its own little one-room cottage. Spacious and comfortable, it is not impressively attractive. It is intended only for husband and wife. There is no kitchen, because all eat in a communal dining room. Children live in their own community—in "children's town." The site of this community in Givat Brenner is on a high hill, and it affords a spectacular view of the surrounding countryside. It brought to my mind the hilly country of Madison County, New York, where I spent my high-school and college years. Undulating hills and low-lying valleys were carpeted with lush verdure. In "children's town" the children eat and sleep and play and go to school and grow up. Evenings, when parents are through with their work, the children come home for a visit. Rest days and holidays they spend with their parents. When mother or father or both go off on a trip to Tel Aviv or to some other village, the children often accompany them. When the parents take their annual vacation of two weeks, the children may or may not go with them. Since the cash allowance is small—about sixty dollars or seventy dollars a year—the range of pleasures or adventures the vacation affords is wider in anticipation than in fulfillment.

For six weeks after the birth of a child the mother stays with it in the nursery. During the first six months after birth the mother works half a day, and the other half she is in the nursery helping to look after her own and other children. Thereafter the child lives in "children's town," save on the occasions of visits to its parents. Relieved of domestic duties and of child care, the mother has more time to do outside work and more leisure to pursue whatever hobby or pleasure she chooses. This is one reason, I was informed, why the co-operative settlement is of particular appeal to the intellectual woman.

Children get the best of care—the best in food, in lodging, in recreation, in medication. Their excellent health is attested to by the fact that the infant mortality rate in settlements like Givat Brenner is the lowest in the world—26 per thousand, as against Sweden's 29 and New Zealand's 31.[1] It is much lower than the rate for all Israel, which is 44 per thousand. The nurseries, the dormitories, the swimming pool, the library, the playgrounds, the indoor games and diversions, the schools are intended to keep the children busy and happy and to enable them to grow into the type of citizen that Israel is striving to develop.

The schools in Givat Brenner are staffed with twenty-one teachers. Education up to the age of eighteen is compulsory. "We believe," said one member, "that a high-school education is an absolute necessity. It is the least we can do to enable our sons and daughters to acquire such an education." Beginning at the age of fourteen, children spend part of their time working on the land or in the cottage industries or both. Nowhere else in Jewish Palestine is labor so much of a religion as in the settlements, and both boys and girls are trained to acquire a wholesome respect for physical work. At the age of eighteen they decide whether they wish to remain in the settlement or seek their fortunes elsewhere. There is parental counsel but no pressure one way or another.

The settlements are particularly well suited to providing homes for orphan children from Europe. The buildings, the schools, the playgrounds, the staffs of trained nurses and attendants, the

[1] I. Kanievsky, *Social Policy and Social Insurance in Palestine* (Tel Aviv, 1947).

home-grown foods—fruits and vegetables, milk products, eggs—
the rich social life, all make it possible to offer these children a
healthy and rewarding life. In Givat Brenner there are seventy-
five orphans, some smuggled out of Europe. When I saw them on
the playgrounds and in the swimming pool I would not have
known, had I not been told, that some of them had virtually been
wrested from death. The Jewish Agency pays the settlement forty
dollars a month for the maintenance and education of each
orphan. They, too, on attaining the age of eighteen, will decide
for themselves whether they wish to remain in the community or
go elsewhere.

There are fifty-five other youths, likewise immigrants, between
the ages of fifteen and seventeen, and the agency contributes
substantially toward their upkeep in the community.

Givat Brenner has its own medical staff—a general practitioner, a pediatrician, a dentist. It has built its own hospital, with
fifteen beds for adults and thirteen for children.

Self-sufficient in material things, the community has not neglected its social and cultural life. Expounding his own philosophy,
the secretary said, "It is easier this way all around. Our security
is assured—a place to live, food to eat, clothes and shoes to wear,
care and education of our children, medical attention—we
needn't worry about any of these things. Unemployment holds no
threat for any of us. We can always live, and when the struggle
for a living and making ends meet is lifted from our shoulders, we
have the time and the opportunity to cultivate individual talent or
to indulge in the social and cultural pleasures that appeal to us."

Another official added, "Besides, the more cash we plow back
into the land, into buildings, and into equipment, the more
prosperous we become as a community and the higher is our
common standard of living."

Culturally, in Givat Brenner the standard of living is higher
than in any rural community this writer has ever known. At the
time I visited it, plumbers, electricians, and carpenters were busy
finishing an imposing new public building—a library. It has since

been opened. For a community of only 1,250 souls, this is an unusually rich library—twenty thousand volumes, half in Hebrew, the others in French, German, Yiddish, English, Italian. It requires the work every night of six librarians to attend to the wants of the readers. Special features of the new building are the seven study halls for children and adults and the new auditorium with a seating capacity of six hundred and a stage large enough to accommodate the Habima or any other dramatic company from Tel Aviv, or the Tel Aviv Symphony Orchestra.

Newspapers come daily not only to the library but to homes, one for several families. So do periodicals. Members who are interested in special studies—politics and psychology are the most popular—organize study groups and carry on discussions at frequent intervals. Those who play instruments have formed an amateur orchestra of twenty-four pieces. They give concerts in the new auditorium and often play in other villages. Other members have organized the choir. Dances are frequent, and so proud are the villagers of the dances that, as one member expressed himself: "Even those of us who are of middle age and older don't mind hopping around. In the old country we did it only at weddings. Now we dance whenever we feel like it." There is a special course in folk dancing under the guidance of an instructor who has made a study of the art. There are also sports for young and old, with swimming, as everywhere in Palestine, particularly popular.

In the last analysis, Givat Brenner appears to be a synthesis of village and town life, so that urban-minded members, which most of them are, may cultivate the interests and the pleasures they have learned to enjoy in the countries from which they have come. By making the community as self-sufficient socially and culturally as it is physically and materially, they rob the city of the lure it often holds to young people on the farm.

"And, of course," remarked a member, an intellectual who had come from Lithuania, "if anyone does not like it, he is free to leave."

He is free not only to leave but not to come. Membership is voluntary. To make sure the applicant will fit into so unorthodox a scheme of living, he spends the first year on probation. The initial half year, I was told, is the most critical. Not only must the new member feel happy to live in a settlement; the membership must feel happy to have him. They want no disharmony of will or temper. The individual, however good a worker, must acquire the talent of easy compromise and agreement, to become an asset to the village. Those who do not manifest such a talent are advised to seek accommodation in a community more suited to their needs and tempers.

Yet at Givat Brenner desertions are rare. In the early years of the settlements they ran from 6 to 14 per cent. Those were the years when members were still learning a new way of life. Now at Givat Brenner departures are from one to two a year, sometimes for unavoidable reasons. A young man or young woman of marriageable age may go off to the city to make new acquaintances among young people. If the girl marries outside the village, she usually does not return, but a young man usually returns with his new wife.

A strong cohesive force is the purely democratic manner in which the village governs itself. There is no one over the members, neither state nor social agency, to impose its will on them. All power is vested in the General Assembly or the Town Meeting, which meets as often as may be necessary. Once a year it elects the executive officers. After these have drawn up the plan for the year's work, the Assembly is convened to debate, alter, and approve it. Labor committees are formed to carry out the plan.

The one subject on which no conformity is ever demanded is politics. Any member may profess whatever political creed he chooses. Let it be noted that the settlement was not created to express political theory or sociological formula, as is the case with collectivization in Soviet Russia. It is not engaged in any crusade to invite others to emulate its example. It is a purely local institution, an outgrowth of purely specific Jewish needs and struggles in Palestine. Its leaders do not perceive in it an agency for the solution of the world's or the farmer's ills. They know it is something new in modern agriculture. They are proud of its achievements. But they do not claim that it fits other peoples, even in the Middle East. They know it does not even fit all Jews. That is why Jewish leaders have established other types of villages and encourage other forms of land ownership. It is an experiment of immense value, and so far it has been found useful in the task of redeeming the Palestinian lands and in offering work and homes to new immigrants, particularly to those who have no funds or capital of their own, and in teaching them to become scientific farmers.

There have been foreign journalists who have spoken of such communities as Givat Brenner as "hives," with no more personal a life for the individual member than that of a worker bee in the swarm. When the members read or hear of it, so they testified, they do not even get angry. "We laugh with amusement," they told me. No doubt to some people so startling a departure from the known modes of rural life in the Western world, so highly socialized a village as Givat Brenner evokes the image of a bee-hive or an ant heap, with the members presumably toiling and sacrificing for the upbuilding of the collective body. Yet to the people who live there the abrogation of certain rights is compensated by the acquisition of certain rewards which they might otherwise be denied. Socialized accumulation of property, they insist, builds up an economic structure which enriches their individual lives. "If I lived on my own little farm," one member remarked, "I should have to go to Tel Aviv to see the Habima players or to hear the Symphony Orchestra. Now both the Habima and the orchestra come to us."

The question inevitably arises: what is the future of so highly socialized a rural community? The answer invites speculation, and this writer can only set down his own opinions.

During the pioneering period the co-operative settlement accomplished its all-embracing purpose only too well. Had the cash been drained out of the treasury for disbursement among members, neither in its agriculture nor in its highly diversified scheme of living would Givat Brenner have attained the triumphs of which it is now so justifiably proud. By leaving the cash in the communal treasury, they acquired an amount of purchasing power which enabled them to lift their once neglected and desolate lands to so high a state of cultivation that, by comparison with their Arab neighbors, their farm is like a world apart, as if dropped from heaven like the manna of yore. The foresight and ingenuity, the diligence and the competence with which the land is cultivated and the livestock tended are all the more astounding when one remembers that the colony, which was only nineteen years old when I visited it, was founded largely by city people with no previous experience in farming. To have converted a village into so highly civilized a community, with its own medical service, its own hospital, its own schools, a community which enjoys theater and music and books, almost as much of them as a city, attests to the extraordinary possibilities that co-operative farming makes possible in the machine age.

No wonder that an outsider like R. A. Palmer, acting president of the International Co-operative Alliance and general president of the British Co-operative Union, was moved to write: "The success of the Jewish settlements in Palestine . . . is one of the outstanding achievements in the history of modern colonization. . . . The Jewish co-operators who set out to colonize Palestine, the ancient land of their forefathers, did not come as conquerors or adventurers in search of gain, they came as workers, as members of a co-operative family in search of a new life, in a new, better society—which they immediately started to establish. The results are certainly encouraging—not only in terms of human happiness, human brotherhood, community life, and community spirit. . . . Before the Jewish colonization experiment, Palestine was to all intents and purposes colonial in character. It is now being transformed into a progressive modern country."

But Givat Brenner is past its pioneering stage. It is coming of age, not only in years but in experience and achievement. It has triumphantly met its severest tests. It is a busy, flourishing community. The toil and the sacrifice have been crowned with rewards which (agriculturally alone) make it a show place not only in Palestine but in the entire Middle East. It may take some time before submerged individual longings, willingly suppressed, reassert themselves. Yet if man does not live by bread alone, neither does he necessarily live by the pleasures and enjoyments that are prescribed by the communal life.

I am convinced that the time will come when the members will want something more in the way of a home than the one-room cottages in which they now live. A larger home implies furniture and furnishings—from draperies to rugs, from a victrola to a frigidaire, from a wineglass to a soupspoon. The members may even tire of the communal dining room. I cannot complain of the food I was served. The mixture of fruits and fish and vegetables would sate any appetite, though it would not tickle the palate of the epicure. There must be times when the members wish they could give dinner parties for friends or guests. Now they must forego such satisfactions. Nothing is more natural than the desire to make a birthday gift to a wife, husband, son, daughter, friend. The meager cash allowances make such pleasurable indulgences trifling or prohibitive. I am mentioning only a few of the distinctively personal wishes or cravings that a cultivated person may seek to gratify.

Cash disbursements are therefore, in this writer's judgment, a question of time. The cashless basis of co-operative settlements like Givat Brenner can only be viewed as something indispensable during the learning and pioneering stage but without permanent basis. It must in time yield to a more abundant gratification of purely individual wants and tastes. Production will no doubt remain co-operative, but consumption is destined to become more highly individualized.

Already leaders recognize certain shortcomings in the highly socialized co-operative settlements. In recent times they have created a new type of village which combines joint tillage with individual home life. They have done so because, with the expectation of fresh waves of immigrants, they want to achieve a more flexible balance between personal needs and social effort.

As I was driving back to Tel Aviv, I was reflecting on the invaluable lessons a village like Givat Brenner affords to countries like Iran, Egypt, and Iraq. The socialized features of living would hardly be acceptable to the peasantry in any of these countries. Rarely do they commend themselves to the Jewish peasant who migrates to Palestine. Yet what an extraordinary demonstration of the multitude of immediate improvements these countries need—in the rehabilitation of their land, in crop rotation, in the breeding of superior livestock, in the selection of seeds, in the fight on disease of man and plant, in the potentialities of cottage industries, in the care and education of their now-neglected children.

CHAPTER XIV

Redemption of the Land

YEARS AGO, WHEN I WORKED ON A DAIRY FARM IN
Madison County, New York, the farmer who was my employer
applied to a New York City employment agency for a man to
help with the harvesting. Though he had specified in his letter
that he wanted "an experienced hand," the youth who arrived
could neither milk a cow nor harness a horse. But because of the
pressure of work, the farmer decided to break in the inex-
perienced youth. Yet one morning when we arose to go to the
barn for our chores, the youth was gone. He had slipped out
during the night, and he never came back.

Nor was this an exceptional incident. Unemployed city boys
often came out to work on farms and soon tired and sickened of
the hard labor and fled back to the city, often without bothering
to collect the wages they had earned. "All them city yahoos is
good far," complained my employer, "is to stuff themselves with
johnny cake and strawberry shortcake. They hain't never learned
whether it's the bull or the cow that gives buttermilk."

It was part of the folklore of the countryside that city men
hated physical labor and that those who came out to work the
land would flee back to the city even as, with the arrival of cold
weather, birds flee to warm climates.

At Givat Brenner the overwhelming majority of Jewish farmers were city-bred. On their arrival in Palestine they did not know the difference between clover and alfalfa, a sulky plow and a cultivator. Yet within a period of only nineteen years they made a spectacular achievement in agriculture. They were living proof of the fallacy of this bit of folklore, which I, too, during my years in Madison County, had considered to be as axiomatic as the ideas that bees would sting sweating horses or that cows would shrink their yield of milk unless at each milking they were stripped completely dry.

Givat Brenner only seemed, but was not, a paradox. Once the city man earnestly resolves on a farming career, particularly if he is a person of some education, he is in possession of advantages which the born farmer often lacks. He need not divest himself of traditions and habits that are sometimes the bane of the hereditary farmer. At Givat Brenner the city-bred colonists were only too eager to learn the latest methods of tillage. They could work with a tool in one hand, a book in the other. They had no past dogmas and values to live down. Instead of resisting, they welcomed the latest findings of science. They were as eager for the newest pronouncements of the experiment stations at Rehovoth, Palestine, or at Berkeley, California, as a woman is for the latest fashions in dress. Passion for the new land to which they had come, financial aid from outside sources, expert scientific guidance, a determination to re-create their own lives in complete denial of the economic though not the cultural attainments they had brought with them—these were priceless assets. Yet nothing would have availed them had they found it beyond their physical powers or their psychological gifts to pioneer for as advanced a system of agriculture as modern science and the modern machine had placed at their disposal.

Their Arab neighbors, also victims of a cruel history, had little to teach them. Dairying, for example, as Westerners understand the word, did not exist in Arab Palestine. Neither the cows nor the sheep nor the goats promised a reward commensurate with the care man might lavish on them. The native cow was as neglected as the land on which it foraged. Neither in milk nor in meat could she serve the demands of a European standard of living. Scrawny and unkempt, she averaged 1,540 pounds of milk a year. Used as a work animal, she dried up five or six months after calving. After hearing of such a cow, an American dairy-man said, "If I had her in my barn I'd cut her throat." "Or your own," a neighbor interposed.

The exceptionally low output of milk of the native Arab cow may be judged by a comparison with average yield of the twenty-five million cows in the United States, which is five thousand pounds a year. This figure is attained by including all the scrubs that wander over the wild hillsides of the most backward agricul-tural regions in the United States.

According to Dr. J. D. Kendrick, of the United States Depart-ment of Agriculture, the business-minded American dairyman can hardly afford to stable a cow that acquits herself with less than 350 pounds of butterfat a year. Translated into milk, this amount of butterfat equals 9,500 pounds in the Holstein and 6,600 pounds in the Jersey. Of the 800,000 cows of all breeds under test and observation by the Department, the average yield of milk is 8,635 pounds.

Only a cow capable of producing at a similarly high level could suit the purposes of the Jewish colonist. There was no such cow in Palestine. In nearby Syria and Lebanon the Damascene or the Beirut cow was superior to the native Arab animal. But she was not good enough. She could serve the immediate family needs of the colonist better than the local Arab strain, but would not pay for herself commercially. Besides, she was difficult to buy. "It is hard to find a few score good cows even in Damascus," read a bulletin of the Jewish Agricultural Station published in 1930, "and even harder to find hundreds." Thousands of cows of the best breeds were available in Europe, but the change of environment involved problems of acclimatization which were difficult to overcome. Their resistance to disease was low, and there was fear that, despite the severe quarantine precautions, European cows would bring with them European diseases.

All manner of European breeds were imported, but they offered no solution. Some of them did exceptionally well, and still do, especially the Friesian breed from the Netherlands. But they could not be transplanted to the Palestinian soil in large numbers and thrive as well as they did in their homelands. It was obvious to Jewish scientists and farmers that they would have to "create a cow" for Palestine, and after much experimentation it was discovered that the Damascene cow from Syria and the Beirut cow from Lebanon held forth the greatest promise. When either cow is bred with a Friesian bull from the Netherlands or North Germany, the offspring represents a complete regeneration. When the secretary of Givat Brenner spoke of "our own breed," he was referring to this offspring, which has now replaced the scrub breeds the colonists were formerly obliged to use.

A creation of Jewish Palestine, this cow averages eighty-eight hundred pounds of milk a year,[1] slightly higher than the average production of the eight hundred thousand cows under observation by the United States Department of Agriculture. Though no pedigreed bulls were imported from Europe during the war years, the milk-producing capacity did not deteriorate. Some of them attained a record of eleven thousand pounds of milk a year, which testifies to the exceptional qualities of the newly created strain.

With such a cow thriving in the Palestinian climate, the Jewish colonists have made an outstanding success of dairy farming. Because they can now grow green forage crops the year around, succulent fodder is no longer a problem. Yet these cows constitute only 8 per cent of all the milch cows in Palestine. Were the Arab farmers to exchange their scrubs for the new breed, the appellation "land of milk" would be as true of Palestine today as it was in biblical times. During the war years some of the effendis and merchants hastened to acquire such cows. Dairy

[1]*Palestine, Facts and Figures* (Tel Aviv, 1947).

foods were so high that the cows proved a lucrative investment. But the venture into commercial dairy farming among Arabs has since subsided. It has not, as it has among Jewish farmers, become a living pattern in Arab mixed farming.

The usual source of milk in the Arab world, as in Persia, has been largely the goat and the sheep. Jews, too, have made use of these animals—of sheep more than goats—but they have not been content with either animal as they found it. The output of milk was too low: an average of 88 pounds for the sheep, 612 pounds for the goat.[2] Without crossbreeding, solely by a process of selection, they have improved the *awasi*—fat-tailed sheep— to a point where it averages 330 pounds of milk a year with an occasional record-breaker that rises to 680 pounds. The figures for goats are equally impressive. The new breeds, attained solely through a process of selection, yield an average 1,575 pounds of milk a year, as against 612 pounds yielded by the neglected Arab goat.

Much cheaper than a cow, a goat or a fat-tailed sheep is often kept as a source of milk by the new settler or the factory worker who lives on the outskirts of the city. Yet both animals have liabilities—they nibble closely, and they contribute toward the disintegration of the land. The goat snaps at everything in sight and chews up saplings to the roots and kills them. The goat is one of the greatest destroyers of forest in the Middle East. Therefore neither sheep nor goats have become as popular with the Jewish as they always have been with the Arab population.

Poultry proved as great a challenge to the Jewish colonizer as cows, sheep, and goats. The native breed was so neglected and debased that it could justify itself only in a lackadaisical economy in which not calculation but chance prevailed. Uncared for and permitted to shift for itself, the native Arab hen was good for an average of seventy eggs a year. She would be no asset on a scientifically managed farm. Finding a favorable substitute that would thrive in the Palestinian climate was perhaps the easiest

[2]*Ibid.*

accomplishment of the Jewish husbandman. The white leghorn answered all purposes. Laying an average of one hundred and thirty eggs a year, it now enlivens many a barnyard. Some settlements have made a specialty of poultry even as they have of dairy farming. Some individual Jewish farmers have done likewise. Poultry is a booming enterprise in the Jewish villages.

The fight for the regeneration of livestock, beset as it often was in the case of dairy farming with aggravation and uncertainty, proved nowhere nearly as stern an ordeal as the battle for the reclamation and rejuvenation of the soil. The good earth of biblical days, with its rich soils, its green pastures, its still waters, its springs and streams, its forests and orchards, had come on evil times. "And God looked upon the earth, and, behold, it was corrupt; for all flesh had corrupted his way upon the earth." (Genesis 6:12) It had become corrupt not in a moral but in a physical sense. Much of its rich substance, which had once nourished a population at least twice the size of today's, had been blown away or washed into the sea. The terraced farming it had once known was no more. Forests and orchards had been ruined or felled. Springs and streams had dried up or had become choked with reeds and rocks and eroded earth, and had discharged their seepage into valleys, turning them into pestilential swamps. Hills were partially or entirely denuded of soils, and only the crevices between rocks and stones held tight the accumulation of sand and dirt. Out of these crevices grew wild trees and wild shrubs. According to Walter Clay Lowdermilk, the American soil expert, over three feet of soil has been carried away from the uplands of Palestine since the collapse of terraced agriculture. Malaria had become as dread a scourge in Palestine as it is in Iran, Iraq, and Egypt. A British report on this subject reads: "The country had been infested by disease for centuries, malaria had decimated the population, epidemics of it at times blotted out in a few months the inhabitants of whole villages and there were few regions that were free from it."[3]

[3]*Palestine Royal Commission Report* (London: His Majesty's Stationery Office, 1937).

Yet no historical-minded person would blame the Arab fellah for the catastrophic collapse of agriculture in Palestine. The invasions and depredations which the little country had for centuries witnessed brought ruin to both land and people. During the two centuries of the Crusades (1094–1291) the devastation never ceased. War made life so uncertain that the Arab husbandman was again and again obliged to flee from his land. Wandering Bedouins looted and plundered. The European warrior was equally merciless. Forests were felled, orchards ravaged.

The devastation of the Crusaders was followed by the depredations of the Mongols. They plundered and terrorized. They pillaged and killed. There was no escape for the helpless fellah. He became more nomad than farmer. With wife and child, tent and flock, he fled from one hill to another, from one shelter to another. Once-growing fields, untilled and unwatered, fell into disuse and became desert and swamp.

The Turkish rule of Palestine, which lasted four hundred years (1517–1918), was as barren of improvement as were the preceding centuries. Constantinople, uncreative and brutally indifferent, was far away, and local officials were little lords who squeezed and plundered the fellah with taxes and with fines. They taught him nothing. They made it undesirable and unprofitable for him to learn anything new. He stagnated, even as did much of the land all around him. The rise of the effendi class (government officials), who bought up the land in the plains and on the hills and who became the landlord class of the country, added to the burden of the fellah's backwardness and helplessness. The Western world, during the second half of the nineteenth century, bored a few cracks into the wall of darkness and isolation that Turkey had built around the Holy Land, but the fellah profited but little from the dribble of light that penetrated it. He was too isolated and too frightened of the outside world. He had nobody to guide him and nobody he could trust. All alone, he continued to battle for his life with tools and weapons which the Western world had long since deposited in its museums.

In 1909, then only twenty years of age, T. E. Lawrence made a journey through Syria and Palestine. He was appalled by the degraded state of those once-flourishing lands. That the degradation in Palestine was remediable became obvious to him from his observation of a few thriving Jewish colonies which he visited. So impressed was he with their achievements that he wrote: "The sooner the Jews farm it all, the better: their colonies are bright spots in the desert." Manifestly unjust to the Arab, this one-sided pronouncement can only be explained on the ground of the author's youth and inexperience. Eleven years later, matured by time and by close association with Arabs, and cognizant of Jewish achievement in Palestine, Lawrence wrote: "The success of their scheme will involve inevitably the raising the present Arab population to their own material level only a little after themselves, in point of time, and the consequences might be of the highest importance for the future of the Arab world. It might well prove a source of technical supply rendering them independent of industrial Europe, and in that case the new confederation might become a formidable element of world power."[4]

Though stripped of its onetime forests and grasses, its once-blooming fields turned into desert, the Palestinian land retains no little of its ancient fertility. *A Survey of Palestine,* which the Mandatory Government prepared in 1945 for the guidance of the Anglo-American Committee of Inquiry, contains the following enlightening sentence: "Whilst the soils frequently show great variations even within narrow limits, they are generally speaking remarkably fertile considering that they have received little, if any, farmyard manure for centuries."

Because malaria was a universal scourge, Jewish colonists from the earliest days set about clearing and draining the pestilential swamps and marshes. Though they exposed themselves to the stings and bites of the malaria-carrying mosquito, they knew that there would be neither health nor hope for them, neither peace nor progress, unless they conquered the dread

[4]T. E. Lawrence, *Oriental Assembly* (New York, E. P. Dutton, 1940).

little insect. The work continued for sixty years, and now, with the exception of the Huleh Plain, there are no more swamps in the Holy Land. The incidence of malaria has all but disappeared. In 1935, though no longer the scourge it once was, it still affected 22.4 per thousand of the population. By 1946 the figure dropped to 2 per thousand.

The Arab was as much the beneficiary as the Jew. No longer in Palestine, as in Egypt and Persia and Iraq, were peasants ravaged by malaria. When I was in the city of Shiraz, Persia, British missionaries told me of whole villages in the province of Fars that had been so badly stricken with the fever that the people could not gather in their precious crops. Government authorities confirmed the report. So vast a catastrophe could no longer happen in Palestine. Whatever the disabilities and the vicissitudes that beset the fellah, he need no longer fear the cruel inflictions of the malaria mosquito.

The clearing of the swamps and marshes accomplished more than the conquest of malaria. Though the area which these swamps and marshes comprised when lumped together was only about eighty-five hundred acres, the lands that were redeemed for settlement in the Plain of Esdraelon, in Samaria, in Galilee and Judea, and in the valleys of Zebulun, Sharon, and Jordan, embraced one hundred and twenty-five thousand acres.[5] In a small country like Palestine the rescue of so large an acreage for human use is an extraordinary performance.

The project for reclaiming the remaining swamps in the Huleh Plain has already been drawn. In antiquity this plain was a rich agricultural region. "It is blessed by nature," wrote Josephus, the first-century Jewish historian, "to such an extent that all kinds of fruits grow there. . . . Nature seems to have gathered together all climates into this one spot." Bound on the west by the Hills of Naphthali in Upper Galilee and on the east by the Hills of Golan and Bashan, the soil of the Huleh Plain has been en-

[5]Joshua Ziman, *The Revival of Palestine* (New York: Sharon Books, 1946).

riched by decayed vegetation. Rains are heavy, and springs, and streams, including Lake Huleh, inundate an area of eighteen thousand acres.[6] The swamps, among the worst in the country, soak an area of nine hundred acres.

Once title to the land has been cleared, the work of reclamation is to start. Upon the completion of the work, the lake will have shrunk to a surface area of twenty-two hundred acres and will have been heavily stocked with fish. The fishing industry alone, according to present calculations, will offer a livelihood to two hundred families. The reclaimed land, of which the Jewish National Fund owns one half, will offer domicile to seven thousand farming families. Because of its soil and climate, the rains, and the streams and springs, the Huleh Plain can regain some if not all of the richness it had in antiquity. Wheat, barley, corn, vegetables, both citrus and deciduous fruits, and grasses, as well as poultry farming and dairying, are well suited to the country. Rising on three sides to heights of from one to three thousand feet, the Huleh Plain might prove inviting to city people and foreign visitors as a place for vacationing. At present only fifteen thousand people inhabit it, one third of them Jewish and the remainder Arab.

While the Huleh Plain is a project for the future, the redemption of other once useless and desolate lands is the accomplished fact of today. From hills, rocks that were imbedded in the soil have been lifted and hauled away. Slopes have been terraced. Eroded lands, such as an area in the vicinity of Ruhama, have been treated so that winds will not blow away and rains will not wash away the soils. On the upper slopes the land has been terraced to a depth of three feet. Along the terraces, trees have been planted. Ravines and gullies have been partially or completely filled up. The long slopes have been broken by ditches. In other places salty lands have been leached and made available for tillage.

While the lands were being rescued, the search for water never

[6]Joseph Weitz, *Palestine's Agricultural Potentialities* (Tel Aviv, 1945).

ceased. There was no real irrigation of fields. Neither the lakes nor the streams nor the springs were adequately utilized previous to the arrival of Jewish colonizers. Save for the shallow wells which the native population had dug, no efforts were made to locate and use underground waters. As early as the 1920s there was still little information about such water sources. There was no science of Palestinian hydrology. When a well was sunk some ninety or a hundred feet, it was deemed a triumphant achievement. Not even the geologists who devoted themselves to the subject imagined that water could be economically obtained from lower levels. Only after new and very advanced methods of prospecting were applied were fresh reservoirs uncovered. By 1936 the Jewish National Fund had made a detailed survey which disclosed that, exclusive of the half million acres of level land in the almost uninhabited Negev Desert, at least four hundred thousand acres could be profitably irrigated. Only about one hundred and twenty-five thousand acres are at present artificially watered, over one half of these on Jewish farms. With fresh sources of water tapped and made available, Palestinian agriculture made a remarkable advance. It ceased to be a one-crop country. Two and three crops a year are gathered from lands that yielded only one. Clover and alfalfa, so essential in dairy farming, are cut from four to seven times a year.

Redemption of the land and the locating of fresh sources of water have been supplemented by a new science of crop rotation and crop tillage. Though oranges had come to Palestine during the Middle Ages (the Bible makes no mention of them), their possibilities, until the rise of Jewish agriculture, remained unexplored and unexploited, like gold in deep rock.

The *shamouti,* as the native orange is called, is in appearance and flavor one of the most attractive and salable in the world. Not even the effendis, always cash-minded, had become aware of the extraordinary commercial possibilities of this excellent fruit. As late as 1922, only seventy-five hundred acres were devoted to oranges. In 1938, the year before the beginning of the war, the acreage had multiplied ten times. It became the foremost cash crop of the country. While the pioneering in sorting and packing, in shipping and advertising had been essentially the achievement of Jewish citrus growers, the Arab growers gained from the export of the *shamouti* no less than the Jews. Between 1922 and 1938, Arab cultivation expanded from forty-five hundred to thirty-nine thousand acres. But whereas the Arab clung to the *shamouti,* the Jews introduced from the United States the Valencia, which had proved so marketable that the Arabs took it up on almost as large a scale as the Jews. Nor did the Jews ignore the grapefruit. They experimented with it, and the results have been so successful that it has become a basic tree in the newer Jewish citrus groves. As yet the Arabs have not given the grapefruit their serious attention.

The war struck the citrus industry a shattering blow. Deprived largely of export markets, some Jewish plantation owners uprooted their trees and planted the land to other crops. About ten thousand acres have been left to nature, receiving but scanty attention. Now that the war is over, citriculture is certain to boom again. Water is cheap. Pests are no serious problem. Frost is never a threat. Climate is excellent, and cost of production is comparatively low.

"Nowhere in the world," says Lowdermilk,[7] "have I found citrus groves cultivated so intensively and scientifically as in Palestine."

To the olive, which, like the fig, is celebrated in the Bible, the Jews have accorded scanty attention. Slow to mature, the olive tree requires twelve years to become fruit bearing. Of the one hundred and fifty thousand acres in olive trees, Jews cultivate only about one per cent. It is as much a purely Arab culture as it was before the arrival of the Jewish colonist. Soil erosion would be worse than it is did not the Arab devote so much acreage to this traditional Palestinian tree.

But deciduous fruits are almost entirely a Jewish innovation.

[7]Walter Lowdermilk, *op. cit.* (New York: Harper's, 1944).

The Song of Solomon praises the apple. "As the apple tree among the trees of the wood, so is my beloved among the sons." But Palestinian scholars do not believe Solomon knew the apple as we know it. They believe Solomon spoke of the pomegranate and that the word has been mistranslated or misapplied. The Jews have imported fine European species of apples and have made them a commercial crop. Large plums, pears, and peaches were unknown until the arrival of Jews. While apples and plums and peaches do well—and plums are especially profitable—pears have so far failed to yield the results anticipated. The banana, which grows in the Jordan Valley, is likewise a Jewish innovation. In recent years Jews have introduced a large array of subtropical fruits—pineapple, mango, avocado, guava, passion fruit, papaya, persimmon, cherimoya, and others.

The variety of vegetables grown in Palestine would content the most exacting housewife—eggplant, squash, pumpkin, cauliflower, radishes, celery, lettuce. Never before have vegetables assumed so significant a place in Palestine agriculture. The Jews have not only improved the native varieties and specialized in the cultivation of select seeds, but have brought in asparagus, rhubarb, red cabbage, and sweet potato. The ordinary potato was not unknown. The German colonist grew it, but only for personal consumption. The Jews made it a commercial crop. It has proven so profitable that Arabs are planting it for themselves and for the Jewish market. Indeed, owing to the example and the stimulation of Jewish farming, Arab agriculture witnessed between 1921 and 1943 the sharpest rise it had ever known, and not only in citriculture. The number of donkeys trebled, the cattle doubled, the amount of vegetables harvested multiplied six times, of olives three times. There has also been a conspicuous rise in the number of domestic fowl. Yet the yields in cereals and vegetables are much smaller than on Jewish farms—of wheat about one half, of vegetables a scarce two fifths.

The reason is obvious. The rich effendi—often an absentee owner, with his residence elsewhere, perhaps in Syria or Lebanon, like landlords all over the Middle East—would rather keep his income than reinvest it in the land. A few have purchased tractors and other modern machinery, but only a few. The ordinary fellah, whose income in 1930 averaged one hundred and forty dollars a year when he worked his own land and only eighty dollars when he was a sharecropper,[8] has not the means to acquire the machinery, to purchase the fertilizers and the select seed, and to bring into action the other features of modernization which Jews invariably employ. Besides, tradition and habit are deep-rooted with the Arab, precisely because he is a hereditary farmer. It is simpler to follow the way of ancestors than to venture into new modes of tillage. It is almost impossible to do so when the Jewish village is remote and the Arab is deprived of the stimulation afforded by example. He plows with his cow or his ox. His plow is a long pole with a steel point—as much a symbol of antiquity in Palestine as "the sharp stick" is in Iran. Though Palestine is not especially suited to cereals, the Arab devotes about 70 per cent of his cultivated lands to cereals—wheat, barley, millet—while Jews seed only one third of theirs to grains. The Arab can hardly be expected to do otherwise, for cereals constitute the most important single item in his food. Since cereals are so important, deep plowing, were he to practice it, and choice seeds, were he to obtain them, would substantially increase his harvest. But his ancient plow digs up only a thin layer of soil. If he is intent on uprooting the weeds, he must plow his land several times. If he does not bury the weeds, which is difficult with a thin slab of soil upturned, or expose their roots to the sun, they germinate again and pollute the planted field.

Unencumbered by tradition and seeking the maximum output of the land, the Jews have gone in heavily for mechanization, for proper rotation of crops, for select seeds, for the practice of growing leguminous plants to fertilize the land, for as great a variety of crops as conditions permit, for only a minimum of cereals and a maximum of alfalfa and clover and other grasses

[8]Robert Nathan, *Palestine: Problem and Promise* (Washington, 1946).

that furnish fodder for livestock, for truck farming, fruit growing. They have learned, if only from the Arab, that so small a land as Palestine is not fitted for extensive agriculture and that only intensive tillage offers opportunities for increasing the numbers of settlers and compensates the tiller for the toil he puts into the land.

The contrast between Jewish and Arab farming is everywhere as sharp as the contrast between the wooden and the steel plow, the ox and the tractor. In consequence the Jewish villages and the Jewish farms bear a closer resemblance to the villages and farms of the more advanced European nations than to those of the Middle East. Science and the machine record a triumph of man over nature which is, with rare and notable exceptions, without parallel in any of the Mohammedan lands.

The abundance of honey, from which the Holy Land was renowned in biblical times, suffered a disastrous slump in the centuries of wars and conquests and stagnation. Now it is being revived. In August 1945 there were on Jewish farms 25,900 beehives. Some of the apiaries are as modern as the cow barns. In a land that is now rich in blossom—in alfalfa and clover fields, in orange grove and apple orchard, in cultivated and wild flower —the bee is as natural as the sun, and performs a double function: enriches the harvest by its profuse pollinization of plant and tree, and produces honey. Already Jewish apiaries account for an annual output of 1,250,000 pounds of honey. It is a new and rapidly expanding branch of farming.

Since it is the aim of Israel to seek out and exploit every possible resource of the country, it is only natural that the Jews should turn their attention to fishing. It was not until 1937 that the first fisheries were started in the Sea of Galilee. The experiment lumbered along without appreciable success until the war years. In 1938–39 the Jewish share of the catch was only fifty-eight tons, or about 4 per cent of the entire catch. The war gave the industry a fresh impetus, and more Jews took up the occupation. Some Jewish settlements have it a part of their subsidiary activities. Fish is now caught not only in the Sea of Galilee but in the coastal waters of the Mediterranean, in inland lakes, and in artificial ponds. Soils unfit for tillage because of too much lime are dug for artificial ponds. With new equipment now available, more fish hatcheries will be started and more ponds will be dug, and it is the estimate of experts that in the future the annual catch can be multiplied five or six times that of 1946 output.

Thus within one generation Jewish colonists have transformed the part of the Holy Land which has come under their cultivation into one of the most flourishing agricultural territories in the Middle East. They have demonstrated that lands, however misused and abused, can be salvaged and rejuvenated. They have strained their backs and sometimes their hearts in this process of rejuvenation. They have fought malaria and have sometimes succumbed to it but have finally conquered it. Provided not all the soil has blown or washed away, they have hoarded it with a miser's passion on the tops and slopes of hillsides, and have clothed those heights with trees and plants and grasses.

Whatever the bitterness of the feud between Jews and Arabs, Jewish achievement in agriculture in Palestine is a historic event, indeed a turning point in the history of the Middle East. Nothing that the Jews in Palestine have accomplished the Moslems cannot achieve, not only in Palestine but in Iraq, Syria, Saudi Arabia, Egypt, Iran. If only there were a force, internal or external, that would lift the pall of apathy and stagnation from the lowly fellah and unleash his creative energies!

I remembered the young Persians, Egyptians, and other Mohammedan youths I had met who were longing to study in the agricultural colleges of Utah, Washington, California, or Iowa. The agricultural schools of America's Northwestern and Pacific states held an overpowering lure for them. A few of them were from families that could afford to send a son to an American college, but overwhelmingly they were sons of the intelligentsia or of shopkeepers whose fathers had not the means to finance their education abroad. They inquired about opportunities to obtain scholarships and other financial help from foundations or private individuals. Usually they were alert and earnest young men, with a fluent command of French or English or both languages, and they would no doubt make excellent students. On their return home, unless they lapsed into the traditional ways of their fathers or neighbors, they might make a significant contribution to the rehabilitation of their country's agriculture. They would be a new voice and might even become a new social force, in their homelands, that would help unleash the creative energies of the rural population.

Because of lack of finances alone, most of them will never see America or Europe. But in nearby Palestine, in the co-operative settlements, they could acquire a practical knowledge of scientific farming and of mechanical skills which is rarely vouchsafed to them in their homelands. What the Jewish colonists have learned, they could learn. If the co-operative settlements could train thousands of city-bred Jewish immigrants from Europe—adults and young people, men and women—to become expert farmers, craftsmen, mechanics, they could with equal facility educate Mohammedan youths in these accomplishments. I realize the difficulties involved, practical, cultural, above all diplomatic. Westerners steeped in power politics will scoff at these suggestions as absurd, naïve, utopian; and, in the light of the prevailing feud between the Arab and the Jewish communities in the Middle East, they do seem without validity. But if the feuds were allayed, if Jewish and Mohammedan leaders would divest themselves of the fears and animosities that have marked their relations toward one another, and if foreign diplomats and military leaders instead of abetting cleavage would further co-operation, rapprochement could result in an educational program for Mohammedan youths that would confer lasting benefit on the Mohammedan countryside.

In the report of the Royal Commission that was sent by the British Government to investigate the Jewish-Arab conflict in Palestine, we find these significant observations:

In Search of a Future

1. *The import of Jewish capital into Palestine has had a general fructifying effect on the economic life of the whole country.*

2. *The expansion of Arab industry and citriculture has been largely financed by the capital thus obtained.*

3. *The Jewish example has done much to improve Arab cultivation, especially of citrus.*

4. *Owing to Jewish development and enterprise, the employment of Arab labor has increased in urban areas, particularly in the ports.*

5. *The reclamation and anti-malaria work undertaken by Jewish colonies have benefited all Arabs in the neighborhood.*

6. *Institutions founded with Jewish funds primarily to serve the National [Jewish] Home have also served the Arab population. Hadassah, for example, treats Arab patients notably at the Tuberculosis Hospital at Safad and the Radiology Institute at Jerusalem, admits Arab country folk to the clinics of its Rural Sick Benefit Fund, and does much infant welfare work for Arab mothers.*

7. *The general beneficent effect of Jewish immigration on Arab welfare is illustrated by the fact that the increase in the Arab population is most marked in urban areas affected by Jewish development. A comparison of the census returns in 1922 and 1931 shows that six years ago the increase per cent in Haifa was 86, in Jerusalem 37, while in purely Arab towns, such as Nabulus and Hebron, it was only 7 and at Gaza there was a decrease of 2 per cent.*[9]

In the same report we read a further significant statement on the rise of wages for the Arab workers in Palestine. "The daily wage paid the Arab for skilled labor is now from 250 to 600 mills and for unskilled labor from 100 to 180. In Syria the wage ranges from 67 mills in older industries to 124 mills in newer ones. Factory labor in Iraq paid from 40 to 60 mills."

If such impressive benefits to the local Arab population could be achieved in the face of constant tension between Jews and

[9]*Palestine Royal Commission Report, op. cit.*

Arabs, how immeasurably higher they would be were the tension abated or eliminated.

No one who has been in the Middle East need underestimate the nature of these tensions. Nor, in this writer's judgment, need they be overestimated. It is not the purpose of this book to propose means and methods of reconciliation. But in the light of the desperate need of agricultural rehabilitation of the Mohammedan Middle East, not only the example but the co-operation of Jews, once enlisted, would constitute a real triumph in international good will.

CHAPTER XV

The Host of Hosts

UNTIL MY ARRIVAL IN TEL AVIV I HAD NEVER heard of Histadrut—the Federation of Jewish Trade Unions of Palestine. The word was as new to me as the sights of the city. Yet I could no more remain unaware of Histadrut than I could of the Mediterranean Sea. It flashed itself on my attention wherever I went. In a multitude of ways, it lapped all aspects of life as ceaselessly as the waves of the Mediterranean beat upon the shores of Tel Aviv.

I had never heard or read of a labor organization like it. In neither the Soviet nor the non-Soviet world had I encountered a trade-union movement that had assumed so gigantic a responsibility or unfolded so prodigious a spirit of creativeness and so disciplined a talent to give it visible form.

Histadrut is spokesman at once of labor and of capital—the protector and the largest employer of labor in Palestine. It not only builds factories, but enters into partnerships with capitalists, individuals or associations, for the promotion of industry and business. Together with a body of private manufacturers, it has created a fund for upbuilding the city of Beersheba—a city which is to provide work and homes for a population of ten thousand. In partnership with a private corporation—the Central Trade and Investment Company—it operates the Nesher Portland Cement Works of Haifa. When a private manufacturer failed to make a success of the Phoenicia Glass Works of the same city, Histadrut bought him out. It remodeled and modernized the plant and is now the most important manufacturer of window glass in the Middle East.

Histadrut has boomed its construction operations into the most gigantic building enterprise in the Middle East. It is the largest manufacturer of shoes in Palestine, of bricks, of soap, of oil, of fats, of cosmetics.

It favors private enterprise for itself and for anyone else who cares to risk his capital in any business venture, old or new. It welcomes and challenges private capital and has mastered capital's own weapons of conquest and advancement: production and distribution, initiative and inventiveness, service and competition. Like any individual entrepreneur, it neither hesitates nor scruples to undersell and outbid a competitor, to displace and absorb him. Whatever advantage Histadrut has won for itself as trader and manufacturer has been derived from its business sagacity, from its ever-mounting power as producer and distributor.

There seems no limit to the fields of endeavor it has invaded and encompassed. It is financier and banker. It promotes mutual savings and loan societies. It publishes books and pamphlets, newspapers and magazines. It has built its own theater in Tel Aviv, yet it imposes no ideological strictures on the plays presented. On the evening I attended a performance, the play was a translation of an old Dutch comedy based on life in Holland during the Napoleonic Wars. Neither in its publications nor in any of its educational and cultural endeavors does Histadrut manifest the slightest resemblance to the late Andrey Zhdanov's inquisitorial pronouncements on the functions of art and culture in the modern world. Unlike the Soviet censors, Histadrut seeks neither to stratify nor to freeze the creative imagination into an instrument of political fanaticism or warfare.

Histadrut encourages sports and fosters all manner of entertainment. It operates technical and educational schools for children, youths, and adults. In association with the Jewish Agency, it trains seamen, builds ships for a merchant marine, maintains an aviation school that teaches flight in both planes and gliders. It constructs and repairs ships. In its own shipyards it has built trawlers and other craft with which to start a fishing industry. It manufactures agricultural machinery, and spare parts for its own and for other makes of machines. It has carved an enviable place for itself in the manufacture of rubber goods, textiles, leatherware.

Histadrut not only buys and develops property but insures it, its own and anybody else's, against burglary, fire, earthquake, against motorcar and maritime risks. It issues life and accident policies. It is, in fact, the leading insurance agency in Palestine. It employs 22 per cent of all the workers and accounts for one fifth of the industrial output of Israel. Its investments have soared to the sum of eighty million dollars.

This unique labor organization will launch into any activity that promises jobs for new immigrants and unleashes a fresh flow of business in the country. Unlike trade unions in other lands, instead of setting itself against immigration, lest it depress wages, dilute labor's bargaining power with employers, or squeeze workers into joblessness, it welcomes new arrivals with open arms. Its leading slogan might be "More and more Jewish immigration for Palestine."

Histadrut is the despair of the Communist, to whom trade unions are an instrument of class struggle for the eventual enthronement of the communist dictatorship. At the masthead of its daily newspaper it prints not the Marxian slogan, "Proletarians of the World Unite," but its own democratic motto, "Freedom of Discussion and Unity." Histradrut is a striking contrast to the conventional trade unions of the West, to whom the chief or sole purpose of labor organization is to wrest from employers ever-increasing advantage for its members.

Labor is a great human ideal for the future, and a great ideal is like the healing sun. We need fanatics of labor in the most exalted sense of the world."

But in many of the lands in which Jews had been living, physical labor conferred on a man social inferiority. Sometimes, as is still the case among the landed gentry all over the rest of the Middle East, the very word "labor" spells social ignominy. Jews, therefore, would need to be re-educated and reoriented toward an appreciation of the dignity and the glory of physical labor. The book and the pen were no longer to be the symbol of civilized accomplishment. The hammer and the spade, the plow and the harrow, would be no less worthy a fulfillment. There would be no future for a Jewish homeland if, as did most of the original settlers, they became shopkeepers or, still worse, landowners who, though supported by philanthropy, were aping the ways of the native effendis. Histadrut would have no traffic with any mode of feudalism, neither with its one-sided economy nor with its perverted social values. The lowly and low-paid Arab peasant was not to be the pillar of Jewish agriculture. Jews themselves would have to cultivate their own lands. The Jewish shopkeeper and intellectual, the Jewish salesman and manufacturer, the Jewish father and the Jewish mother would have to become labor-minded. Palestine was to be a land not only of artists and scientists, of traders and manufacturers, but of bricklayers and plumbers, of mechanics and ditchdiggers, of porters and stevedores, of fishermen and plowmen. Love of land, work on the land, life on the land, and love of all that it grows and ripens would be emulated and exalted as in biblical times. To be not gentlemen farmers but dirt farmers was to become the urge and the passion of the colonist. It was not only biblical inspiration but immediate urgency that gave fresh meaning to the Bible's words: ". . . He will . . . bless the fruit of thy womb, and the fruit of thy land, thy corn, and thy wine, and thine oil, the increase of thy kine, and the flocks of thy sheep, in the land which he sware unto thy fathers to give thee." (Deuteronomy 7:13)

Therefore Histadrut conceived it as its function not only to defend and protect labor and to fight for an eight-hour labor day, for collective bargaining, for vacations on full pay, for consultation with trade-union representatives on the discharge of workers, and for other purely material labor aims, but to transform the non-laboring immigrants into laborers, to rip to shreds the aversions to and contempt of labor which they may have acquired in the European and Near Eastern lands from which they came. It was only after I delved extensively into Histadrut literature that I realized what the term "conquest of labor" meant and what a significant revolution in Jewish psychology the word "Palestinization" signified.

Yet had the Mandatory Government, in the twenty-eight years of its rule, displayed an earnest desire to promulgate social reform as the British Government—even when Conservative—had done in Britain itself, it is doubtful that Histadrut would have become the hydra-headed institution that it is today. Again and again Histadrut, as spokesmen of labor, demanded action for the protection of labor, Jewish and Arab. Invariably the response was tardy and halfhearted. The British colonial mind was no more responsive in Palestine to social trends at home than it was in other parts of the colonial world. It would pilot its way with as little embarrassment to native rulers and with as little favor to the peasantry and the laboring population as it comfortably could.

The labor legislation which the Mandatory Government saw fit to enact was a vast advance on anything the Arabs in Palestine had ever known, but was barely a shadow of what even the Conservative party in Great Britain had been promulgating. In 1925 the Mandatory Government invoked a ban on the use of white phosphorus in match factories, which was only in compliance with international agreements on the subject. To discourage the Arab practice of hiring out daughters under seventeen for long periods of menial labor, it limited such contracts to one year. The only obligatory social protection it fa-

Yet the Histadrut Sick Fund has not shut its doors to Arabs. The Arab peasantry who live in villages far from towns are medically the most neglected people in the country. Of the 2,520 authorized medical practitioners in the country, 210 are Arabs, 125 are non-Arab Christians, the others Jews. None of them are located in villages. The reason is quite understandable. Life in an overwhelmingly illiterate peasant community offers the university graduate few if any of the physical conveniences and the social amenities to which he has become accustomed. In czarist Russia, in the days of "going to the people," nurses and physicians, young men and young women, seized with a tender sentiment for the muzhik, made their way to the villages and did not mind the physical discomforts and the lack of cultural stimulation. Nor, in the days of the czars, did the zemstvo, or district, physician refuse to settle in a rural community however far away from town or city. But the pre-Revolution intelligentsia of Russia had a fervor for the common man, particularly the muzhik, which the intelligentsia of the Middle East has only recently begun to manifest. There is as yet little of it in Arab Palestine. Otherwise physicians would not have isolated themselves so markedly from the Arab peasantry.

Arab members of the Labor League, wherever they may be living, receive the same medical services as Jewish members, either free or on payment of a nominal fee. Those Arabs who have been won to the idea of paying a lump sum for medical aid, as do the Jewish workers, pay no fee when the services are required. But many of them prefer to pay for services as they need them. In factories in which Jews and Arabs work together, the Arab workers are well provided by Histadrut with medical care, since the employers pay for it. In the Arab villages, Histadrut clinics and physicians treat cases calling for first aid and accident cases without a fee or sometimes on the payment of a nominal sum for medicines. Infant welfare stations in several settlements offer free services to Arab mothers and children. Histadrut efforts to organize mutual-aid societies among Arabs have failed to materialize. Neither Arab physicians nor Arab political leaders would countenance so close a relationship between Arabs and Jews.

Yet its welfare work—medical aid and other social services, as well as labor benefits and all the other improvements which trade unions customarily seek—is only one aspect of Histadrut philosophy and action. No less energetically has it applied itself to the upbuilding of the Jewish community in other ways, physically and culturally. Hence its manifold industrial and commercial enterprises. Hence its schools and playgrounds, its books and magazines. Hence its acceptance and fostering of Hebrew as the working and living language of the Jewish population.

Yet since I was chiefly concerned with the subject of land and the people who derive their living from work on land, I sought to inform myself on Histadrut's contribution to the phenomenal achievements of Jewish agriculture in Palestine.

I did not need to probe deeply into the subject to become aware that without its far-reaching services and ever-present encouragement, there would have been no such settlement as Givat Brenner, or at least not in its present flourishing state. The colonists of such settlements and of the small farmers' villages are members of Histadrut. Automatically they are beneficiaries of its multifarious services, most impressively the medical. There are resident physicians and nurses, local clinics and hospitals. In a country of short distances, with good roads and telephones, the specialist is within easy reach of the village. In an emergency, the resident physician may invite the specialist to come to the settlement, or he may easily take the patient to the city hospital. If the medical care of the colonists, and especially of their children, rivals that of the city resident, it is solely because of the accomplishments of the Histadrut Sick Fund.

To facilitate the development and advancement of the colonist, the Histadrut financial institutions, wholesale and retail co-operative societies, and industrial enterprises are ever at his service. Home-manufactured implements, imported machinery, spare parts for both, technical journals, training schools for skilled technicians and agricultural specialists are as much the solicitude of Histadrut as medical care. It has been the chief and never-tiring champion of the two forms of farming most widely prevalent in Jewish Palestine—the co-operative settlement and the small farmers' village. Without Histadrut, there would not have been 195 such settlements in 1947.

Histadrut has been, in fact, the vanguard in the creation of a Jewish farmer class. It is always prospecting for fresh opportunities to settle Jews on land, principally by its own preferred pattern of rural life. It plans everything in advance. The teacher, the nurse, the physician follow in the footsteps of the plowman. It seeks to make the new pioneer as comfortable as possible in his new pursuit. It lifts from him much of the fret and worry over food and shelter, over children and civilized recreation. It consults with the new community and offers its expert counsel on practically every phase of the new life, including, of course, agriculture. With the great store of accumulated experience at its disposal, Histadrut protects the new community from the errors and pitfalls into which it might otherwise have lapsed.

Under Histadrut's guidance and with its blessing, a group of young men and women started off for the coast country of the Dead Sea. Not since the days of Sodom and Gomorrah had vegetation grown on the land there. The minerals in the soil prevented plant life. The young men and women set to work leaching the land. Their arduous efforts were rewarded by the flourishing community, Bet-Haarava, which has since been destroyed by Arab troops in the summer of 1948.

Ever in search of new lands to bring into cultivation, Histadrut in 1943 shifted its attention to the much-contested Negev region, which British diplomacy has striven to detach from its once-mandated territory. A triangle of desert land in southern Palestine, the Negev composes some three million acres, or almost half of Palestine exclusive of Trans-Jordan. Water is scarce and vegetation is sparse. Along its more fertile strips, Bedouins wander as in ancient times with their black tents and their flocks. Now and then, when water is available, they dig up a patch of ground and sow it with wheat and barley. Once the scene of a substantial civilization, the Negev has in the course of centuries lapsed into dreary disuse.

Three scouting parties recruited largely from Histadrut ranks had started off on an expedition in the Negev to gather information on soils, climate, water, plant life, and all else that would facilitate the establishment of new villages. The prospecting was largely confined to territories the Jewish National Fund had acquired through purchase. And one fine October day in 1946, fourteen new settlements were established, as if sprung out of the earth. For the immediate future, twenty-one more villages are projected in the Negev.

Lands which had witnessed neither cultivation nor civilization save that of the wandering Bedouin for centuries, and not only in the Negev, have with the aid of Histadrut been cleared and plowed and now flourish with plants and trees and grasses and grains.

Histadrut more than any other agency has sought out and championed the cottage industries. Givat Brenner, which derives three fourths of its income from these industries, is an exception. But there is hardly a farming village now that has not installed some subsidiary industrial activity. In countries where there is constant pressure of population on the land, the potentialities of such non-agricultural sources of livelihood are as priceless a gift as water. The learned Ahmed Hussein in Egypt has perceived it as clearly as any leader in Histadrut. Iran, especially in the Caspian region, abounds in a multitude of raw materials that lend themselves to such efforts. There is, in fact, no nation in the Middle East but could, with much profit to itself, apply on a large scale this newly exploited mode of enriching the rural community. Cottage industries absorb idle hands. They enable farmers to manufacture, at lower cost to themselves, commodities they need and to dispose of the surplus in the local or nearby market. Bringing consumer and producer together has ever been the hope of farmers everywhere, and Jewish farmers in Palestine have demonstrated that the goal, however limited in scope, is more easy of achievement than politicians and officials imagine.

Though co-operation has been the watchword and the life-blood in all its plans and efforts, Histadrut has not committed itself to any doctrinaire theories or policies. Therein lies its chief merit and its greatest strength. Socialist in sentiment, it is not a political party. At its sixth General Convention in January and February 1945, ten of Palestine's twenty-five political parties, each professing its own political creed, were represented. Yet the Mapai (Labor party) predominates in Histadrut as it does in all Jewish Palestine. It is as close to being Social Democrat as any such party in the world.

The Communists, who until Russia's recent reversal on Zionism had invoked disfavor and discredit on themselves for their militancy against the Zionist ideal, having even at one time loudly voiced their support of Arab anti-Semitic rioters, are an inconspicuous influence. Neither the Jewish intelligentsia nor the overwhelming mass of the laboring population, and least of all the colonists, have forgiven or forgotten their past record of militancy and intransigence. In the last general elections in Palestine, in 1944, the Communists obtained 3,948 votes, which is less than 2 per cent of the entire electorate. No other political party in Palestine has such a "hard row to hoe" in order to live down its unsavory past.

Despite ideological differences and clashes of the parties it embodies, Histadrut has faced no critical impasse because of politics. So far it has successfully avoided strife and skirmish over political doctrine. It is seeking to make the Jew a natural man—not in the sense of Rousseau, Tolstoy, or Gandhi but in terms of Palestine environment, ancient heritage, and modern scientific accomplishment. It is indifferent to all mystical conceptions of Judaism. It is willing to let rabbis and talmudic scholars battle over the issue, provided they do not encroach on its own empirical domain.

Pre-eminently practical and business-minded, it is striving first and foremost to re-educate and re-form the Jew into a laboring and labor-minded citizen. It is seeking to rid him once and forever of the internal perturbations and of the external pressures which he has known in Diaspora. Its proudest boast is that it has been one of the chief instruments in creating a Jewish farm class which constitutes about 7 per cent of the population, or about the same as in the United Kingdom or Belgium.

Because of its large membership, its vast economic power, its eminent social prestige, Histadrut has often been spoken of as "a state within a state." In more than one sense, it was that under the Mandatory Government. Having assumed functions of state which the Mandatory Government shirked, it could not help becoming its own legislative and executive body.

Will it continue to be a state within a state now that Israel has achieved statehood?

Only time will answer the question. Israel is as splintered politically as so many of the nations in Europe from which the Jews in Palestine have come. There is no evidence as yet that, in spite of its triumphs over swamp and desert, over disease and adversity, Israel will fuse itself in the manner of the English-speaking nations into limited if unwieldy political groupings. Twenty-five political parties for a nation so small and so young —only on the threshold of independence—may loom as a foreboding rather than a promise. Israel's ultra-nationalistic factions, which in their fierce underground battle against the Mandatory Government have acquired an image and a power all their own, are in this writer's judgment the chief threats to Jewish national unity. If frustrated in their efforts to achieve their own concept of an all-inclusive Palestine, will they battle the new state with the same weapon of terror with which they fought the Mandatory Government? This question is the darkest specter that hovers over Jewish Palestine. Yet were the worst to happen, Histadrut, by virtue of numbers and the magnitude of its efforts, will prove the most steadying force in the land.

CHAPTER XVI

Re-Creation or Catastrophe

AT LAST I WAS BACK IN SWITZERLAND. DESPITE THE
raw and cloudy weather, Geneva sparkled with tidiness and
animation. It was all so different from the Middle East. Here
one sensed no particular urgency for anything new, no particular
challenge to anything old. Here civilization has grown up in its
own way, brick on brick, with the finished edifice revealing to
the casual eye neither startling beauty as in Cairo, for example,
nor, again as in Cairo, startling ugliness. It was a harmonious
whole, symbol not of struggle but stability, not of doubt but self-
confidence.

Geneva was a good place to collect my thoughts and to shake
together the impressions and experiences I had gathered in the
various lands I had visited. I emptied my voluminous notebooks
and the published material that I had bought or that had so gen-
erously been given me, especially in Cairo. I pored over my own
written words and the printed words of others. Against the back-
ground of leisurely and cultivated Geneva, the cities of the
Middle East, each so different from the other, each reflecting in
its very bricks and pavements and in the surge of traffic in the
streets its own image, so old and so new, so harassed and so

buoyant, seemed even farther away in spirit than in space. Even
Tel Aviv, with all its energy and creativeness, all its faith and
enthusiasm, was, in the light of the international tempest gathering over its skies, more legend than reality, more hope than fulfillment. Yet this remarkable city, by its very site on the once
swirling sand dunes of the Mediterranean shores, supplied a
multitude of answers to a multitude of questions which I had
asked and which were asked of me, which every foreign journalist and every foreign diplomat asks and is asked in the Mohammedan lands of the Middle East.

As I read and reread my notes, it came to me with astonishment that some of the wisest words I had heard, full of tender
sympathy for the people, were the utterances not of diplomats
but of missionaries. It was a memorable experience to know Dr.
Charles Lamm, of the Presbyterian mission in Tabriz, and Dr.
William Sharp, of the Anglican mission in Shiraz. Unpretentious
men, both of them, each distinguished in his own field—Dr.
Lamm in medicine, Dr. Sharp in Arab-Persian scholarship—the
stories of their personal relations with the people were as enlightening as they were moving. They were both aloof from, and
beyond, the power politics of diplomats. Ministering to human
beings, they, more than any scientists or diplomats I had met,
perceived the magnitude of the human problem of the Persia
they were serving. They offered no solutions. They were hoping
for the best, but where the best would come from they did not
know. Nobody really knows.

Among the books I had brought with me was Dr. Lowdermilk's *Palestine, Land of Promise,* which I had picked up in
Tel Aviv. Soil conservationist, biblical scholar, he had put much
into this book that had escaped my observation: there was much
that I had not Dr. Lowdermilk's trained eyes to see. Still, with
the glow of satisfaction that comes to a man who finds his own
judgment confirmed in the utterances of a personage more
eminent than himself, I paused and pondered the following
sentence: "In their Palestinian settlements Jews have shown the

way for the reclamation and restoration of the decadent Near East." He was speaking not only of Palestine but of "Mesopotamia, which is now known as Iraq, Syria, Arabia, Lebanon, Trans-Jordan, Sinai, and Egypt." I use the more comprehensive term Middle East, and include Iran. Despite differences in language and culture, Iran and the Arab world have more in common with each other than just the Moslem faith. In its way of life, in the agricultural implements it fashions and uses, in the methods of tillage it pursues, sometimes in the crops it grows, the Arab village is different from the Iranian only in geography. The sheep and the goat, the donkey and the camel are features as distinctive of the landscape of one as of the other. Both are victims of the same brutal neglect, the same unspeakable incompetence for which the peasant in either is no more to blame than for the color of his eyes or the shape of his mouth. Not he but others fashion the compulsions to which he must submit, and from which he cannot escape.

Devastation of the land, overgrazing, pestilential marshes, poverty, disease, illiteracy, these are as common to the Persian as to the Arab village.

In both, absentee landlordism, in the words of William Vogt, "demanding its pound of the soil's flesh every year, had brought disaster to millions of acres"[1]—and to millions of human beings, the author might have added. Echoing these sentiments in his own dispassionate language, Charles Issawi, formerly of Magdalen College, Oxford, in speaking of the Egyptian landlords, writes, "Few classes have justified their existence so little as the Egyptian landlords, who have all the defects of a privileged class unredeemed by any of the virtues of a ruling class."[2]

Despite their outward gallantry and their extraordinary hospitality to foreigners, the absentee landlords of the Middle East, with all the political power they have mustered and all the elo-

[1]William Vogt, *Road to Survival* (New York: William Sloane Associates, 1948).

[2]Charles Issawi, *op. cit.*

sheep a year should die from preventable diseases and that pests should damage and destroy crops to the value of thirty million dollars. Nor does it make any sense that the peasantry should be ravaged by malaria, when (even if his prediction should fail of complete fulfillment) Dr. Hayden's suggestion for a nation-wide effort to wipe out the scourge within three years at a cost of only five dollars a family goes unheeded.

And what shall be said of the perverse plight of a nation which is fat with oil, the fourth largest oil producer in the world, yet heats its homes and cooks its meals with the charcoal that comes from burning of the forests or, as in the village, with the animal dung that should enrich the earth with the humus that has been drained out of it, and where the overwhelming mass of the peasantry retire shortly after sunset because they can afford no kerosene for their lamps?

In Egypt, garden spot of the world, where only seven and a half million acres are available for cultivation, nearly two million are still sun-scorched desert. Only now, spurred on by the voices of rebellion, especially of the college youth, is the Egyptian Government, largely an instrument of landowners and their lawyers, beginning seriously to concern itself with bringing water from the Nile to these lifeless acres. That about three fourths of its rural population should be afflicted with bilharziasis and with hookworm is of itself the saddest commentary on the plight of the Egyptian village.

In Syria, with a population of over three million, of whom two million live in villages, three fifths of the land is in the possession of absentee landlords. Of its twelve and a half million acres of arable land, only about one third is in cultivation. The sharecropper peasant has not even the legal right to demand or receive compensation for the improvements he may have made with his own labor and his own meager funds, in the event that he is forcibly evicted.

In Iraq, with a population of over four and a half million, only one fifth of the cultivable land is under plow. British scientists have done yeoman work for Iraqi agriculture, for its dates and its wheat, and for its irrigation projects. Yet sharecropping persists, and the average life span of the Iraqi is only twenty-seven years.

Almost a century ago the Russian satirist Saltykov-Shchedrin, in a burst of bitter indignation over the lot of the muzhik, wrote: "Why does our peasant go in bast slippers instead of leather boots? Why does the muzhik seldom or never eat meat, butter, or even animal fat? Why is it that you rarely meet a peasant who knows what a bed is? Why is it we all perceive in all the movements of the Russian muzhik a vein of fatalism devoid of the impress of conscience? Why, in a word, do the peasants come into the world like insects and die like flies?"

One feels like asking: why does the fellah come into the world like an insect and die like a fly? Russia has paid for her serfdom and the abuse of her peasantry with the most violent revolution the world has ever known; and one wonders about the Middle East.

To the author it is not the eloquent spokesman of the newly inflamed nationalism of the Middle East, but the lowly fellah, who is the central though voiceless character in the crisis that has come upon that part of the world. His physical condition alone deprives him of the first requisite—soldierly health—for an effective military force. The dismal showing the Arab armies made in fighting against the Jews in the summer and autumn of 1948, despite all the modern equipment they brought into play, must have been as rude a shock to the Arab leadership as to the British Middle East Command, which had reckoned that within ten days the campaign would be over and the Arabs would unfurl their banner of victory over Palestine. Had the British officers in the Middle East Command not been exclusively military- or rather victory-minded, but even slightly land-minded, with an elementary grasp of the relationship between the tiller of the soil and absentee landownership in the Arab countries, they would have tempered their self-assurance with a sense of reality

259

Marx or Thomas Jefferson. The language they speak is alien to him; their words carry no meaning. But he will listen to anybody (in time he will, and secretly if he has to, even as the Persian peasant in the Caspian provinces and in Azerbaijan has already been listening to Tudeh spokesmen) who speaks to him of land and a new life. If he will not find or be shown a genuine solution of the land problem, he will reach out for a false one. He will listen to anybody who, honestly or not, mistakenly or not, offers him the land without which he cannot live. If the West will not help him while it still can, the East eventually will. If Western democracy fails to meet the challenge of the landless or land-poor peasant, communism will run away with the triumph, even as it did in the peasant Russia of yesterday and is now doing in the peasant China of today.

Dressing up the countries in the Middle East with foreign loans, while leaving the fellah to his agonies, is like putting rouge on the cheeks of a cancerous patient to give him the illusion of health. While the malady persists, there can be no real glow of health in the face. Damascus and Beirut, Bagdad and Mecca, Teheran and Cairo, above all London and Washington, await the prophet who, armed with social purpose and a scientific knowledge of the land, will cry out with Isaiah: "Awake, awake, put on strength!"—strength on the fellah, before it is too late.

have done yeoman work for Iraqi agriculture, for its dates and its wheat, and for its irrigation projects. Yet sharecropping persists, and the average life span of the Iraqi is only twenty-seven years.

Almost a century ago the Russian satirist Saltykov-Shchedrin, in a burst of bitter indignation over the lot of the muzhik, wrote: "Why does our peasant go in bast slippers instead of leather boots? Why does the muzhik seldom or never eat meat, butter, or even animal fat? Why is it that you rarely meet a peasant who knows what a bed is? Why is it we all perceive in all the movements of the Russian muzhik a vein of fatalism devoid of the impress of conscience? Why, in a word, do the peasants come into the world like insects and die like flies?"

One feels like asking: why does the fellah come into the world like an insect and die like a fly? Russia has paid for her serfdom and the abuse of her peasantry with the most violent revolution the world has ever known; and one wonders about the Middle East.

To the author it is not the eloquent spokesman of the newly inflamed nationalism of the Middle East, but the lowly fellah, who is the central though voiceless character in the crisis that has come upon that part of the world. His physical condition alone deprives him of the first requisite—soldierly health—for an effective military force. The dismal showing the Arab armies made in fighting against the Jews in the summer and autumn of 1948, despite all the modern equipment they brought into play, must have been as rude a shock to the Arab leadership as to the British Middle East Command, which had reckoned that within ten days the campaign would be over and the Arabs would unfurl their banner of victory over Palestine. Had the British officers in the Middle East Command not been exclusively military- or rather victory-minded, but even slightly land-minded, with an elementary grasp of the relationship between the tiller of the soil and absentee landownership in the Arab countries, they would have tempered their self-assurance with a sense of reality of the proprietor, of the landlord, and the agent, who, in too many cases, would, if he dared, exterminate them. Don't let us disguise it for ourselves; there is a war between landlord and tenant—a war as fierce and relentless as though it were carried on by force of arms."

More than a century earlier, in 1729, Jonathan Swift, having lived in Ireland and witnessed the immense wretchedness of the Irish tenant farmer and the city poor, wrote his *Modest Proposal,* which is the most biting protest and the most savage outcry against landlords that any writer has ever penned. In despair of the expediency "of teaching the landlords to have at least one degree of mercy toward their tenants," he satirically advances the proposal that the quickest and most assured way of ridding Ireland of the hungry mouths it could not feed was to market one-year-old infants for meat. "I believe no gentleman will repine to give ten schillings for the carcass of a good fat child, which as I have said, will make four dishes of excellent nutritive meat. . . . Thus the squire will learn to be a good landlord, and grow popular among his tenants, the mother will have eight schillings of net profit, and be fit for work till she produces another child."

The shadow of landlordism shrouds the Middle East of today as darkly as the Ireland of yesterday.

The United States knows but little of this tumultuous and terrible struggle for land. The America which would have neither king nor a hereditary aristocracy placed at the disposal of the common man a vast domain of free land (up to June 30, 1946, 285,000,000 acres have been homesteaded). This was one of the most spectacular events in all history. Free land, as much as or more than any other circumstance, has been the mighty pillar of American democracy and American opportunity. The needy, the disgruntled, or the adventurous citizen could always sally forth and stake out for himself a claim of free land. With a quarter section or more in his possession, he commanded—even when the capital was borrowed from a bank or an insurance company—purchasing power which stimulated the financier to span the continent with railroads and the industrialist to pioneer for new agricultural implements, new household gadgets, and a multitude of other commodities with which to ease and enrich human life. Without free land, there would have been no Sears, Roebuck catalogue and no Model-T Ford, both aimed at the rural rather than the town dweller and both symbols of a prosperity that has not its equal anywhere in the world.

The case of Denmark is equally illuminating. At the beginning of the nineteenth century the Danish peasantry did not own any land. The system of farming was as primitive as the life of the people in the countryside. Crop rotation was not science but a habit—five to ten years of pasture followed by a period of equal length in cereal crops. Dependent on landlords for their livelihood, without education and without any skill, the peasantry were lethargic and sullen. A bare existence is the most they eked out for a living.

Then came the change in land ownership. By 1850, 42.5 per cent of the land was still leased. By 1930, Denmark was a nation of small farmers, with 90 per cent of the land cultivated by the men who owned it. Though Denmark has no natural pastures of any significance, no rich lands, and not even a salutary climate, it is for its size the foremost dairy country in the world, producing butter that is appreciated with equal relish in Europe's East and in Europe's West. The Denmark of today, still essentially an agricultural nation, is one of the freest and most stable in the world. But who knows what Denmark would have been like had the peasant still been a tenant farmer, nursing a fierce grudge against the outside world, his gifts and energies as effectively throttled as those of the fellah in Iran and in the Arab world?

The Jews in Palestine have learned much about dairying from Denmark. Now Jewish Palestine is the only country in the Middle East with a highly modernized, completely sanitary though still calculable potentialities of the cottage industries; the schemes of co-operative effort, so diverse and so flexible; the never-ceasing search for fresh contrivances with which to tame a sullen nature and coax out of it hidden and neglected treasures; the mastery of scientific schemes to conserve and enrich the soil—in all these performances, the Jewish colonists have pioneered for a renaissance not only of their own land, but for all the Middle East.

The failure—or the reluctance—of British diplomacy to exploit this momentous achievement in its own interests and in the interests of the peoples of the Middle East is not so much a Jewish and Arab as a world calamity, and a calamity for Great Britain perhaps more than for anybody else. It would of course be eminently unfair to lay all the blame on the British. The reconciliation of the intense Arab and Jewish nationalisms, so boldly arrayed against one another, would have taxed the wisdom of a Solomon. But there is no record that British diplomacy has earnestly attempted to seek a reconciliation. Most illuminating is the comment of the so-called Peel Commission on the subject: "The National [Jewish] Home is a highly educated, highly democratic, very politically minded, and unusually young community. It is conceivable, though we think improbable, that it would acquiesce in a dictatorship if the dictator were a Jew of its own choice, but it can never be at ease under an alien bureaucracy. Crown Colony Government is not a suitable form of government for a numerous self-reliant progressive people, European for the most part in outlook and equipment, if not in race."[4] And again: "The Government of Palestine is of the Crown type, unsuitable in normal circumstances for governing educated Arabs and democratic Jews."[5] The question arises: why did not British diplomacy abrogate the Crown type of government in Palestine and, with the aid of some of its best minds, unencumbered with the traditions and habits of colonial rule, and as responsive to the new conditions in the Middle East as to those at home, create

[4]Palestine Royal Commission Report, *op. cit.,* p. 32.
[5]*Ibid,* p. 121.

266

a political administration which might make an earnest effort to cope with the admittedly herculean dilemmas the Arab-Jewish conflict presented?

The author has no answer to the question, any more than, while in Prague at the time of the Munich crisis in 1938, he, like so many other writers who reported the event, could understand what prompted the late Neville Chamberlain to cry out jubilantly, "Peace in our time!"

The power politics which dictated the abandonment of Czechoslovakia spelled disaster. The power politics which dictated the policy of the Foreign Office toward Palestine was no less shortsighted. Josiah Wedgwood had once proposed in the House of Commons that Jewish Palestine be made a Dominion of the British Commonwealth. At the time the proposal was made it would have been welcomed by an overwhelming majority of the Jewish settlers. As a Dominion, Jewish Palestine would have been an enormous asset economically and politically to the British Commonwealth. Now the opportunity Great Britain had to benefit herself and the entire Middle East through the creative performance and the creative energies of Israel has been hopelessly shattered. The miscalculations of Ernest Bevin are as complete as were the miscalculations of the late Neville Chamberlain when he signed the Munich agreement with Hitler in September 1938. The gamble for a conjectural advantage at the sacrifice of a realizable asset has been as fruitless in the one instance as in the other.

Now that the Jews have attained statehood, it is their responsibility, despite all the external pressures bearing on them, to fulfill themselves as friendly and helpful neighbors of the Arab world. They face no more arduous a task and no greater a historical challenge. If they fail, they can hope for no peace, nor can the Arab nations.

Coming back to the United States, I found myself in a world of glittering abundance such as no country I have visited knows,

Marx or Thomas Jefferson. The language they speak is alien to him; their words carry no meaning. But he will listen to anybody (in time he will, and secretly if he has to, even as the Persian peasant in the Caspian provinces and in Azerbaijan has already been listening to Tudeh spokesmen) who speaks to him of land and a new life. If he will not find or be shown a genuine solution of the land problem, he will reach out for a false one. He will listen to anybody who, honestly or not, mistakenly or not, offers him the land without which he cannot live. If the West will not help him while it still can, the East eventually will. If Western democracy fails to meet the challenge of the landless or land-poor peasant, communism will run away with the triumph, even as it did in the peasant Russia of yesterday and is now doing in the peasant China of today.

Dressing up the countries in the Middle East with foreign loans, while leaving the fellah to his agonies, is like putting rouge on the cheeks of a cancerous patient to give him the illusion of health. While the malady persists, there can be no real glow of health in the face. Damascus and Beirut, Bagdad and Mecca, Teheran and Cairo, above all London and Washington, await the prophet who, armed with social purpose and a scientific knowledge of the land, will cry out with Isaiah: "Awake, awake, put on strength!"—strength on the fellah, before it is too late.